Acts of identity

Acts of identity

Creole-based approaches to language and ethnicity

R. B. Le Page
Department of Language,
University of York

and

Andrée Tabouret-Keller
Section de psychologie, Université Louis Pasteur, Strasbourg

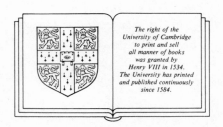

The right of the
University of Cambridge
to print and sell
all manner of books
was granted by
Henry VIII in 1534.
The University has printed
and published continuously
since 1584.

Cambridge University Press

Cambridge

London New York New Rochelle

Melbourne Sydney

Published by the Press Syndicate of the University of Cambridge
The Pitt Building, Trumpington Street, Cambridge CB2 1RP
32 East 57th Street, New York, NY 10022, USA
10 Stamford Road, Oakleigh, Melbourne 3166, Australia

First published 1985

Printed in Great Britain by the
University Press, Cambridge

Library of Congress catalogue card number: 84–28481

British Library cataloguing in publication data
Le Page, R. B.
Acts of identity: Creole-based approaches to
language and ethnicity.
1. Psycholinguistics   2. English language –
Dialects – West Indies
I. Title   II. Tabouret-Keller, Andrée
401'.9   P37

ISBN 0 521 30260 9 hard covers
ISBN 0 521 31604 9 paperback

UP

Contents

'These are facts. Afterward I'll try to connect them – if it's possible, for it's difficult to say what effect is produced by what cause. An angel's intervention would suffice to change everything, so it isn't surprising that one thing cannot be proved to be the cause of another thing. Even if one must always try, as I am doing.'

'Yours is a difficult life,' I said.

'But I found Brunellus,' William cried, recalling the horse episode of two days before.

'Then there is an order in the world!' I cried, triumphant.

'Then there is a bit of order in this poor head of mine,' William answered.

Umberto Eco, *The name of the rose*,
trans. William Weaver, pp. 207–8
(London: Secker and Warburg, 1983;
New York: Harcourt Brace Jovanovich)

Acknowledgments

The research on which this book is based was financed primarily by the then University College of the West Indies, the University of York, and the Université Louis Pasteur, Strasbourg; by the Carnegie Corporation of New York, the Ford Foundation, the Social Science Research Council in London, the Direction générale de la recherche scientifique et technique and the Conseil national de la recherche scientifique in Paris; and by the Mary Glasgow Educational Trust.

The book has been written in York, in the British Museum, in Strasbourg, in the French Alps, in the Caribbean and in Singapore. Our indebtedness to informants and colleagues over the years is great; they are too numerous to mention individually, but in particular our fellow members of the Society for Caribbean Linguistics, whose work we have occasionally pillaged, have given generously of their help and friendship, as have former students and members of staff of our two departments. We would like to convey our thanks to all those informants who helped us in various Caribbean territories, many of them becoming life-long friends. Finally, long-suffering secretaries, in particular Susie Roberts, have typed innumerable drafts of this book, and our respective spouses have put up with it as a topic of conversation and argument since about 1968.

There is one group of colleagues to whom particular thanks are due, in that they read all or part of the penultimate draft of the book and made detailed observations which we have done our best to take into account. They include Ian Hancock, Suzanne Romaine, Mark Sebba, James Walvin, Anthony Warner, Mark Williamson, and an anonymous reader for the Cambridge University Press. Le Page would like to acknowledge also the very friendly encouragement at a much earlier stage of Rebecca Posner and, above all, of the late, still greatly missed, Sugath De Silva.

Thanks are due to those who gave generously of their time to make possible the monthly seminar which Le Page was able to conduct with the help of the Multi-Ethnic Inspectorate of the Inner London Education Authority and of the Mary Glasgow Educational Trust; in particular, to Urmi Chana, Carlita Daniel, Kean Gibson, Joan Goody, Elaine Gordon,

Roger Hewitt, Steve Hoyle, John Lee, Joyce Little, Alex McLeod, John Richmond and Jim Wight.

The book owes its origins to Randolph Quirk, who commissioned Le Page in 1965 to write a volume on 'The English language in the Caribbean' for a series he was editing for Longman. This book completed, Le Page made the mistake of going back to the Caribbean to check his facts, and of asking friends their opinion of the book. As a result he came to the conclusion that it was not worth publishing; it had in any case been overtaken by the Chomskyan revolution, and by the work of William Labov. Meeting Andrée Tabouret-Keller at the Airlie House Conference in 1966 and again in Moncton in 1967, they decided to form a team, with a social anthropologist, to carry out research and explore ways (a) of providing help and guidance for teachers caught up in the post-colonial problems of education for children in multilingual countries and (b) of resolving the problems of sociolinguistic description which had led Le Page to abandon the earlier book and which were outlined in his 1968 paper to the Philological Society in Cambridge, 'Problems of description in multilingual communities'.

Whatever insights there may be in the book which follows stem thus from many years of trying to grapple coherently with creole and contact languages and with the problems of multilingualism. At least we can claim that our way of looking at things derives from close contact with the data. It may be, of course, that we have developed a squint.

R. B. Le Page and Andrée Tabouret-Keller

July 1984

1 Introduction

The approach to people's linguistic behaviour, and to their expressions of belief concerning language and concerning ethnic identity, developed in this book, is the outcome of thirty years' work on creole and contact varieties of English in the former British colonial empire undertaken by Le Page, with the collaboration over the past fifteen years of Andrée Tabouret-Keller, whose work has also been concerned a great deal with psychological and social aspects of plurilingualism in France and in the former French colonial empire. What has evolved in the course of this work is a way of looking at the phenomena we have observed which seems to provide some general explanatory insights. From the outset Le Page has had as a main concern the problems of helping children growing up in multilingual communities to profit best from the educational opportunities available to them – and of helping to improve those opportunities and the understanding of teachers. More recently, we have turned our attention to the behaviour of immigrant communities in Britain and France, and of their children. We hope that our way of looking at language may be helpful, therefore, both to teachers and to those concerned with the training of teachers.

In recent years a subject or conglomeration of subjects loosely labelled 'sociolinguistics' (usefully surveyed in, e.g., Hudson 1980, or Downes 1984; the word goes back at least to André Martinet's preface to Weinreich 1953) has had as its central concern the ways in which linguistic variation within a community, or from contact between communities, can be correlated with social factors of one kind or another, once the variation due to internal systematic factors is allowed for. 'Variationist' studies, therefore, have started from the supposition that there are languages in the use of which members of a community vary. The languages themselves have been objects of theoretical and descriptive study, as has variation in their use. But 'languages' and 'groups' have been taken as given, the starting-points.

This book is not a critique of such variationist studies, nor of variationist theory, within which so much very valuable work has been done. Rather, it views variation in linguistic behaviour as the norm, approaches language as essentially idiosyncratic, and seeks to throw some light upon the ways in which such concepts as 'a language' and 'a group or community' come into being through the acts of identity which people make within themselves and with each other. We exemplify our approach primarily from the history and behaviour of various Caribbean communities and their immigrant descendants in London.

The word *identify* has at least two meanings. The first is 'to pick out as a particular person, category or example'. In this sense a person can identify a child as his/her own child in a crowd of children, by some idiosyncratic feature. The second is 'to recognize some entity as a part of some larger entity'; in this sense, we can identify ourselves with a group or a cause or a tradition. In this book we are concerned with both of these meanings, trying to exemplify how acts of identity in the first sense are in a symbiotic relationship with those in the second sense – in other words, how the individual's idiosyncratic behaviour reflects attitudes towards groups, causes, traditions but is constrained by certain identifiable factors; and how the identity of a group lies within the projections individuals make of the concepts each has about the group.

Again, a good deal of work has been done in recent years which relates to our own concerns. We refer in some detail to the work of Lesley Milroy in Belfast. Among social psychologists, we recognize our indebtedness to Roger Brown; we have long recognized also that Howard Giles and his various associates (see the Bibliography) have taken an approach which is strikingly similar to our own in certain respects, in their work on accommodation theory. Nevertheless, although there are important similarities (and differences) between Giles's approach and our own, we are not here concerned with a critique of that work – we see it as valuable, but our own central concerns are different. Generally speaking, accommodation theory has been concerned with interactive behavioural events, and the ways in which people can be seen to accommodate linguistically, as in other ways, to their perceptions of each other; we are much more concerned with the ways in which people perceive groups, whether in immediate contact or not, and clothe those perceptions with linguistic attributes. Both approaches have led, in their own ways, to considerations concerning ethnicity.

We would agree with a number of the formulations made in, for example, Giles (1979), including his preferred definition of ethnic group as 'those individuals who perceive themselves to belong to the same ethnic category' (p. 253); but we fundamentally disagree with others – for example his statement that 'it is usually only in formal, institutionalized settings that members of different ethnic groups encounter one another' (pp. 255–6). This latter statement would seem to disregard the slave trade, and ships' crews, and a hundred other situations central to our concerns, and in any case his approach from 'given ethnic groups' and 'given languages' appears to be susceptible to less fundamental formulations than our own. We do not intend, therefore, to do more than refer the interested reader to this alternative literature, selected items of which are listed in the Bibliography. Giles's own opening statement in his 1979 paper as to the awesomeness of the task of examining the ways in which people mark their ethnic group membership is one we would echo, and one which makes clear the need for the toleration of alternative approaches.

It is a not very controversial, but sometimes disregarded, part of our own approach that everybody's (layman's and scholar's) theories and suppositions about language and society are powerfully conditioned by the culture and tradition within which he/she works – conditioned, that is, either positively or negatively. It would be incorrect for us to claim that we have chosen to exemplify our approach from the Caribbean and other communities within which our work has lain; rather, our way of looking at things has grown upon us as we struggled to come to terms with the social and linguistic processes we observed going on around us in those communities. But whereas in the case of Andrée Tabouret-Keller's work in Alsace (see Tabouret-Keller 1985a, b) it was not too difficult to 'identify' such entities as 'Alsatian' as opposed to 'French', it was even there already impossible for there to be agreement as to whether a bilingual education policy meant teaching both 'French' and 'Alsatian', or whether it must mean teaching 'French' and 'German', since 'Alsatian' was not identified as 'a language'; and in the Caribbean the task of such identifications was much more difficult. It is for this reason that we have felt obliged to illustrate many different facets of 'creoleness' in Chapter 3, to show linguistic similarities and differences at local and at regional levels and to show what the individuals in our surveys of Belize, St. Lucia and London Jamaicans might conceivably think they were identifying with. To borrow from sociology the concept Lesley Milroy (1980) has so successfully employed, we have seen West Indians in terms of their membership of networks, many of which are in process of formation; and it is the process of formation which interests us, as well as the development of the stereotypes which are the concomitants of membership. The very fact that Mervyn Alleyne (1980) could write a book called *Comparative Afro-American*, thus radically re-orienting what are usually referred to as the

'Anglophone Creoles'; or that today Rastafarianism as a supranational cult can be so widespread both geographically and socially; or that a language called Kwéyol can have become the object of such overt nationalistic cultivation in some of the French Creole-speaking islands (e.g. Guadeloupe, St. Lucia), shows how necessary it is to pay attention to the processes of emergence and the processes of disintegration of identities, and the processes we refer to below as *focussing* and *diffusion*. Our historical survey in Chapter 2, and the discussion of our survey results in Chapters 5 and 6, are intended to shed light on such processes. The history, the sociolinguistic observation and the recording of people's attitudes towards and about language and ethnicity, all march hand in hand.

Sociolinguistic research is often represented as having successfully demonstrated certain correlations. Our experience over the years – since 1951, in fact, when Le Page started work on the Linguistic Survey of the British Caribbean – must in this respect be acknowledged to be one of comparative failure. It would be very difficult to provide rigorous statistical confirmation for our insights. Nevertheless, we have felt it more valuable faithfully to record the difficulties, out of which those insights grew. Others have been much more successful than we have, their techniques being more closely derived from their models of society and sometimes more sophisticated. Our conviction remains that it is extremely hard to carry out sociolinguistic work in a rigorously hypothesis-testing manner when one comes to a society as an outsider and tries, as we tried, to make no prior assumptions about the social divisions within that society. It may be of value to those who come to the literature of sociolinguistics as laymen – and it is, as we have said, to these that the book is addressed – to have at least one experience recorded where the social class assumptions which underlie the work of, for example, Labov in New York or Trudgill in Norwich do not apply: this we have done in Chapter 4. There is, however, a more positive reason for the fairly detailed description of our attempted statistical analysis in Chapter 4: this is that the technique of cluster analysis appeared, and still appears, to us to offer a useful analogue for the social processes we are concerned with, those by which individuals locate themselves in the multidimensional space which is the social universe as each perceives it, and the focussing or diffusion of the rule-systems by which they define their position in relation to each other, so providing the foundation for those concepts such as 'a language' and 'a group or community' with which we are concerned.

For Le Page it is essential to stress that groups or communities and the linguistic attributes of such groups have no existential locus other than in the minds of individuals, and that groups or communities inhere only in the way individuals behave towards each other. Unless he manages to convey this point right at the outset the reader is likely to misunderstand the purpose of the book. For Tabouret-Keller such a formulation would not be sufficient: linguistic items are not just attributes of groups or communities, they are themselves the means by which individuals both identify themselves and identify with others; hence the existential locus of *homo*, be it individuals or groups, is in language itself. It is Le Page's point of view that has been accepted both for carrying out the research and for writing this book.

1. Linguistically heterogeneous situations

Typically, the communities in which we have worked have shared at least three characteristics. Firstly, the vernacular behaviour of most of the population has been looked down on, stigmatized, in comparison with a linguistic standard set by the education system which has acted as a yardstick for formal social acceptability and prestige. Secondly, the linguistic behaviour of many of the people has shown a great deal of apparently unpredictable irregularity quite different from the kind of monolingual homogeneity imagined by many linguists and non-linguists to be the norm. Thirdly, the question of what linguistic standards should be prescribed has been a controversial and touchy one within these societies. Several of the communities have been in a state of flux as they have worked out their new identity with new social patterns and structures in their post-colonial independence. In case it should be thought that we are in all this dealing with unusual and atypical societies, we would point out that the above characteristics apply to virtually the whole of Africa, of India, of South-East Asia, of the Caribbean and a large part of the Americas. In this book, however, we concentrate on parts of the Caribbean and on the children of West Indian immigrants in Britain, with some incidental insights offered by Malaysia and Singapore, and by some other countries of which we have experience.

Predictability. Predictability would seem to be a condition of successful communication, since the speaker has to take a chance on the hearer sharing his linguistic rules and values. Among tightly-knit and closely-interactive communities – those which we shall refer to as *focussed* – the sharing of rules, and the regularity of rules, can be considerable. However, it is not difficult to illustrate the extent of unpredictability among users of 'the same language', for example, those who regard themselves as 'English speakers'.

The following list of words allows us to exemplify a pattern of

pronunciation which to some extent distinguishes in British minds speakers
of northern from speakers of southern dialects:

bath   lath   pass   grass   alas!   dance   Mass   purple
asters   elastic   plastic   plaque   castle   Newcastle   half
staff   Lady Astor   Doncaster   laugh   daft   ass   asterisk
aunt   Bewcastle   Pakistani   elastoplast   rather   plantation
chant   nasty   Cornish pasty   'last chance garage'   Tadcaster
Dover Castle   dastard   bastard   transport   Mohammed Ali
transitive   Rockefeller Plaza   gymnastic   substantial   lather
blather   saga   moustache   translate   photograph   graph
aftermath.

It is felt that speakers of northern English dialects have the same vowel,
generally described as a low central [a], in nearly all these words whereas
speakers of southern dialects divide them between those pronounced with
a low back [ɑ] and those pronounced with a front [æ]. However, if one takes
any group of, say, 50 or 60 people from various parts of the British Isles
one finds that it is most unlikely that they will use the same kind of vowel
in each of these words consistently, and it is very unlikely that everyone
in the group would agree on the pronunciation of any one of these words
(unless it is *saga*). Moreover, if the experiment is being done in the north
of England with a group which includes people who have come from the
south, the southerners will tend to modify their pronunciation depending
on how long they have lived in the north, how belligerent they feel towards
northerners or how much they wish to identify with the north, what they
are talking about and so on.

Then, there are a number of loan words from other languages in the list,
and proper names of foreign origin, and different members of the group
will deal with these items differently. Some will feel that, for example,
Mohammed Ali can be naturalized and completely integrated with other
words of their own dialect while some will want to continue to give that
name some kind of 'foreign' pronunciation. There are also some old-
fashioned words in the list, which the younger generation today might not
use at all or might be familiar with only through old-fashioned fiction,
whereas older members of the group might be familiar with them and have
a pronunciation assigned to them. The changing habits from one generation
to another can be illustrated by reference to the flowers, purple asters; the
only pronunciation given for the name of these flowers in the *Oxford
English Dictionary* is the [ɑ] pronunciation, presumably reflecting either the
polite usage of the 1870s, when the first volume of the *OED* was being
compiled, or the usage of its editor, Murray (who was a Scot).

There are a number of words in the list which a lot of people would rarely
use unless they were specialists; for example, *lath* and *plaster*; users then

tend to hesitate over *lath*. This method of constructing a wall is in any case known in the north of England as *stoothing*. Pronunciation of the place names may be conditioned by whether or not the speaker knows where they are – if he is an adaptable newcomer to the north of England he may be impelled to pronounce Doncaster with [æ], and yet retain his low back vowel [ɑ] for Bewcastle if he happens to know that it is in Cornwall. He is less likely ever to use [æ] for Dover Castle; he may not use it for the northern Newcastle either because he will then also need to shift the stress to the second syllable, Newcástle. Some people make a distinction between two pronunciations of the word *bastard*, depending on whether they are using the word vituperatively or descriptively. One could go on listing factors on which the particular choice of vowel in particular speech acts involving one of these words would depend. Nevertheless, a great many northerners, having the same vowel in most of these words except the foreign loans, also have a stereotype southerner in their imagination who will use a low back [ɑ] in all of these words; so that the northerner who wishes to behave like this stereotype southerner will tend to say things like ['ɑ:stə]. The situation outlined here in respect of the pronunciation of words spelt with *a* among British speakers is similar to that studied by William Labov among speakers of English on the Lower East Side of New York in the 1960s and described in his (1966) book, *The social stratification of English in New York City*. In order to accommodate within a description of a single language 'English' the behaviour of speakers as they shifted from less formal to more formal modes of behaviour and changed their pronunciation of certain features accordingly, Labov introduced the concept of the 'linguistic variable' (Labov 1966: chs 4, 5). In respect, for example, of the presence or absence of some kind of [r]-like consonant in words such as *work* which are spelt with an *r* after a vowel, Labov described the /r/ as being there in the language system but as having a variety of exponents in the performance of his speakers, including a zero value (∅). A similar line was taken by Peter Trudgill (1974). Trudgill followed Labov's methods fairly closely in his survey of Norwich speakers. Both Labov and Trudgill reflect the underlying assumption that there is a language called 'English', and that the people they are dealing with are speakers of that language; variation in their behaviour, therefore, must be accounted for in terms of variation in units which nevertheless remain discrete and identifiable units in the underlying system, a system which all speakers of the language share. Whereas, however, both Labov and Bickerton (1975) have treated the variation they observe as a linear progression from a less formal or broader dialectal form towards a single educated model, the most formal or standard language, Trudgill has envisaged rather the possibility of movement in a number of different directions as his speakers adjust themselves to a variety of dialects of English within Norwich. Nevertheless, he claims that since they all understand one another they must have the same underlying phonological system, a diasystem in which the differences of performance arise from the use of rules peculiar to each dialect group but comparatively superficial in their differences as compared with the underlying system which the speakers all have in common.

It is clear that we can formulate certain 'linguistic' rules which constrain an individual in his selection of a value for the vowel in the list of words on page 6, rules which relate to the linguistic environment; but it is clear that the selection is constrained also by a host of other considerations, including the stereotypes which the individual has about other people.

The problem of defining 'a language'. Labov (1966) and Trudgill (1974) have both wished to preserve the underlying identity 'the English language' while explaining variation in the use of the system in terms of variables which are socially marked in the community. Let us, however, immediately raise just one problem posed by such an approach. One very broad generalization divides dialects of English into those which are rhotic and those which are non-rhotic. That is, there are speakers who do in some sense 'pronounce the *r*' in words spelt with an *r* following a vowel and coming before another consonant (e.g. *work*), and there are other speakers who never do. And as Labov's work in New York has shown, there are many who sometimes pronounce it and sometimes do not. When we turn to those dialects – Received Pronunciation (RP) is one, broad Jamaican Creole another – from which this /r/ has disappeared, we have to face the question of whether speakers of these dialects who sometimes *do* pronounce the *r* are then using variables of one underlying phonological system, or switching between two systems. In the case of RP the problem may be solved by pointing out that the underlying variable (r) reappears in forms derived from /r/-less words with no final consonant such as *wear* (e.g. in *wearing*); but this solution does not hold good for words such as *work*. When we turn to broad Caribbean Creole dialects we may find that speakers who lack (-r) also lack derived forms. We then have to face the problem, which Labov has discussed in respect of Black English Vernacular (1972b), as to how to know when to speak of separate systems. If we start from the concept of an underlying system this becomes an extremely difficult, if not insoluble, problem; if however we approach it from the point of view of the degree of coherence evidenced in the behaviour of a group of individuals, the problem is seen to be one of relationships and of stereotypes inherent in each individual. We do not ourselves then need to put a boundary around any group of speakers and say 'These are the speakers of Language A, different from Language B', except to the extent that the people think of themselves in that way, and identify with or distance themselves from others by their behaviour.

Grammaticality and acceptability. There are many people who say, 'Well, of course, accents vary, but otherwise we all speak the same language.' This may be reasonably true of the formal usage of a highly literate group of, let us say, academics; but to illustrate the degree of variability in what even such a group may judge to be 'grammatical' (whatever that may mean) in 'English' (whatever that may mean), we can look at the results of an experiment carried out by William Labov with a group of 52 university students in New York (Table 1). They were asked to say whether they regarded ten sentences (presented in written form) as 'Grammatical', 'Questionable' or 'Ungrammatical'. It is unlikely that any other group of speakers would agree exactly with the judgments passed by Labov's informants, among whom there was in any case a fair amount of disagreement. It would be possible to make certain crude statistical generalizations about the group as a whole, but not to use them as the basis for a prediction about the judgment of any individual member of the group. Moreover, anybody asked to judge the grammaticality of these sentences may well feel that his/her judgment in each case will depend on whether he/she can provide a context in which the sentence could occur, and that of course depends on a decision as to what the sentence would mean in that context, and what the appropriate prosodic pattern (of stress, pitch levels, and spacing) would then be. (To consider how in fact we arrive at decisions about what utterances mean would take us far beyond the question of 'grammaticality'.) For example, the first sentence (which 95 per cent of the sample regarded as 'ungrammatical') can be made acceptable to most people by stressing the first word: '*Anyone* doesn't eat in my mother's restaurant'; in other words, you have to be *someone* to eat there.

It is clear that it is possible to be uncertain whether a sentence is acceptable in one's own language or not, and also that some people will use a sentence which others would not use. We return to this question in Chapter 5.

Labov carried out this experiment (Labov 1972a: 779–81) as part of the

Table 1. *Grammaticality judgments of 52 subjects on conditions for obligatory negative attraction (from Labov, 1972a : 781, table 1)*

	Grammatical %	Questionable %	Ungrammatical %
1. Anyone doesn't eat in my mother's restaurant.	0	4	96
2. I expected anybody not to eat in my mother's restaurant.	4	8	88
3. It's not true that anybody doesn't eat in my mother's restaurant.	35	29	36
4. Anybody's not eating in my mother's restaurant is a shame	31	55	14
5. I hated anybody's not eating in my mother's restaurant.	56	33	11
6. It's OK that anybody doesn't eat in my mother's restaurant.	56	42	2
7. For anybody not to eat in my mother's restaurant is OK.	65	35	0
8. For anybody not to eat in my mother's restaurant is a shame.	73	27	0
9. It's OK for anybody not to eat in my mother's restaurant.	79	17	4
10. It's a shame for anybody not to eat in my mother's restaurant.	85	15	0
(N = 52)			

work he did to unravel the problem of how Black English speakers in Harlem could use double negatives – or even four negatives, as in the reply given to a question about whether pigeons in coops on the roof would be safe from cats:

> It ain't no cat can't get in no coop

This kind of negation, strongly stigmatized by schoolteachers and at a formal level both in our own society and in other parts of the English-speaking world, is nevertheless the norm among speakers of many vernacular varieties of English, in London English as in the English of the lyric *Ah still suits me* from the film of *Showboat* (lyrics written by Oscar Hammerstein in 1936):

Queenie: You don't make money!
Joe: Ah know that, honey.

Queenie: Ah never see none!
Joe: Ain't gonna be none,
          But that don't worry me none, no sirree!

The rule we are taught at school is an algebraic rule, that two negatives make a positive, but this rule was introduced into the prescriptive rules of teachers in England only in the sixteenth century, when 'grammar schools' were turning from the teaching of Latin grammar to the teaching of English grammar on a Latin model. And so Chaucer, in the second half of the fourteenth century, could say perfectly elegantly about the Knight among his pilgrims (Prologue to *The Canterbury Tales* l. 70.):

> He nevere yet no vileynye ne sayde
> In al his lyf, unto no maner wight.
>
> 'He never yet no rudeness did not say
> In all his life, unto no kind of person'

Shakespeare's elder contemporary Sir Philip Sidney was able to say in 1586 (*Arcadia*, l. 323): 'A vow...that I would never marry none...'; and Shakespeare himself could still use it, though he did so infrequently.

Today, however, the schoolboy who says 'I never had none' will be corrected by the teacher to say 'I never had any', and the latter is the rule that prevails when people wish to be considered 'educated'. Again, we have to face the problem of whether 'English' consists of just one linguistic system or more than one, and what 'system' then implies.

The creativity of speakers. Another aspect of language which emerges from studying the behaviour of the communities we have been concerned with is the creativity of speakers, not just in the Chomskyan sense of using a finite set of rules to make up an infinite number of sentences, but in the sense of being able to make up the rules as one goes along. In the contact situations in which pidgin languages develop any ploy is tried which may make for communication under difficult circumstances – language is, as Roger Brown (1958) once called it, a game, in which the players invent the rules and, we would add, also act as umpires. Dr Elton Brash of Papua-New Guinea (personal communication) has described the pleasure with which speakers of New Guinea Tok Pisin try out new grammatical arrangements or new words on one another to see if they can make them stick. A similar phenomenon may be observed (see Chapter 4) among London teenagers trying to 'talk Black'. In our data from the West Indies we can see that, even though there may be several fairly highly focussed broad creole vernaculars with fairly regular rules, Creole speakers coming

into contact with speakers of more standard varieties of English will
nevertheless try a variety of code-switching or code-mixing or modifying
devices, adjusting their Creole to meet the needs of the situation. In some
societies, for example modern Malaysia, purists become seriously
concerned at what has been called the 'pollution' or 'bastardizing' of 'the
language' because of the freedom with which speakers switch codes and/or
pidginize. In fact, in any community we find that language use ranges from
the highly inventive and idiosyncratic to the highly conventional and
regular. Each one of us is liable to be inventive and idiosyncratic, but poets
and writers generally are particularly inclined to be so, since they feel more
strongly than most the uniqueness of their insights and the urgent necessity
to draw on every possibility language affords in order to achieve accuracy
about those insights. T. S. Eliot (1944) has described the process as
'trying to get the better of words', and sees the poet as only achieving that
when he no longer wants to say what it is he has managed to say:

> So here I am, in the middle way, having had twenty years—
> Twenty years largely wasted, the years of *l'entre deux guerres*—
> Trying to learn to use words, and every attempt
> Is a wholly new start, and a different kind of failure
> Because one has only learnt to get the better of words
> For the thing one no longer has to say, or the way in which
> One is no longer disposed to say it.
>
> (*East Coker*, Stanza v)

There have been a number of well-known exploiters of the linguistic
possibilities of English, James Joyce among them (he looked back ad-
miringly and sometimes enviously to his predecessor Lewis Carroll in this
respect):

> The babbelers with their thangas vain have been (confusium hold them!) they
> were and went; thigging thugs were and houhnhymn songtoms were and comely
> norgels were and pollyfool fiansees. Menn have thawed, clerks have surssurhum-
> med, the blond has sought of the brune: Elsekiss thou may, mean Kerry piggy?:
> and the duncledames have countered with the hellish fellows: Who ails tongue
> coddeau, aspace of dumbillsilly?
>
> (*Finnegan's Wake*, p. 15)

In such writing it is clear that the author is trying to make use of every
kind of echo that he can evoke in our minds, every kind of analogy, every
kind of relationship between the sounds and between the meanings of
words in close or more distant proximity to each other, in order to convey
with his metaphors levels of meaning which he presumably feels cannot
be conveyed in any other way. It is part of our case that Joyce only provides
a somewhat extreme example of what we all do with language.

2. Data and questions to be answered:

It is clear, therefore, that whatever views we may hold about the nature of linguistic systems and the 'rules' they embody, about 'correctness' in pronunciation, in grammar, in the meanings of words and so on – and most educated people do have views, sometimes very strong views, on these subjects – in our actual behaviour we are liable to be somewhat unpredictable. De Silva (1979) has examples (see also Palmer 1924, cited in Mencken 1963: 517) of people doing the thing they say is 'wrong' in the very utterance in which they forbid it. Examples of this can be found in the conversation with a Belizean teacher in Chapter 6. Our concern in this book is to explore the relationship between these types of behaviour in people: how do norms, and concepts about standards, and stereotypes about the behaviour of groups (whether prestige or stigmatized) come into being? What is their relationship to the way people actually behave linguistically?

The behaviour of the old lady telling the story in Belize (see Chapter 3) provides us with a case in point. She began by using her most standard English; that was because she was talking directly to two visitors whom she knew were not Creole, and whom she assumed to be English. She started telling the story in what was more or less Creole English, and at a particular point where she related some crucial dialogue she switched into Spanish, finally reverting to Creole to finish the story off. Some of the characters of her story – for example, the carpenter, who evidently is a somewhat superior tradesman – speak in more standard English than others. But her most standard English was not the same as ours; her Creole was not exactly that of Belize City, on the coast; her Spanish was not exactly that of Guatemala City or Mexico City or Castile. Down on the coast, what was once regarded as the idiosyncratic rule-less broken Negro English of the logwood cutters and fishermen who settled at the mouth of the Belize river, is today coming to be regarded by some as the real language of a new nation, with its own rules which are distinct from those of English. This has come about through various processes but partly because of the close everyday interaction of the descendants of those settlers within the confines of a small city on the delta of a river; partly also because of the recurrent threat of invasion from Guatemala or Mexico, which if successful would reduce the political and social status of the Creoles in the eyes of the lighter-skinned and straight-haired Spanish-speaking 'conquerors'.

We have chosen this community and others like it in the Caribbean precisely because their identity as newly independent communities in a post-colonial epoch is still to be finally resolved. The very powerful polarizing forces which exist in older communities such as some of those of Europe or India or China, which impose prescriptive norms hallowed by centuries of tradition upon the members of the community, and a sense of identity or belonging which is very powerful, do not yet exist here. During the colonial period these polarizing forces were those of the European or North American nations; now new identities are emerging within the Caribbean countries themselves, as they are elsewhere in the post-colonial world. Even within Belize itself there is a variety of choices apparently open to the people. The country has been settled partly by Creoles but also by Black Caribs expelled from St. Vincent, and partly by migrants from surrounding Spanish-speaking countries – Mexico to the north, Guatemala to the west, Honduras to the south; various Amerindian peoples who were there before the European settlers arrived have also remained within the country. Although the close daily interaction of the coastal city has provided norms of behaviour recognized and labelled by the Creoles who live and work there, the more sparse and more mixed population of the interior lacks even those norms. The old lady who tells the story shares with those in her community a capacity for more Spanish-like or more Creole-like or more English-like or more American-like behaviour; she can shift her identity according to her company and she and her friends vary from one to the other according to the degree to which they are prepared to shift in any particular direction to proclaim their political and cultural identity. Here we introduce, then, the concept which is the theme of this book, that of linguistic behaviour as a series of *acts of identity* in which people reveal both their personal identity and their search for social roles. In the case of Belize it seems that the coastal Creoles have made their act of identity; they are waiting for this old lady and her neighbours to throw in their lot – politically, culturally and linguistically – with them. But the people of the interior are subject to rather different pressures from those of the coast; they still reveal themselves as being more or less Spanish, more or less Creole, more or less educated and so on; they still move quite considerable distances within a multidimensional sociolinguistic space in order to accommodate to different encounters and different topics of conversation. We do not see evolutionary linguistic processes taking place within such communities as being describable in terms of a linear progression from a broad dialect towards a model language, nor even from one dialect towards another; but rather as the evolution of newly-focussed norms with each group of each generation and within each political entity according to their needs for various identities.

Moreover, we see these processes not as peculiar to new communities, though more easily observable there, but as the common processes through which mankind has evolved its languages and its sense of linguistic identity.

Since claims about ethnicity are often closely involved with linguistic questions, we have examined those too, and the nature of the relationship of ethnicity to language. Here we have taken the statements made to us in our 1978 follow-up study of 40 of our 278 1970 informants in Belize about the ethnic identity of themselves and their families; we have related them to the criteria used by students in York for assigning people to ethnic categories, and also to the claims made both by our informants and by their parents in 1970. We find processes at work here similar to, and interrelated with, those we have described for the language. Thus it seems as if our way of thinking about these two kinds of 'acts of identity' may provide a more general framework of value to linguists, to sociologists, social psychologists and social anthropologists – with some of whom, as we are aware, we already have a good deal in common.

Our linguistic data consist of conversations and story-telling recorded in Belize, in St. Lucia and in London; we set these against the recorded results of using a grammar questionnaire in three Caribbean territories, Jamaica, St. Vincent, Grenada, in the 1950s. We are concerned to throw what light we can upon the data, accepting it as it stands, not discarding any of it as deviant or abnormal. We are interested both in what our informants said about themselves and their language, and in their language itself. We are interested also in the fact that our informants felt themselves to be part of some certain community, though members of different subgroups within that community, while at the same time their linguistic behaviour was so clearly variable— each person varied in any one conversation or story, they varied from one to another, they themselves changed over time. In Belize, younger members of the community intermarry ethnically more than their elders; in the face of hostility from Guatemala all draw closer together; social change and linguistic change are constantly taking place. In London too, some younger members of the West Indian community, whether from St. Lucia or Jamaica, draw closer together in the face of hostility from their surrounding circumstances; again, social change and linguistic change are constantly taking place. How can we best understand it? What common model will accommodate both the search for identity in social terms (ethnic, racial, national), any linguistic symptoms of that search and the stereotyped views we all have upon some aspects at least of the subject?

3. Summary: the programme of the book

Thus, a concern which originated with observation of the educational disadvantages of children in the Creole-speaking Caribbean has led to an investigation into how that and similar situations came about, how they can best be described and what insights they afford us into social and psychological aspects of linguistic behaviour and the stereotypes we all have about ethnic and linguistic identity. We believe those insights have important implications for general linguistic theory, perhaps also wider implications for social anthropology.

The book is organized as follows. In Chapter 2 we survey the settlement history of the Caribbean from Europe and Africa from the fifteenth century on, drawing attention to those factors which seem to have played a major part in forming the non-indigenous languages spoken there today and concluding with a brief glance at migration from the Caribbean to Britain in the 1950s and 1960s. In Chapter 3 we present sample West Indian texts; these are organized partly to show coherence and variability within the grammar of the English Creoles, and partly to exemplify the linguistic relationships of our data from Belize, St. Lucia and London. In Chapter 4 we give an account of our sociolinguistic survey of those three territories, with some samples of the kind of results we hoped (but sometimes failed) to achieve. In Chapter 5 we discuss the linguistic significance of our data, both in terms of internal structure and in terms also of the way people construct stereotypes about language (their own, and that of other people and groups of people) and in doing so establish what they feel to be their relationships to others. In Chapter 6 we try to show that similar analytical procedures can be applied to reveal how people feel about their ethnic or tribal or racial relationships, and we examine the complex role of language in these stereotypes.

In the course of the book mention is made of other studies which have utilized our general theoretical framework. To these we would like to add a series of recent studies in India which have come to our attention as the book goes to press; they will be found in the Bibliography under Mukherjee (1980), Satyanath (1982), Agnihotri, Khanna and Mukherjee (1983) and Sahgal (1983).

2 Some Pidgin- and Creole-speaking communities and their histories

1. The need for case-histories

We shall be concerned in Chapters 5 and 6 with the processes through which communities come to develop a sense of having a language of their own, and with the reification and totemization of that concept. In this chapter we examine in some detail case-histories of Pidgin- and Creole-speaking communities. We sketch in outline the general background of the European voyages of exploration and colonization of the Caribbean, after which we examine in more detail the demographic history and related linguistic history of the West Indian territories of Barbados, Jamaica, St. Vincent, St. Lucia and Belize. Later in the book we shall describe the processes at work in Belize, in St. Lucia and in London today, as they have been revealed by our linguistic fieldwork there. The texts in Chapter 3 provide a general sample of the linguistic outcome of the history we are concerned with here, as it affected the former British Caribbean territories.

This rather extensive treatment of the general demographic background to the settlement history of the Caribbean is needed in order to throw light upon various disputed aspects of what has gone into the making of a regional culture. It is an essential part of our case that out of many common elements (such as European settlement, slavery, later immigration, education) each Caribbean territory has evolved a clear and distinct sense of its own identity. It is clear, nevertheless, that there are also distinctive regional identities (Afro-Caribbean, Anglo-Caribbean, Franco-Caribbean, Hispano-Caribbean; mainland vs. island, Western vs. Eastern) and that to understand these as they impinge upon the people of each individual territory it is necessary to know about the settlement history of the region in some depth.

We accept the general premise that a pidgin language is one which develops as a *lingua franca*, a trade or common language, between speakers of different languages when they meet under certain conditions. Chapter 5 discusses this process in much greater detail, together with the fact that creole languages are generally held to develop in situations where children are born into a community in which the Pidgin has become more generally useful than any of the original native languages of the members of the community. For the moment it is sufficient to repeat the general hypothesis and riders which, we maintain, provide the framework within which the actual linguistic behaviour of any individual is determined: that individuals create the patterns for their linguistic behaviour so as to resemble those of the group or groups with which from time to time they wish to be identified, subject to the constraints dealt with at length in Chapter 5.

The link between the individual and the community is provided by the processes of projection and feedback; the evolution of communal norms by the focussing provided by the models in the community, by the interactive processes of daily life and by the inherent properties of linguistic systems. The processes of focussing are discussed in Chapters 5 and 6. In this chapter we must therefore provide as much background information as possible for our subsequent illustration of these processes.

The general background to our case-histories

From one point of view, history is the story of successive localized civilizations, their rise, achievement and decline. Those that are known to us, a fraction of those which have come and gone in man's history, are known either through archaeology or from their art and literature. Those which have left behind any kind of writing are known to us from that writing; and by an analysis of written remains we have reconstructed what we call the 'languages' of past civilizations, and have given them names such as Sanskrit, Greek, Latin, Gothic, Chinese. Those reconstructions have been helped by extrapolating back into the past from the evidence of modern dialects; comparative linguistics and dialectology compare modern French, Spanish, Italian, Romansh and arrive at some idea of the relationship of the concept 'Latin' to the actual behaviour of the people who used some form of it in different parts of the Roman Empire, either for speech or writing. 'Primitive Germanic' is a reconstructed language whose form has been conjectured by comparing texts in Anglo-Saxon, Gothic, Old Norse, Old High German and so on. It is not generally supposed to represent, except in a very attenuated and abstract way, the actual linguistic behaviour of prehistoric Germanic tribes, whereas a grammar of classical Latin will be based upon an analysis of the actual sentences written by a fairly small group of authors whose work has chanced to survive and who are thought to be close enough to one another in time and place and usage to constitute a language community. (We can in this respect compare the group of Middle Scots writers examined in detail in Romaine 1982.)

From another point of view, however, history is the story of the human migrations which have taken place, migrations which have generally had a lot to do with climate and the pressure of population on resources, and with the adventurous, enquiring and acquisitive instincts of men. From this point of view, a civilization is a way of life that evolves in response to a particular set of circumstances; it may, like the language which evolves with it, be highly focussed, or it may be diffuse. Most migrations have led to contact and contests between different groups, to colonization, very often to conquest. The linguistic symptoms of contact initially may be the development of a *lingua franca* or pidgin, accompanied by increased diffuseness in the older linguistic systems in use. This can be seen, in the case of Britain, in the effects of both Norse and Norman colonization (see, for example, Poussa 1982; Warner 1982; Le Page, to appear). Indeed, the dialects of modern Britain continue to reflect migratory processes, most recently the immigration of Irish, Asians and West Indians into certain industrial areas. On the other hand, if the contact is one which appears to threaten a community they may well respond by drawing closer together, identifying more closely with their cultural norms, in which case their linguistic behaviour becomes more highly focussed. This happened in England in the fourteenth century and is happening in Belize today. The migrations with which we are for the moment concerned, however, are those of the colonial expansion of European populations along tropical trade routes from the fifteenth century onwards, and in particular the establishment in tropical countries of Portuguese, Spanish, Dutch, French and British plantation colonies with Amerindian, African and Asian labour.

An example: Jamaican English

If we examine the *Dictionary of Jamaican English* (Cassidy and Le Page 1980) we find there words in use in Jamaica, today or in the past, the vast majority of which come ultimately from one dialect or another of English – although sometimes so changed in form or meaning, or from such an unfamiliar or archaic dialect, as to be scarcely recognizable as 'English' words. There are a number of seafaring terms. In addition, however, we find a fair number of words from Portuguese and Spanish; many from African languages, especially from those spoken in what is today Ghana; some from French; some from Hindi; a few from Chinese; and a number

from American Indian languages – either borrowed directly or via Spanish.
Here are some examples of each.

From Portuguese:

pickney or pikni	a small child	Pg: *pequenino*
pimento	the allspice tree	Pg: *pimienta da Jamaica*
sampata	a sandal	Pg: *sapato*

From Spanish:

barquadier	an export wharf	Sp: *embarcadero*
bobo	a fool	Sp: *bobo*
maaga	thin, lean	Sp: *magra* (but also in Germanic languages)
palenque	a stockade	Amer. Sp: *palenque*

From West African languages:

adru	a medicinal herb	Twi: *adúru*, Ewe: *adrú*
afu (yam)	a common variety of yam	Twi: *afúw*
agidi	a cornmeal pudding	Yoruba: *àgidi*
budum	the noise of falling heavily	Twi: *bŭrùm*
hangkra	a hoop or rack for hanging meat or fish on above the fire to cure	Twi: *hã́ŋkáre*
himba	an edible wild yam	Ibo: *mba*
John Canoe (dancer)	a kind of masked dancer	Ewe: *dʒoŋ'kɔ-nu*
kaba-kaba	rough or roughly-done	Yoruba: *kábakàba* (perhaps also < Eng. *cobble*)
nana	grandmother or nurse	Twi: *nãnã* (also English *nan*, *nanny*)
packy or paki	a calabash	Twi: *apákyi*

From Bantu languages:

dingki	a funeral ceremony	Kongo: *ndingi*
dundus	an albino	Kongo: *ndundu*
kumuna	a dance of spirit possession	Kimbundu: *kumona*
		Common Bantu: **-min*

From French:

bateau	a rough raft	Fr: *bateau*
leginz	a bunch of vegetables for a stew	Fr: *légumes*
Maroon	a runaway slave	Fr: *marron* Sp: *cimarron*

From Hindi:

beti	a little girl	Hindi: *beti*
roti	a kind of bread	Hindi: *roti*

From Chinese:

ho senny ho	a greeting ('How's business?')	Cantonese: *hóu sangyih hóu*
tai shiin	a book of gambling tickets	(etymons uncertain)

From American Indian languages:

taya	an edible root (coco)	Tupi, Carib: *taya*
hicatee	a land turtle	Sp: *hicotea* < Island Arawak

Among the English words we find such dialect words as *calaban*, from a Somerset word (*EDD* callyvan) for a bird-snare (although F. G. Cassidy has proposed an alternative etymology in the second edition of *DJE*), and *gaulin*, from a West of Scotland word for a sea-bird; among seafaring terms, *leeward*, *windward* and *galley* (for a cooking-pot); among the archaisms, *pass* for 'passing' or 'surpassingly', as in *pass ugly* for 'extremely ugly'; *hige* ['haɪg] preserves an old dialectal pronunciation of *hag*; *higgler*, the common term for a market-woman in Jamaica, is now obsolete in most parts of England. Many English dialect words and phrases, especially those from seventeenth century south-western dialects, may have reached Jamaica via Barbados (see Niles 1980).

We have now already introduced many of the parameters of variability in the provenance of West Indian 'English'. In the first place, it will be evident that the kind of English which would serve as a departure-point for the migration-languages we are going to consider was itself by no means homogeneous – the speakers of English who engaged in the slave-trade or formed colonies overseas did not all go at the same time, nor did they all come from the same place or have the same level of education or social status.

Secondly, the travellers either encountered a West African trade already formed to some extent by other nations (West Africans and Arabs, West Africans and Portuguese, West Africans and Dutch and so on) or they went straight to the Americas from Britain. In the latter case, they sometimes went first to the mainland colonies (such as Virginia or South Carolina) and found their way south to the Caribbean, sometimes the reverse.

Thirdly, the slaves who were taken to the New World were captured and enslaved from many different parts of Africa (and even from Madagascar) and were shipped in ever-increasing numbers; they reached their destinations by a variety of routes, sometimes sailing direct from a West African, Congo or Angolan port to the New World port where they were sold to a plantation owner, sometimes spending time in one or more slave depots on the African coast or in the Americas. The manner of the trade has been described in some detail for Jamaica in Le Page (1960), and more generally for the Americas in Curtin (1969) and Rawley (1981).

Fourthly, since the *Dictionary of Jamaican English* was first compiled studies of many other West Indian and American varieties of Creole have shown the extent to which Jamaica shares its Creole. (The second edition is annotated for shared vocabulary with five other territories: Guyana, Trinidad, Barbados, Nicaragua and Belize. See also Le Page 1978b.) One of the most recent studies (Hancock 1980a) is a study of the Creole of the Afro-Seminoles of Brackettville, Texas. These are the descendants of slaves who escaped from the plantations of Georgia to settle with the Seminole (= Maroon, < Sp. *cimarron*) Indians of Florida; their language, although dying out from lack of use today, is very similar indeed to Jamaican. A much earlier study showing similarities of structure and vocabulary is Lorenzo Turner's pioneer work on the Gullah of the Sea Islands off the coast of Carolina (Turner 1949). The fact that 'Jamaican Creole' was described and named and thus given a separate identity to match that of the people of the island in which it is spoken, before a more general description of Creole English in the Caribbean could be made, is to some extent an accident of the history of linguistics (see Le Page 1980a) which masks the wider truths of the history of the slave-trade and of colonial America. Finally, there is a distinct difference between the contribution of the American Indians of the Caribbean islands, who were there before the Europeans arrived but who were eventually virtually exterminated by the Europeans, and that of the Madeiran Portuguese, Chinese, freed West Africans, and East Indians, who arrived as indentured labourers only in the nineteenth century. Each kind of social contact has had a particular kind of linguistic outcome. We shall discuss samples both of social contact and of linguistic consequences, some in more detail than others.

2. Voyages of exploration and processes of colonization

The Portuguese

Voyages to the Americas in the fifteenth, sixteenth and seventeenth centuries were only part of a much wider process of European exploration in search of trade which was led by the Portuguese. They had been attracted southwards along the coast of what is today Saharan Mauritania initially by the fishing. It was from the vantage-point of their knowledge of the coast as far south as the Gambia river that they participated in the great era of discovery which led Europeans between the middle of the fifteenth and the late seventeenth centuries in one historian's words, to learn 'to think of the world as a whole and of all seas as one' (Parry 1963: 1). By 1475 the Portuguese had rounded the bulge of the Guinea coast, explored as far east as Benin, and established a series of trading posts and contacts with African villages and towns ashore from the Senegal river to the island of Fernando Po (modern Bioko) in the Gulf of Guinea. Papal bulls of 1454 and 1456 granted to Prince Henry the Navigator and the Order of Christ 'the sole right and duty of converting the natives' of the Guinea coast (Parry 1963: 134), and to this the Portuguese added a claim to the monopoly of trade. They defeated their Spanish rivals at sea in the war with Castile over the rival claims of Isabella and Juana to the throne, and in 1481 secured from Spain a treaty recognizing their monopoly in fishing, trade and navigation along the whole West African coast. In 1482 they leased from the local African chiefs the site for a fortress at what became known as Elmina, to protect their Gold Coast trade in gold, slaves, pepper and other local commodities. They garrisoned the fort with Portuguese soldiers and an African village grew up around it, as around their many other missionary/trading settlements. Thus by the time they were expelled from Elmina by the Dutch in 1642 the Portuguese had had settlements on the Gold Coast for 160 years, and those settlements had close contact with those islands in the Gulf of Guinea from which they were to some extent victualled, São Tomé, Principe and Fernando Po. (For descriptions of the Creole Portuguese of these islands see, e.g., Schuchardt 1882, 1889; Günther 1973; Ferraz 1974, 1979.)

It has been argued that the Creole Portuguese which became the *lingua franca* of these settlements was the mould in which the trading Pidgin used by all the subsequent European nations on the West African coast was formed. One's view about this claim will depend to some extent on one's view about the acquisition and transmission of linguistic characteristics generally, and our own view is argued in Chapter 5. Nevertheless, nobody can deny the considerable extent of Portuguese influence around the slave-trade coasts before the arrival of the ships of other European nations. In the course of the sixteenth and seventeenth centuries the Portuguese introduced to West Africa from their Far Eastern possessions oranges, lemons, limes, rice and sugar-cane; and from Brazil, maize, tobacco, pineapple, cassava and guava. The Gold Coast historian W. E. F. Ward (1948) noted among Twi loan-words from Portuguese: *asepatere* (compare Jamaican *sampata*, above) for 'shoe', *krata* 'paper', *asekan* 'knife', *prako* 'pig' (found among the Jamaican Maroons as *bracho*, q.v. in *DJE*); and in Gold Coast pidgin: *palaver, piccin* (cf. Jamaican *pickney*), *fetish* and *dash*. Other African languages (e.g. Kongo) have similar Portuguese loan-words. However, we must see the Portuguese activities in relation to later events. The population of Portugal at this time was only one million; the population of their garrisons and settlements strung out around the trade routes could not have amounted to more than a few thousand; their trade in slaves, prior to the development of colonies in Brazil, was to be numbered in hundreds rather than in tens of thousands.

In the 1480s Diogo Cão explored as far as the Congo, and took Congolese Africans back to Lisbon with him; and Bartolomeu Dias, after him, rounded Cape Hope and Cape Agulhas (without sighting them) and entered the Indian Ocean. After this it was ten years before Vasco da Gama again entered the Indian Ocean, sailed north along the African coast to Mombasa and Malindi, and there fell in with the Gujerati navigator Ahmed ibn Majid, who guided the expedition across the Indian Ocean to Calicut. In the meantime, not only had Columbus returned to Portugal from his first voyage across the Atlantic, but the Portuguese traveller Pedro da Corilha had reached Calicut overland via Cairo and Aden.

Early Portuguese arrivals in India found the Arabs and the Malays active across the Indian Ocean in trade and proselytizing for Islam just as they themselves had been active in the Atlantic for Christianity. The linguistic consequences of these activities have many similarities. The Swahili language, Kiswahili, is used today not only as the native language of Arabized communities in Mombasa and Zanzibar but as the national language of Tanzania and the major trade language of East Africa; whatever its ultimate Bantu origins, it developed primarily as a *lingua franca* between Arab traders and Bantu in the trade in slaves and spices up through the Gulf of Aden and the Red Sea. Malay, whatever its Austronesian origins, became established alongside Arabic as the *lingua franca* of the Malay peninsula and the Indonesian archipelago, leading to its use in the creolized form, Bahasa Indonesia, as the national *lingua franca* and official language of Indonesia today. Sometimes these trade languages themselves came into contact, as happened with Malay and Pidgin Portuguese on the east coast of South Africa (see Valkhoff 1966), in the Straits of Malacca and in Macao. Today the Creole Portuguese called Papia Kristang ('the language of the Christians') is still spoken by a Malayo-Portuguese community in Malacca (see, e.g., Hancock 1969 *et seq.*; Baxter, to appear), and a recording of it which we made in about 1962 and then sent to Macao was readily understood by the Malayo-Portuguese community there (for whose vocabulary see Batalha 1977), although they found it 'old-fashioned'. Varieties of 'Creole Portuguese' have been described also in, for example, Java (Wallace 1978) and Sri Lanka (Smith 1977).

At the beginning of the sixteenth century the Portuguese (Parry 1963: 142) obtained permission to build a factory (trading post) on the Indian coast at Cochin, so avoiding to some extent the established Muslim traders at Calicut; but by 1502 the two trading religions were at war. Under Afonso d'Alboquerque the Portuguese set out to establish themselves more securely in the Indian Ocean with fortresses and permanent bases ashore and a fleet at sea; they established their main base at Goa, which continued as a Portuguese possession until annexed by force by India in 1961. Their base at Malacca, commanding the Straits through which the spice trade from Indonesia had to pass, was set up in 1511; it was 1556 before they were able to establish a base at Macao, down river from Canton, and so develop their trade with China. That settlement survives today. Before their arrival in Malacca there were already Chinese living there under the Sultan of Malacca and using a pidgin Malay for trade. There is still today a 'Baba' Chinese/Malay population in Malacca, as well as the Creole Portuguese settlement (see Clammer 1979). Their furthest penetration to the east was to the Moluccas, spice-islands of the Indonesian archipelago.

By this time Portuguese was undoubtedly among the most international of languages, in use from Brazil to Indonesia; it was followed in this respect by Arabic and Malay (Valkhoff 1975). Documentation of creole and contact varieties of Portuguese from many parts of the world dates back at least to the early part of the nineteenth century (see, e.g., Berrenger 1811) and scholarly or semi-scholarly descriptions to the second half of the century. They are carefully recorded in Reinecke *et al.* (1975).

Trade languages and Creole Portuguese. We should notice that none of the trade languages so far mentioned came into being as a completely new linguistic start, nor in a linguistic vacuum. Theoretically we could have a *lingua franca* or common language evolving in the extreme case of a man and a woman each swimming ashore to the same desert island from different wrecks and there living together; if they had children those children might use the Pidgin of their parents as their own language and develop it into a Creole. (The nearest we get to this kind of new beginning is in the case of Pitcairn Island, as narrated in, e.g., Ross and Moverley 1964.) The Portuguese settlements in which a trade pidgin developed and was then creolized – taken as the basis of their native language by the children of miscegenation – were made by men some of whom were already familiar, from Mediterranean usage and from their own earlier contact with Moors and West Africans, with the *idea* of a trade pidgin; and in the places they visited they found others before them also familiar with the same concept. We shall discuss this point again in Chapter 5.

A number of writers (e.g. Hancock 1972) have drawn attention to the importance of the language of British ships' crews, themselves often linguistically heterogeneous, in the formation of English pidgins and creoles. General maritime usage seems to be the source of a number of words recorded in the *DJE*; Hancock has drawn attention to phonological parallels between modern Krio pronunciations and those reflected in the logs of seventeenth- and eighteenth-century seamen analysed by Matthews (1935, 1937). The influence of maritime usage is also clearly visible in the development of Pacific Pidgins and Creoles (see, e.g., Charpentier 1979). It is not necessary to postulate any kind of direct 'descent' of modern maritime usage or of Pidgin English from the *sabir* or *lingua franca* of the Mediterranean; similar conditions – the focussing of the usage of a polyglot or linguistically diffuse ship's crew, and of ships' crews in general – produce similar results, and it iş reasonable to suppose that similar conditions produced similar results among the Portuguese crews.

During the period (late fifteenth to early seventeenth centuries) when the Portuguese maintained a near monopoly of the West African trade, their small demand for slaves was quite easily met by the long-established slave trade which was in the hands of various Moslem traders such as the Mandinka. The crusading Islamic armies which conquered, converted and colonized North Africa between the seventh and fourteenth centuries did not penetrate into the forests beyond the Niger; but the Arabs did take slaves from that region (brought to such markets as that of Timbuktu) back to the Mediterranean coast, just as they took them by sea from the East African coast to the Red Sea coast. By the time the Portuguese reached Senegal the trade was well established on the trans-Saharan caravan routes from Senegal to Algeria, Libya and Egypt. The Senegal and Gambia rivers allowed the European ships convenient penetration a little way into the interior, and sheltered anchorages. The African slave-traders began to reverse some part of their trade, to supply the newcomers. To begin with, these slaves were taken to Portugal and Spain. When Ovando went as Governor to the Spanish possession of Hispaniola in 1502 he was allowed to take with him some Christian Negroes born in Spain or Portugal. By the end of the first quarter of the sixteenth century slaves were being sent to the Spanish islands in the Caribbean in some numbers, to replace the native Indian labour which was rapidly dying out under forced exploitation. The Spaniards did not themselves ship slaves but bought them from the Portuguese. It is worth noting here that under the union of the crowns of Portugal and Spain under Ferdinand and Isabella in the seventeenth century the Portuguese acted as merchants for the Spanish even in the Spanish colonies of Mexico and Peru, frequently to the disgust of many Spaniards who identified all Portuguese as Jews and complained that trade was in the hands of non-Christians and non-Spaniards (see, e.g., Boxer 1957: 102). By the middle of the sixteenth century Brazil, Portugal's own colony, was becoming a large market for slaves. As the demand grew in the New World so also the Portuguese extended their trading from Senegambia first to the Gold Coast, then to the Bight of Benin and south to the Congo and Angola; but as the trade grew so also it began to attract more and more interlopers from the other European nations, in particular the Dutch.

Without wishing to over-emphasize the role of Creole Portuguese as an element in the formative processes of other Creoles, it is necessary to draw attention to the role of the island of São Tomé and its neighbouring islands in the Gulf of Guinea in the focussing of Creole Portuguese itself. The subject has been dealt with by Ferraz (1974, 1979). His 1974 study deals in particular with São Tomense – the three islands São Tomé, Principe and

Annobón yielding four varieties of Creole. He quotes Father Alonso de Sandoval's 1627 description, published in Seville about 160 years after the first Portuguese settlers arrived:

and we call them Creoles or natives of São Tomé. With the communication they have had with such barbarous nations in the time they have been living in São Tomé, they understand nearly all of them by means of a very corrupt and broken Portuguese speech which they call the language of São Tomé...(p. 3)

The name, today, Ferraz says, is still (in São Tomense) *'lungwa san'tome*, meaning a Portuguese Creole. Today, Portuguese is said to contribute 93 per cent of the lexicon, while the substratum, which has contributed most of the remaining 7 per cent and a great deal to the phonology and grammar, derives from Kwa and Western Bantu languages.

The first major contingent of settlers, about 2000 of them the young children of Castilian Jews, arrived in the island in 1493. In addition, 'up to 1535 most of the convicts sentenced in Portugal for serious offences were sent to São Tomé' (Ferraz 1974: 25). Each convict was allowed a black slave woman, and slaves were imported from the Kwa-speaking areas of the Bight of Benin. In 1500 the citizens of São Tomé were allowed to extend their trading operation on the mainland down to the Kingdom of the Congo. The island was being farmed and produce exported to the mainland; it was also a major entrepôt for the slave trade. Ferraz states that the period up to 1566, when the island developed towards prosperity, also saw the important development of a free section of the African population and its acquisition of wealth. In 1567 a French attack on the island heralded its decline. The French captured the island in 1614 and lost it again in 1644. But meanwhile many of the Portuguese planters had left for Brazil, and removed from the community Portuguese as a model language for a Creole which by then, according to Ferraz, was 'reaching its maturity'. We quote the final paragraph of his third chapter in full:

This severance of Portuguese at this point in time could possibly account for the high African component in the lexicon, phonology, and grammar of São Tomense. If the Portuguese settlers had remained in large numbers, it is natural to expect that the Creole would have moved considerably closer to Portuguese. As it was, as Negreiros writes, 'the white race had moved away, and the mixed race, consequently, gradually diminished, until it was almost extinguished'. Regarding the African population, Negreiros writes: 'Even the Portuguese blood which ran in their veins was gradually lost in the constant crossings with the races of the mainland opposite, because Portugal no longer even sent her convicts there' (1895: 37, 40). The linguistic corollary of these observations is that the Portuguese language was virtually removed from the social situation, and presumably the Portuguese of the Portuguese-speaking free Africans was lost, only the Creole remaining.   (1974: 30, 1979: 19)

Before leaving the Portuguese voyages, mention must be made of their colonization of Madeira, the Azores and the Cape Verde Islands (see, e.g., Valkhoff 1975). Not only did these islands provide stepping-stones for the colonization of Brazil, and so lead to the enormous development in the slave-trade necessary to develop the Brazilian sugar plantations; it was in these islands that sugar cultivation itself was developed by the Portuguese with canes brought from Sicily. It was sugar which made the fortunes of so many European planters and led to the deaths of so many hundreds of thousands of migrants, both African and European, in the centuries before slavery was abolished and tropical diseases controlled. Finally, although many Portuguese peasant farmers and Portuguese Jews went to populate the New World from Portugal itself, many also went from Madeira and the Azores, especially in the mid-nineteenth century, as immigrant labourers. In Jamaica there was still in the 1950s an identifiable community known as 'The Portos' near Montego Bay, and the descendants of such Portuguese labourers are to be found throughout the Caribbean and in Guyana, generally through intermarriage with the coloured population. The language of these peasant labourers who came from the Cape Verde Islands was, as Valkhoff has shown, Portuguese Creole.

The Dutch

Although occasional French and British ships (like those of Sir John Hawkins in 1562) broke through the Portuguese-West African-American trade monopoly during the sixteenth century, it was the Dutch, arriving on the scene towards the end of the century, who first made a major bid to take over trade. And paradoxically, although the Dutch seem linguistically to have been the most accommodating traders, their arrival had far-reaching linguistic consequences. It seems that they, in contrast to the British and French, must have made full use of the Portuguese Pidgin or Creole. There was at one time a Dutch Creole (Negerhollands, or Creol) now almost extinct, spoken in the Virgin Islands (see Reinecke *et al.* 1975). We are indebted to Ian Hancock for the information that Gilbert Sprauve has presented the Smithsonian Archives in Washington DC with a contemporary tape-recording of a native speaker. Goodman (1982) has traced this Creole back to the Windward Netherlands Antilles, particularly to St. Eustatius and St. Martin. Today, however, apart from Afrikaans and the language of a small community in Guyana (see Robertson 1974), there are comparatively few surviving traces of Dutch trade languages (although a number of contact varieties of Dutch are listed by Reinecke *et al.* 1975) other than in a number of seafaring terms (such as *drogher*, 'a coasting vessel'); and Williams (1983a) has cast doubts on Goodman's historical evidence for the importance of Dutch Creole in St. Eustatius (see below). Curaçao, the island off the coast of Venezuela which they seized in the 1630s and made into a slave depot from which they supplied the plantation colonies of every European country (either legally or illegally), is one of a group of three islands which today speak a creole language, Papiamentu, which although now strongly hispanized because of the proximity of Venezuela, may originally have been a creolized Portuguese. It is not clear whether, or why, the Dutch ships' crews adopted Pidgin Portuguese readily, but the following are possible contributory reasons. Firstly, as members of a small community which lived by maritime trade in a multilingual region of Europe they could not afford to be other than linguistically adaptable. Secondly, the prosperity of Amsterdam had originally been built on salting herrings, the salt for which was brought by Dutch ships from Portugal and supplied not only to the fish trade but to northern Europe generally. Thirdly, as members of a republic which had been (until their Act of Abjuration of 1581) part of the Spanish empire and until a few years earlier occupied by Spanish troops, they were accustomed to dealing with (even if violently hostile to) Iberians. Fourthly, they were the first of the interloping nations to arrive in any numbers, and had direct dealings with the Portuguese both in West Africa and in Brazil.

In the 1580s Dutch smugglers were visiting Brazilian ports; in the next twenty years they extended their activities northwards, to Cuba, Hispaniola, and Trinidad. They found in the Araya lagoon off the coast of Venezuela a salt-pan from which they could replace the supplies of salt from Portugal, interrupted by war. In 1621 the Dutch West India Company was chartered and its warships soon dominated the Caribbean. In addition to Curaçao, Bonaire and Aruba, island bases were established in St. Martin, St. Eustatius and Saba (in what are today the Virgin Islands). In the 1630s and 1640s they established themselves on the Brazilian coast. During this period they became the chief maritime traders of the Caribbean, moving slaves, trade goods and settlers from colony to colony. They pursued the Portuguese not only in the West Indies but, with even greater resources, in the East; they destroyed a powerful Portuguese fleet off Malacca in 1606 (Boxer 1957: 2) and it was eventually the Dutch East India Company which founded the most extensive overseas colony, that of Dutch Indonesia. It is, however, the West Indian trade and settlements which concern us here.

By the time the Dutch West India Company was chartered the Dutch already aimed to supplant the Portuguese as the chief Gold Coast traders. They minted all their coinage with Guinea gold. Dutch merchants estimated that through their factories and agents (many of them Portuguese) in Brazil they had taken over more than half the trade between Brazil and Europe. There were 25 sugar refineries in Amsterdam alone. In 1624 a Dutch expedition of 26 ships and 3,300 men sailed for the conquest of Bahia and established themselves for a time before being dislodged by a joint Spanish-Portuguese armada the next year. In 1628, among other captures at sea, the Dutch commander Piet Heyn captured the Spanish silver fleet from Mexico in a Cuban harbour and took back to the United Provinces such vast treasure (177,000 pounds of silver, 66 pounds of gold, a thousand pearls, 2 million hides, in addition to silk, musk, amber, bezoar and other items) that capital became available for an attack on Pernambuco, the most important centre of sugar production in Brazil. By this time the Dutch were showing considerable determination in their efforts to establish themselves as a major colonizing power along the coasts of South America. (For more detailed accounts see Boxer 1957, 1965; Curtin 1969; Goslinga 1971; Rawley 1981.)

The case of Pernambuco : Dutch against Portuguese. Since the early part of the seventeenth century Pernambuco had been the centre of a very rich sugar industry, sending large quantities of sugar back each year to Lisbon and importing a great deal of luxury goods (wine, cloth etc.) and manufactures of all kinds. It was importing about 4,000 slaves a year from Angola by the 1620s. In 1630 a large Dutch fleet attacked and managed to seize Olinda and Recife, but it was soon bogged down in guerilla warfare outside the towns and a good deal afflicted by disease. Early in 1631 both Dutch and Portuguese received reinforcements, and a tremendous but indecisive sea battle ensued, leaving the situation much as before. The Dutch then withdrew from Olinda and concentrated on sending out expeditions from Recife. By the early part of 1632 they had with them hundreds of slaves who had deserted from the Portuguese, and also a Mulatto, Domingos Fernandes Calabar, who had an intimate knowledge of the country.

More reinforcements came from Holland, and by 1635 the Dutch controlled an extensive stretch of coastline around the 'hump' of Brazil. They captured Paraiba, where a leading Jesuit priest threw in his lot with them, and attacked Porto Calvo under the leadership of Admiral Lichthart, who had lived in Lisbon and spoke good Portuguese. Gradually they extended their hold on the coast and the local planters and townspeople submitted to West India Company rule. The Dutch themselves occupied ruinate plantations. They called their colony New Holland. But the cost of defending it against Portuguese and Spanish guerilla attacks was proving greater than the revenue it brought in to the Company when in 1636 they sent out a fleet under Johan Maurits. He extended and consolidated the colony and sent back glowing reports about it; he sought to bring together Portuguese, Amerindians and Dutch into one homogeneous nation with mutual tolerance. Attempts were made to attract emigrants from Holland. The Dutch had not until now played a major part in West Africa in the slave-trade; their interest in the Gold Coast had been primarily in its gold. Their Negroes in Pernambuco were in the first place those imported by the Portuguese from Angola; but they now found they could not work their own sugar plantations without large numbers of slaves, and in the 1630s they began to increase very considerably their exports of slaves from Elmina. There, in 1637, they first dislodged the Portuguese from their fortress. By this time they controlled half the Portuguese captaincies in Brazil, and were once again casting their eyes on Bahia. One unsuccessful attempt to capture the town, in 1637, was repulsed.

Over the next few years the Portuguese and Spanish combined forces to send a fleet to dislodge the Dutch entirely from Brazil, where conditions in all the towns were by now very bad. The constant warfare at sea and inland between Iberian and Dutch forces and between the settlers of both sides became a running sore to the economy of both. Policies of revenge, of burning plantations and murdering prisoners, led to the countryside being terrorized by bands of deserters, both European and Negro. The split between Spain and Portugal which led to the accession of John IV as king of an independent Portugal created conditions which contributed to a fresh start in diplomacy. The Prince of Orange and leaders of some of the other United Provinces wanted a truce with John IV, and, against the opposition of the merchants of the East and West India Companies, a ten-year truce was signed in 1641. In spite of the truce, on the other side of the Atlantic Maurits continued his campaign to extend the Dutch colony, and moreover sent an expedition to capture the Portuguese slaving ports on the coasts of Angola, the Congo and the Bight of Benin, in order to supply the colony with slaves more amenable than those from the Gold Coast and in far larger numbers. By 1642 Luanda, Benguela, São Tomé, Annobón and the last of the Portuguese Gold Coast forts, at Axim, were in Dutch hands.

The Dutch West India Company. The early 1640s represent the zenith of the Dutch Atlantic empire, with settlements in Guiana, the islands of Curaçao and Aruba off the Venezuelan coast, control over North-Eastern Brazil, New Amsterdam (now New York) and a considerable degree of control over the slave coasts of West Africa. The Dutch West India

Company regarded Brazil as its most important possession, and in Johan Maurits it had a remarkable Governor General there. After his departure in 1644 the fortunes of the Company declined. Nevertheless, his short period of government in Pernambuco is of considerable importance from our point of view.

In the first place, he sought to encourage good race relations and good relations between the various Christian denominations in Brazil. The eventual failure of the Dutch to colonize Brazil was due to their failure to attract in sufficient numbers immigrants from northern Europe as settlers; Maurits's vision of these co-existing on the land with the Portuguese, intermarrying and producing a new Brazilian race did not come to very much, but a number of Dutch mercenaries (among whom were many English, Scots and French) did marry local women, and a number became converts to Roman Catholicism. The rebellion of 1645 brought this close association to an end.

In the second place, under his protection sugar production methods were greatly improved, with the encouragement of Portuguese and Portuguese-Jewish factors, and Dutch slave suppliers introduced these improved methods to the planters in Barbados, to whom they wished to sell the slaves which a change in the crop from tobacco to sugar would necessitate. Barbadian planters went to Pernambuco to study the sugar processes and the trade at first hand. New Holland became notable in other ways as a cultural and scientific centre, and its existence encouraged the French and British to increase their efforts to colonize in the tropical sugar-belt.

Thirdly, the development of sugar in Pernambuco brought the Dutch into the slave-trade in a big way, and led to them establishing slave depots in Curaçao and St. Eustatius from which, as we have noted, they for a time supplied the colonies of all the European nations. The importance of the Dutch slave depots as centres of the linguistic dispersion of varieties of English and Dutch has been dealt with by Williams (1983a, b) – see below, pp. 35, 41. Their slaves came predominantly from Angola and the Congo, and were Bantu-speaking, whereas later on in the West Indian islands slaves were in theory linguistically mixed on the plantations to lessen the risk of revolts being plotted in African languages which the overseers could not understand. In Brazil, however, linguistic homogeneity seems to have been valued as it enabled the older generations of slaves to teach the new arrivals. Perhaps the medium of instruction was in any case Creole Portuguese. The slaves known as 'Ardras' (from the place of shipping them) were less valued; they worked harder than the Bantu, but were less amenable. Slaves from Sierra Leone and Cape Verde, particularly women, were valued as domestics. During the years of unrest in Pernambuco before 1641 many slaves escaped to the bush or were given their freedom, and formed agricultural settlements. However, it is relevant for our purposes that just at the time when the Dutch were persuading Barbadian planters to turn over to sugar, and were building up their slave depot in Curaçao to supply the British and French Antilles, they were also entrenching themselves on, and increasing their slave exports from, the Gold Coast.

In all this story the Jewish merchants played an important role. As already noted, they were said to have captured the Iberian trade everywhere from Mexico to Peru. In 1644, out of a total white population (excluding servants of the Dutch West India Company) in Pernambuco of 3,000, 1,450 were said to be Jews. They were said to monopolize business because they were good linguists. According to Boxer, relatively few of the Dutch learnt to speak Portuguese fluently; virtually none of the Christian Portuguese learned Dutch. Later, in Surinam, we find a variety of Creole being called 'Jew-language' (*Dju-tongo*; see Voorhoeve 1973). It must, however, be remembered that after the forcible conversion to Roman Catholicism of Portuguese (and refugee Spanish) Jews in 1497, and the subsequent high rate of assimilation of their descendants into the general population of Portugal, many writers tended to regard all Portuguese as Jews (see Boxer 1969: 266).

The Dutch as agents for the spread of Portuguese and English Creoles. Whether or not the Dutch themselves used and spread some knowledge of Portuguese or of Portuguese Creole, they were the agency through which the Portuguese and Portuguese-Jewish trading network spread into the Caribbean in the first half of the seventeenth century; through which also sugar planting spread throughout the Caribbean islands. They supplied the slaves, the equipment and the know-how, advanced the capital and bought the crop. By this time they had had many years of very intimate dealings with the Portuguese. Dampier, who visited Curaçao in 1681, published the following account:

Querisao is the only Island of Importance that the *Dutch* have in the *West Indies*...it is a very secure port for ships, either to careen, or lye safe. At the East end are two Hills...The rest of the Island is indifferent level; where of late some rich Men have made Sugar-works; which formerly was all Pasture for Cattle: there are also some small Plantations of Potatoes and Yams, and they have still a great many Cattle on the Island; but it is not so much esteemed for its produce, as for its Situation for the Trade with the *Spaniard*. Formerly the Harbour was never without Ships from *Cartagene* and *Portabell*, that did use to

buy of the *Dutch* 1000 or 1500 Negroes at once, besides great quantities of
European Commodities; but of late that Trade is fallen into the Hands of the
English at *Jamaica*: yet still the *Dutch* have a vast Trade over all the *West-Indies*,
sending from *Holland* Ships of good force laden with *European* Goods, whereby
they make very profitable returns.   (Dampier 1697, ed. Penzer 1927: 40–1)

In a recent paper Williams (1983a) presents arguments to offset those
of Goodman ('The Portuguese influence in the New World Creoles')
given at the same 1982 Society for Caribbean Linguistics conference.
Goodman had emphasized the role of Dutch and Jewish refugees from
Brazil in spreading Portuguese Creole influences in the Caribbean, in
particular the Dutch Creole of the Virgin Islands which was, he claimed,
taken there by Dutch colonists from St. Eustatius and St. Martin.
Williams, on the other hand, emphasizes the early and sustained influence
of English in St. Eustatius and Saba:

By all accounts, a multilingual situation existed on St. Eustatius in the seventeenth
and eighteenth centuries...The English influence on the early histories of the
Windward Netherlands Antilles has been previously underestimated...Evidence
presented in this paper suggests that St. Eustatius served as a distribution point
for Guinea Coast Creole English in the West Indies.

The two points of view are not, however, necessarily contradictory; both
processes may have taken place. Our knowledge of the precise extent and
nature of inter-Caribbean trade and migration during the seventeenth
century – particularly in view of the large amounts of contraband trade and
covert migration – is not yet sufficiently detailed or accurate.

3. Disputed settlements and their outcome

British interests in Barbados and the Leeward Islands

The Guiana coast was explored initially in search of the fabled El Dorado
in the interior; it was an inhospitable coast and early attempts to colonize
it failed. There were, however, French settlements on the coast by 1613,
and Dutch settlements on the Essequibo River by 1616 and on the Berbice
River by 1624. The survivors of English attempts to colonize Guiana and
parts of Central America returned to try their luck in the Caribbean
islands. By contrast, in 1605, 'sixty-seven Englishmen en route to the
Guianas put ashore at Vieux Fort Bay [in St. Lucia] and formed a
settlement of huts purchased from the Caribs'. They were mostly
slaughtered by the Caribs; 19 survivors left for Venezuela (Jesse 1966).
These men had already made a landing in Barbados and had claimed it
for King James, although by that time both Barbados and Trinidad had

been known to the Spaniards for over 100 years. As we shall see later, the attempted settlement of the Windward Islands in the seventeenth century was generally delayed by the fierceness of the Carib Indians, but in the Leewards and Barbados settlements were made in the 1620s and the scene was set for the English and the French to dispute possession of the Antilles for the next 180 years, both as sugar colonies and as naval bases of great value. By this time the French and the English were beginning also to establish their colonies in North America. To supply all the consequent plantations, they were forced to develop their own supplies of slaves from the West African coast, which thus similarly became an area of dispute (Rawley 1981: Chs 5–7).

The starting point : St. Kitts. The dispute was scarcely evident in the early history of St. Kitts (St. Christopher) in the Leeward Islands (referred to by Burns (1954: 187) as 'The Mother Colony of the West Indies'). To begin with French and English settled amicably there, without slaves, side by side. On the English side, the island was first settled in 1624 by Thomas Warner, son of a Suffolk gentleman farmer, who had previously spent nearly two years in Guiana; he took his wife and eldest son and a few settlers he had recruited on the way in Virginia. The island was inhabited at the time by Caribs, and by three Frenchmen; after some individual tensions the Europeans all settled together to plant tobacco. Reinforcements came from England the following year. Various disasters overtook the island, including a large Carib raid from other islands and the inevitable hurricanes, but French and English continued to make common cause, and settlers continued to come in small numbers not only to St. Kitts but also to the neighbouring island of Nevis.

The Carib population was virtually eliminated in a massacre, after which there was a fairly rapid increase in the number of settlers, so that by 1629 there were about 3,000 from Britain or North America alone. This number was, however, greatly reduced by a Spanish attempt in that year to clear the settlers out. Nevertheless the colony prospered on tobacco planting, extending to the neighbouring islands of Nevis and Montserrat and attracting many more settlers, especially British.

Early settlements on Barbados and the mainland coast and offshore islands. Barbados had been claimed for the King of England not only by the crew of the *Oliph Blossom* in 1605, but also by John Powell, the captain of a ship returning from Brazil to England in 1625, though again without settlement. His brother, Henry Powell, went back with a party of about 80 men in 1627 in a ship belonging to the Anglo-Dutch firm, Courteen Brothers. The ship sailed on to the Dutch settlement on the Essequibo and returned to Barbados with tobacco, cassava roots and the seeds of other crops, together with a group of about 30 Arawak Indians to teach the settlers how to plant. Courteen Brothers sent out more men, and by 1628 there were nearly 1,600 people in the island. As in St. Kitts and Nevis, at first tobacco was the cash crop grown. The island became the object of a disputed claim between the younger John Powell (Henry's nephew) and Courteen Brothers on the one hand and a Governor sent out by the Earl of Carlisle with 80 settlers in 1628. The following year Henry Powell brought a ship with more settlers and arrested and took back to England many of Carlisle's men. The consequent legalities were decided by the King in favour of Carlisle.

Meanwhile other settlements were being made. In 1629 a Puritan colony settled on the island which is today known as Providencia, off the coast of Nicaragua. A privateering crew had already been put ashore to garrison its neighbour, now San Andrés, and Providence Island was known also to Dutch ships which used it as a base or for watering. The colony degenerated into a pirate base and an entrepôt where Dutch ships called to buy cargoes (including slaves) seized from the Spaniards. By 1635 the town of the island, New Westminster, contained about thirty wooden houses and a brick church (Burns 1954: 207); it was defended by about 40 guns in batteries, and had a population of about 500 Englishmen, a few Dutch, about 40 European women and children and about 90 Negro slaves. Some of the slaves had come from another pirate base, Tortuga, off the coast of Hispaniola, when the English re-occupied that island after the Spaniards broke up their settlement there in 1634. The Providence Company formed a subsidiary to develop trade with the Miskito Indians along the mainland coast, a venture joined by a Dutch sailor called Blauvelt (or Blewfield) who is commemorated in the names Bluefields Bay and Bluefields Town. When the English were finally driven out of Providence Island by the Spaniards in 1641 those who escaped went to the Miskito Coast, some going on later to Roatan, one of the Bay Islands in the Gulf of Honduras; others to Tobago and St. Kitts. The Spaniards captured 600 slaves. Today after a long period of being ruled from various Spanish-speaking countries (now from Colombia) a Creole English is still spoken in Providencia and San Andrés very similar to that of various pockets of Creole English settlements all along the mainland coast, including Belize. Thus it is reasonable to consider Barbados, Guiana, the coastal islands and the mainland coast of Central America as the scene of a joint Anglo-Dutch seaborne culture of the 1630s, touching and harassing the fringes of the

Portuguese and Spanish mainland empires and carrying Negro slaves with them as they moved westwards. The case of the Miskito Coast illustrates the importance to general Caribbean developments of early settlements on the mainland coast of Central America and its offshore islands.

The origins of Miskito Coast Creole have been explored in some detail by John Holm (1982a). He shows that the Providence settlers established good relations with the Miskito Indians and especially with their women-folk, and that this close relationship of Indians and British continued after the Providence Company established settlements on the Miskito Coast itself. Of the Pidgin English which developed among the Indians alongside that Miskito Coast Creole which was the product of contact between this Anglo-Dutch-African westward sweep and the Indians, Holm comments (pp. 23–4):

> Historically – and possibly linguistically – the importance of this Miskito Coast Pidgin (MCP) can scarcely be overemphasized: it is likely to have been one of the first pidginized varieties of English to become established anywhere ...either in the Caribbean or West Africa...MCP is unique in its survival as the simplified English spoken as a second language by the Miskito people today.

Holm finds Miskito Coast Pidgin immediately distinguishable in phonology and syntax from the Creole.

The British interests continued to be developed most rapidly in Barbados (Le Page 1960). Lacking any indigenous Indians, or forbidding mountains; having a climate tempered by Atlantic breezes, an excellent supply of water beneath the coral rock, the rock itself as a building material, and a fertile soil, Barbados rapidly increased its population, aided by great poverty in parts of Britain, especially Ireland, and by Cromwell's habit of sending into exile any political prisoners (and particularly Irish prisoners) he needed to get rid of. He was described by a contemporary as 'very apt to "*barbadoes*" an unruly man, – has sent and sends us by hundreds to Barbadoes, so that we have made an active verb of it...' Writing from Dublin in 1644 Cromwell himself described his treatment of his Irish prisoners thus: 'When they submitted, their officers were knocked on the head; and every tenth man of the soldiers killed; and the rest shipped for the Barbadoes. The soldiers in the other Tower were all spared, as to their lives only; and shipped likewise for the Barbadoes.' After the Battle of Worcester in 1651 a great many Scottish prisoners were transported.

The gaols of England were regularly emptied to provide indentured labourers and servants for the American plantations, including the West Indies. In addition, the ports of London and Bristol supplied indentured servants, men and women, of whom some at least were tricked aboard outward-bound ships and some were running away. Ligon (1647) speaks of the prostitutes and other women from Bridewell prison and Turnball stew in London who were on board his ship to Barbados and who had been consigned thither; the passengers took some of these women ashore in the Cape Verde Islands to wash their clothes for them. Niles (1980) has made a study of the provenance of these poor Whites and white servants in Barbados, linking their origins to the evident influence of English dialectal morphology and lexis on Bajan. Although every part of Britain was represented among them, the labouring classes and the poor of London and its purlieus, and, even more, of Bristol, Somerset and the south-western counties generally, evidently predominated.

Meanwhile, the French were also busy planting colonies, extending their presence both in the Antilles and taking over from the buccaneers what became their large colony of Saint Domingue (Haiti) on the island of Hispaniola. Negro slaves were by this time being brought to St. Kitts and Nevis, and both French and English tried to enlarge their respective shares of the islands. The French Compagnie des Iles d'Amérique was established in 1635, to be responsible for French colonies in the Antilles; de Poincy was sent out as Captain-General of St. Kitts and Lieutenant-General for all the French American islands. In 1635 the French had colonized both Martinique and Guadeloupe, the Martinique settlers coming from St. Kitts; and the company's colonies were then extended to Grenada and St. Lucia in the Windwards and to some of the small islands north of St. Kitts. It was some time before either Grenada or St. Lucia had secure colonies. Guadeloupe and Martinique on the other hand, two of the largest islands in the Lesser Antilles, have remained and grown as prime centres of French, and of Creole French, influence in the region. In 1660 de Poincy made a treaty with the Caribs promising that they would be left undisturbed in St. Vincent and Dominica if they left the French unmolested in the other islands.

Immigrants to and emigrants from Barbados. The build-up of the white population of Barbados was quite rapid, and for nearly twenty years kept pace with the increase in Negro slaves, whose importation on a large scale was made necessary in the 1640s by the switch to sugar. The relative size of this white population, its provenance, and the fact that it was to a large extent a population of field labourers and artisans, are important factors linguistically. So also is the historical fact of continuing high population density on, and consequent endemic emigration from, a small flat and fertile sugar-island, contributing powerfully to the *focussing* of 'Bajan', and its convergence with standard varieties of English on the one hand, and the export of 'Bajan' influence around the Eastern Caribbean on the other.

In his study of the population of Barbados Lowenthal (1957) divides the island's demographic history into five periods, the first being one of rapid growth up until the 1680s. Men of all ranks flocked to Barbados from Britain and Ireland to plant tobacco and cotton; but with the switch to sugar the smallholders among them were squeezed out by the rich, and after 1650 the white population declined steadily both proportionately and in absolute numbers:

> 1642   37,200 Whites
> 1650   c. 50,000 (the figure claimed by Ligon for 1647)
> 1684   23,624
> 1851   15,824
> 1951   less than 10,000

The period up to 1650 was the formative one for Bajan ways of speaking.

Between 1650 and 1690 there was a major exodus of Whites, mostly 'small planters and yeomen' and indentured servants; they went to New England, Virginia and Carolina, to Jamaica (see Le Page 1960), to the Windwards (including the French islands), to Surinam and Curaçao and Bermuda. (Dunn, 1973: 111, lists the destinations of 593 who were granted tickets to leave in 1679.) Later, when Negro slaves so greatly outnumbered Whites as to constitute a threat, attempts were made in Barbados, as elsewhere, to attract more white settlers. In the eighteenth century the population as a whole was relatively static despite large annual importations of slaves; in the years 1712–62 slave deaths exceeded births by 120,000. In the nineteenth century, after the abolition of the slave-trade, and then of slavery in the island, the black population began to increase sharply; this was mainly through natural increase, although Barbados received some share of the freed Africans captured from the continuing slave-trade of other nations and, like other islands, experimented with indentured labour from Malta, Madeira and the Azores, China and India. From the beginning of the present century, with the recruitment of labourers both for work in St. Lucia (see below) and – on a much larger scale – to dig the Panama Canal, the male black population declined again. The decline continued after 1914 through emigration to North America, and the departure of so many young males also led to a decline in the birthrate at home. In the interwar years opportunities for emigration were greatly reduced and population pressure increased. During the 1950s and

1960s there was again considerable emigration, mostly to England in response to recruiting campaigns on behalf of, for example, London Transport; but this outlet was closed in the 1970s. Barbados has therefore been a labour exporting island since 1650; it has also exported (as we shall see when we consider the Windwards) schoolmasters and administrators in sufficient numbers to have had an appreciable affect on the English dialects of other islands in the Eastern Caribbean.

The case of Bajan. Although the Barbadian English vernacular shares a number of features with other, broad creole, varieties of English, it is much closer to British English in its grammar, and contains far fewer Africanisms (as the second edition of *DJE* reveals) than does, for example, Jamaican or Belizean or Guyanese Creole. Moreover, it contains some features of pronunciation and grammar which are closely associated with the West of England and Ireland. Bristol was the chief port for Barbados; white indentured servants embarking (or being tricked aboard) there came mainly from the surrounding counties (Le Page 1960: 12). Ligon speaks of loading donkeys to carry sugar across the steep Barbadian gulleys after the Devonshire fashion 'for there we learnt it'. Among the texts in Chapter 3 we have transcribed and translated a Bajan story by a Barbadian raconteur, the late Mr Joseph Tudor, giving his impression of a court case in which the plaintiff sued him because Mr Tudor's dog had rushed out and bitten him. Those familiar with West of England dialects will have no difficulty in recognizing some characteristic features in Mr Tudor's speech. There remain today in Barbados communities of so-called 'Red legs', or 'poor Whites' – the descendants of white indentured servants who have kept themselves comparatively aloof from the black and coloured population. Williams's study of White Saban English (1983b) allows us to compare in this respect the two islands and others with similar histories:

Study of the social and demographic history of early white indenturement in the Lesser Antilles indicates that periods of sociolinguistic history should be differentiated. In the early period, prior to 1660, indentured white servants were in the numerical majority and those African slaves imported during this time were learning English as a second language, modeled on the regional English dialects spoken by the white population. Modern descendants of the original indentured population are still found in Saba as well as other scattered, isolated areas of the Caribbean.
(Williams 1983b: abstract)

The question has been asked as to whether or not one or other variety of pidgin or creole usage is to be seen as the common progenitor of Bajan as of, for example, the Creoles of St. Kitts, of Providencia and San Andrés, of Jamaica, of Belize, of the Afro-Seminoles of Brackettville, and so on. We hope to show in Chapter 5 that this is not a very profitable question to ask and that it derives from a misunderstanding of the stereotypical genetic metaphor commonly applied to languages, so that, for example and as we have already noted, French, Spanish, Portuguese and Italian are all misleadingly said to derive from one 'parent language', some variety of Latin. There can be little doubt that among the earliest shipments of slaves to Barbados were some, in Dutch ships, who had spent some time in a Portuguese Creole-speaking environment, either on the African coast, or in Brazil, or in Curaçao. (In 1643 a Dutch captain even offered 50 Portuguese, prisoners from Brazil, as slaves in Bridgetown, though the Governor of Barbados set them free.) Ligon, describing his voyage to Barbados in 1647, tells how his ship's captain was supposed to buy slaves for Barbados in the Cape Verde Islands *en route*. Ashore in these islands it seemed to Ligon that the governing class spoke Spanish, but he used Portuguese to try to converse with the free Negro girls whom he found so attractive drawing water from the well (p. 16). Later (p. 52) he refers to some of the Barbadian Negroes 'who have been bred up amongst the *Portugalls*' as having some extraordinary talents in singing and fencing.

It was not until the 1640s that the switch from cotton and tobacco and other smallholder crops to sugar took place on a large scale. At the beginning of that decade the population of Barbados was about 35,000, of whom white field labourers, small peasant farmers, artisans and white servants were still very much in the majority. When Ligon arrived in 1647 sugar making was new there; by the time he left in 1650 it was much better established. Looking forward to our general hypotheses in Chapter 5 about the factors governing the way in which individuals create their linguistic systems, and the way in which communities in close daily interaction identify themselves linguistically, we see that Negro slaves entering the Barbadian community in the 1640s had ample daily access to the vernacular of the island as spoken by a labour force of predominantly West of England, Irish and lower-class London provenance; it was not until the 1650s that the tide of slavery began to assume the proportions of a flood. By this time the characteristic features of Bajan usage were probably well established and recognized, just as the characteristic features of Mauritian Creole French have been shown to have been formed within 50 years of the first continuous settlement of the island (Baker, in Baker and Corne 1982: 248).

Ligon wrote that in 1647 the population of Barbados was not less than 50,000 in addition to the Negroes; the island was able to muster a militia of 10,000 foot and 1,000 horse soldiers. A little later, however, he claims

that there are twice as many Negroes as 'Christians' in the island; 'they
are fetch'd from several parts of *Africa*, who speak severall languages, and
by that means, one of them understands not another: For, some of them
are fetch'd from *Guinny* and *Binny*, some from *Cutchew*, some from
Angola, and some from the River of *Gambra*' (p. 46). Curtin (1969) seems
to have missed this statement, which, numerically, is very much out of line
with his own estimates.

Drawing on various sources Curtin has estimated that annual slave
imports into Barbados increased from about 1,300 to about 2,100 after
1645; that the slave population of Barbados in 1645 was only 6,000,
whereas 10 years later it was 20,000 and by 1668 40,000. Thereafter it seems
to have increased more slowly throughout the eighteenth and into the
nineteenth century, before slavery was finally abolished. But by the
beginning of the nineteenth century slaves so outnumbered Whites as to
make the latter very harsh in their insecurity; and the general slave uprising
of 1804 was only put down after 1,000 slaves had been killed. 'Thus' says
Harlow (1926: 327) 'the transformation was complete. A populous British
colony had become a settlement of African negroes, ruled by a small band
of European overseers, nervous for their safety.' Rebellions were indeed
endemic in all the Caribbean colonies, as were the attempts of runaway
slaves to form Maroon settlements which, where successful, became
centres for the conservation of both language and culture. The most serious
slave rebellion in Barbados was Bussa's rebellion of 1816; this and others
have been chronicled for the whole British West Indies by Craton (1982).

Patterns of the slave-trade. We know very little about the pattern of the
Dutch slave-trade to Barbados, how many ships came direct from Africa,
how many from Curaçao or St. Eustatius, how many from Brazil (but cf.
Rawley 1981: chapter 4). As Goslinga comments:

The regularly quoted numbers of imported slaves does not include the many
blacks clandestinely introduced into the area by English, French, and Dutch slave
traders. That this illicit traffic was increasing and perhaps assuming even vaster
proportions than was the legal trade is suggested by the fact that in 1678 the
Governor of Puerto Rico appointed a special official to put a stop to the
contraband in slaves between Jamaica, Curaçao, and his own island

(1971: 340).

It seems likely that a high proportion of the Barbadian slaves in the 1630s
were from Angola, but that as Dutch control on the Gold Coast tightened,
more Gold Coast slaves may have been supplied in the 1640s and 1650s
(these being preferred by British planters). In either case, Barbados is, of

those we are concerned with, the island whose earliest slaves are those most likely to have had close contact with Creole Portuguese in slave depots. There is no evidence that the linguistic influence of that contact was of any great importance in the formation of Bajan usage. It is also probable that contacts were close between Barbados and the Providence and Miskito Coast settlements mentioned above, and that some early settlers (both black and white) in Barbados came from those settlements.

As to the provenance of the slaves, again a perhaps critical date or series of dates separates the Barbadian from the Jamaican story. These dates are those of various attempts by successive British merchant venturers, sometimes with a royal interest, to secure the monopoly of the supply of slaves to British colonies. (The history of these, and particularly of the Royal African Company, is given in Davies 1957.) The first company to receive a monopoly licence, The Governor and Company of Adventurers of London Trading to Gynney and Bynney, was formed in 1618; it set up a permanent base on the Gold Coast in 1631. Among the ethnic stereotypes commonly accepted in the British slave-trade and plantation colonies was one that Gold Coast slaves, or Cormantins (Kormantyn, Kromantin, Kromanti and other spellings), were superior in strength and character to those of other nations, more liable to rebel and run away if badly treated, but hardworking, loyal and courageous if well treated. The British monopoly was difficult to enforce in the face of competition both from the well-established Dutch and the many private traders or interlopers. Until the Barbadian sugar expansion began in the 1640s their slaves had been supplied almost entirely by the Dutch. The Dutch did not yield quietly a market which they themselves had developed; nor during the civil disturbances in England were the English monopoly holders able to secure much support to enforce their claims. However, the companies chartered in England after the Restoration (in 1662 and 1663 The Royal Adventurers in Africa, and in 1672 its successor The Royal African Company) fared rather better, at least until about 1690, when the Charter was recognized to be partially defective.

By the time Jamaica was colonized by the British (in 1655) the tide of slavery from Africa was well under way; the linguistic outcome in Jamaica is clearly distinguishable from that in Barbados, and the demography of a community in its formative years is thus clearly an important factor in determining such an outcome. It may be that it is more misleading than helpful to speak of a Creole English in Barbados; although Bajan certainly deserves the term in the sense of being 'locally-born', it does not seem that any prior Pidgin had anything more than a minor role in forming the way Barbadians developed their local English dialect. It has, however, been argued that Bajan does preserve a number of features similar to those of other Caribbean Creoles (Burrowes 1983).

The case of Jamaica

Aspects of the settlement history. The settlement history of Jamaica has been told in *Jamaican Creole* (Le Page 1960). The expeditionary force which sailed under General Venables in 1655 contained, according to his own account (see Bibliography), 2,500 men raised from various regiments and from the streets and gaols of England, and 1,200 seamen; also 1,851 horse and foot volunteers from St. Kitts, Nevis and Montserrat. Thus about one-third of the total force had been raised in the Leewards and Barbados. It is probable that a high proportion of these were men from the West of England or from Ireland, with some Scots: men whose indentures or sentences had run out and who were landless. About 1,000 of the force were lost in the fruitless attack on Hispaniola, the capture of which had been the original object of the expedition; the remainder reached Jamaica. There the Spanish colonists and their Negro slaves fled to the hills, and for the most part the survivors subsequently made their way to Cuba; they left behind them fewer than 40 Spaniards and a few hundred Negroes, most of whom (about 250) were in three isolated Maroon settlements in the interior. Some Portuguese settlers and Portuguese-Jewish merchants may possibly have submitted to the English forces and stayed in the island, but they could not have been very many.

The indigenous Arawak Indians of Jamaica had all been killed or had died some years before the English invasion. Their few legacies to modern Jamaica, transmitted via the Spaniards, are some place-names, a few rock-carvings and a number of middens. We have at present no means of knowing where the Negro slaves who replaced them under the Spanish came from. As has already been noted, the Spanish colonies did not at this time normally import slaves in their own ships, but were supplied by the Portuguese. The Spaniards in their turn left behind them place-names, their small towns such as their capital of Santiago de la Vega (modern Spanish Town), the abandoned north coast harbour of Sevilla la Nueva (St. Ann's Bay), Las Chorreras (Ocho Rios) where the Spanish defender Yssassi was finally defeated; and their *hatos* or grazing lands and arable farms. What language the Maroon Negroes in the mountains used among themselves we do not know, but it is quite possible that they had some knowledge of Portuguese Creole, and among those very few modern Maroon words which we have identified as having a special provenance, *bracho* 'pig' seems to be from Portuguese via the Gold Coast (see Chapter 1). Otherwise one must assume that they spoke their African languages and some form of Spanish. But the small Spanish element in the modern Jamaican vocabulary is most frequently due to migrant workers returned e.g. from Panama or Cuba or the Spanish-speaking areas of Belize or from Costa Rica within the present century.

Within a few weeks of their arrival about half of the British expeditionary force in Jamaica were sick. The high mortality rate from tropical diseases (Dunn 1973: Ch. 9) and personal excesses was one of the constant factors in the demography of the Caribbean until very recently; it affected Blacks and Whites – the excesses affecting the Blacks, however, being mainly those of white behaviour towards them.

At the end of 1655, 780 fresh soldiers came out from England. The next year 1,000 settlers and their slaves came from Nevis to plant lands assigned to them at Port Morant, under a guard of Scottish and Irish soldiers. By 1658, according to the Jamaican historian Edward Long, the population was about 4,500 Whites and 1,400 Negroes. In 1660 it was decided to encourage men from all the other Caribbean islands to move to Jamaica to take up land; women were to be sent out from England as planters' wives; King Charles was to contract with the African Company to deliver 100 Negroes. An Act of Parliament of 1661 required the arrest of Gypsies for shipment to Virginia, Jamaica and Barbados, and there is evidence that many were so deported over the next half-century (Hancock 1980b, 1982).

Inter-island movement. The movement of men around the various colonies at this period is worth noting, as are many of the other implications of this quotation from a petition to King Charles from the Barbadians in 1667:

[The island contains] not above 760 considerable proprietors and 8,000 effective men, of which two-thirds are of no reputation and little courage, and a very great part Irish, derided by the negroes as white slaves; and indeed except the proprietors, merchants, tradesmen, officers, and their dependants, the rest are such as have not reason to discern their abuses, or not courage to leave the island, or are in debt and cannot go; for 12,000 good men at least formerly proprietors are gone off, and tradesmen, wormed out of their small settlements by greedy neighbours, are thus computed: – Between 1643 and 1647, to New England, 1,200; to Trinidado and Tobago, 600; between 1646 and 1658, to Virginia and Surinam, 2,400; between 1650 and 1662, to Guadaloupe, Martinique, Mariegalante, Grenada, Tobago, and Curaçao, 1,600; with Col. Venables to Hispaniola and since to Jamaica, 3,300 ... Of men born on the island few are gone off ...   (CSP Col. 1661–8, No. 1657)

In Jamaica by 1673, according to Long (1774), the white population was 8,564; the slave population for the same year has been estimated (see Curtin

1969: table 14) at 9,500. By 1746 there were approximately 10,000 Whites and 112,000 slaves. The low ratio of Whites to slaves was so alarming to the Jamaican House of Assembly that it regularly passed Deficiency Acts, fining those planters who failed to keep a due proportion of white servants so as to meet the costs of extra soldiers as guards against slave rebellions.

The provenance of the black population of Jamaica. In Le Page (1960) an attempt was made to establish the provenance of the slaves brought to Jamaica. It was not possible to do so with any exactness. Nevertheless it is clear that slaves from the Gold Coast could never have made up more than one-quarter of the annual total, and that during the second half of the eighteenth century, when the total trade was more than treble what it had been 100 years earlier, the vast majority of the slaves were coming from the Bight of Benin, Bonny, the Calabars and Angola. In the middle of the nineteenth century, when a number of West Africans freed from supposedly 'illegal' slave-ships by the Royal Navy were recruited as indentured servants in both Jamaica and the Eastern Caribbean, the largest single number of any one language community seems to have been Yoruba speakers. In spite of these facts, the largest number of Africanisms recorded in *DJE* are from the Akan (Gold Coast) languages, especially from Twi, and Ewe. There is an appreciable number of Bantuisms, most readily identified through the Kongo forms (see *DJE* 1980).

In view of very early contacts between Surinam and Jamaica it is significant, as Hancock (personal communication) has pointed out, that the Africanisms in the Saramaccan (Bush Negro, or Maroon) language of Surinam are also 'overwhelmingly from Ewe and Kongo'. It is quite possible also that planters and slaves who left Surinam for Jamaica in 1675 (the former territory was ceded to the Dutch in 1667) and who took up land at what became known as Surinam Quarters in Jamaica (Le Page 1960: 17) brought with them many Portuguese words in their Creole; many are preserved in Saramaccan.

Cultural and linguistic focussing in Barbados and Jamaica. Today the identity 'West Indian' certainly means something both to West Indians from the former British colonies and to people in Britain among whom many of them have settled, in terms of shared physical, cultural and linguistic characteristics. Nevertheless, among West Indians a Jamaican is distinguished from a Trinidadian or a Barbadian by cultural and linguistic differences, and each territory has its stereotypes about the inhabitants of each of the others. When one considers the common origins of so many of these physical, cultural and linguistic characteristics the differentiation which has taken place in the course of 300 years is remarkable, and the reasons for it are of great interest. We may say that each island has 'focussed' differently. If we now compare Barbados with Jamaica we can already see three important contributory factors at work. First, there is the fact that for a period of twenty years Barbados developed with a predominance of West of England men and Irishmen among its Whites, comparatively few slaves, and a close working relationship between labouring Whites and slaves. Jamaica, on the other hand, found its white population – of similar provenance – swamped within ten years by large numbers of slaves, and no such close working relationship developed, the Whites to a large extent dying or withdrawing from field labour. Secondly, Barbados is small and comparatively level; although internal communications were poor there were never any estates so remote from one another or from a town as in the riverine valleys of Jamaica, cut off from one another by mountain ridges. In 1647 Ligon said it was advantageous to have an estate near the sea in Barbados because then you could unload perishables from a ship and store them all in the space of a night, whereas if you lived inland the night would not suffice. In the early nineteenth century it took 'Monk' Lewis five days to travel from one of his estates in Jamaica to another at the far end of the island (Lewis 1834). Jamaica, because of its terrain, was more likely than Barbados to contain centres of linguistic conservatism.

Thirdly, planters on the whole did not like to educate slaves; as Ligon explains, schooling tended to lead towards Christianity; it was widely believed that a Christian could not be made a slave and therefore planters were reluctant to help slaves become Christians. But for 'free people of colour' it was a different matter; it was the children of mixed African/ European unions who formed the backbone of the 'creole middle class', who identified most strongly with their native island and who also received at least rudimentary education, very often becoming tradesmen, craftsmen, and urban merchants. Their survival rate was generally higher than that of any other class, and they became a well-established and numerous class quite early on in Barbados.

Finally, the evidence of the Twi and Ewe words in Jamaica points to the dominance of Gold Coast slaves both culturally and as linguistic models in the formative stages of Jamaican Creole, and in the transmission of oral culture via folk-stories in Jamaica – with the Maroons perhaps playing a particularly significant role here (Le Page 1960: Ch. 7).

One can therefore understand both the greater homogeneity of Bajan than of Jamaican Creole and its closer similarity to a particular regional variety of British English. Moreover, Barbadians have always taken pride in their level of education. In contrast, one can understand the extreme conservatism of the varieties of Jamaican Creole preserved on remote plantations, in mountain villages and in the Maroon settlements, and the extent to which the latter in particular, and the island population as a whole, have preserved identifiable African elements both in their culture and in their language. These geographical and demographic considerations will be seen to be important when we examine the dialects of the other territories, as will also the colonizing activities of the Barbadians and the Jamaicans themselves.

French interests in the Windward Islands

Whereas Barbados, Jamaica and most of the Leeward Islands have had a continuous history of African and English-speaking settlement since the seventeenth century, the Windwards, as we have already noted, were the focus of French colonization with African slaves in the seventeenth century. They were disputed prizes of war between France and Britain, changing hands many times over until the end of the eighteenth century. Moreover the Carib Indians, natives of these islands, resisted European colonization far more vigorously and successfully than the more northerly Arawaks (whom they themselves had often dispossessed, enslaved or eaten). Each of the Windwards and Trinidad have at one time shared with Haiti in the north and French Guiana (Guyane) on the South American mainland a French Creole 'Patois'; shared not only in the sense of similarity of provenance and of linguistic structure but also by reason of inter-territorial migrations of both planters and slaves, and family visiting. Today a variety of Patois (or Kwéyol) remains the first language of most of the population of Haiti, as also of the population of Guadeloupe, Martinique, Marie-Galante and Guyane which are now Departments of metropolitan France and use French for all official purposes and for education. It is also the first language for a large proportion of the population of Dominica (Christie 1969) and St. Lucia (Carrington 1967). It is only a part of the distant past in St. Vincent (Shephard 1831), and of the more recent past in Grenada and Trinidad (where there are still some French Creole speakers to be found among the older generation). In these islands, in the Grenadines, and in Dominica and St. Lucia, English has been the official language and the language of education since the beginning of the nineteenth century.

The case of Haiti (St. Domingue). Haiti is an Arawak (Taino) name applied now to the western third of the island which Columbus named La Isla

Española, later Hispaniola; as St. Domingue it was ceded by Spain to France in 1697, since French settlers (originally those driven out of St. Kitts by the Spaniards in 1627) had already established themselves there. Its gold (some of which the natives gave to Columbus on his first voyage) and the docility of the Arawak Indian inhabitants, made it a prized colony, whose value was subsequently increased by sugar and coffee cultivation. Its comparative proximity to the Gulf of Mexico provided it with a link with French settlements in Louisiana which began in 1698; and it was a prosperous and powerful base for the French colonization of the Windwards in the eighteenth century. As a large and important sugar colony during the eighteenth century its African slave population greatly outnumbered the free people of colour and the Whites, and its mountainous terrain provided, as in Jamaica, pockets of linguistic conservatism.

The French Revolution affected all the colonies of the European powers, leading to demands for political equality and freedom, but the inevitable differences of economic and political interests between planters, 'petits blancs', free people of colour and slaves led to rioting and bloodshed in both St. Domingue and the Windward Islands. According to the 1788 Census, the population of St. Domingue in that year consisted of 28,000 Whites, 22,000 free people of colour and 405,000 slaves. In 1792 the French Assembly gave full political rights to all groups, and in 1794 abolished slavery. One result of this was that many French planters left for the various British islands or for Trinidad to which, since 1783, Spain had been welcoming Roman Catholic settlers and their slaves from all nations friendly to her. Another result was the fruitless British expedition of 5,000 troops sent from Jamaica to Haiti; yet another result was that when Napoleon reimposed slavery in the French colonies of St. Domingue, Guadeloupe and Martinique in 1802 further fierce rebellion by the former slaves broke out in St. Domingue as well as in the Windwards. In each colony except St. Domingue the rebellion was crushed, but the St. Domingue Blacks, outnumbering the Whites and coloured people by about 7 or 8 to 1, found a leader of genius in Toussaint L'Ouverture and forced the surrender of the French army in 1803. When its independence was formally declared on 1 January, 1804, the country took again the Arawak name of Haiti. These events incidentally deprived Napoleon of the secure base for the repossession of Louisiana which he had hoped to make of St. Domingue (Geggus 1982).

The subsequent history of Haiti has been tragic. Its tremendous prosperity as a colony exporting indigo, cotton, sugar, coffee and other primary products to France while importing much of its food did not long survive the eclipse of France as the colonial power and the destruction, ordered by Toussaint, of almost the entire class of free people of colour, as a consequence of which irrigation works vital to sugar production were also destroyed. Civil war now became endemic. The dictators of the country who have come to power in succession during the nineteenth and twentieth centuries, with one or two honourable exceptions (e.g. Fabre Geffrard, 1859–67, Paul Magloire, 1951–6), have simply exploited it for their own ends. Haiti has been regarded by the peoples of other Caribbean countries with great ambivalence. They view it with pride on the one hand, as the black republic which emerged when a black leader defeated the armed forces of the European colonizing powers, including those of Napoleon (although it was yellow fever which killed off most of his huge expeditionary force). On the other hand, they view it with trepidation, as an example of the 'relapse from civilization into barbarism' which the Whites of the region have always dreaded as a consequence of black rule. In fact, Haiti has, in spite of the sufferings of its poorer people, produced far more cultural activity – especially in painting and music – than most other Caribbean countries; but the sufferings have also been much greater. A tiny, French-speaking urban elite exploits the urban and rural poor, who remain for the most part Patois-speaking, uneducated and unprovided-for. On the other hand, Haiti has until recently been the scene of the most serious attempts yet made to provide for literacy and education through the medium of Patois, and has thus provided some orthographic and literary models for the rest of the Caribbean. For example, the Roman Catholic liturgy and creed in Creole French being used experimentally in St. Lucia during our survey had been produced in Haiti.

The cultural and linguistic similarities which link Haiti with Guadeloupe, Martinique, Dominica and St. Lucia today and, in the past, St. Vincent, Grenada and Trinidad, are not due to any coincidence of settlement history. Rather, they owe a great deal to the rapid growth of Creole folk culture in Haiti in the late seventeenth and early eighteenth centuries and to the dispersal of population, frequently retaining kinship ties, from that centre to the Windwards and Trinidad in the middle and late eighteenth century. The 'Cric? Crac!' stories which we recorded in 1974 in the mountains of St. Lucia are very similar to those published by Georges Sylvain from Haiti in 1901. Since 1804 Haiti has retained a role as a cultural model in relation to the other islands, linguistically conservative partly because of its poor communications and partly because of the lack of schools.

British rule and education in the Windwards, and 'the Patois'. One of the most interesting sociolinguistic problems of the region is why the outcome

of over a century and a half of British rule and British education should
be linguistically so different from island to island in the Windwards. As
we shall see, some clues are embedded in the following over-optimistic note
in the 1921 Census Report for Grenada and Carriacou (p. 16):

English is the vernacular or mother tongue of the people – 97.79 per cent of whom
speak that language. The patois speaking element comprise 2.01. Since the
prohibition in 1884, of the speaking of patois in the Primary Schools, the dialect
has been slowly dying out and is now spoken only among the small number of
the adult population of the rural districts. The highest percentage of the
English-speaking section reside in the Chief Town (St. George's) and Carriacou.

The Patois was still in fact in vigorous use among the older generation of
rural Grenadians when Le Page was doing fieldwork in the island in the
early 1950s. Moreover, the prohibition referred to was in force also for
many years in St. Lucia, and teachers could be dismissed if heard using
the Patois; but the rule was quite ineffectual there. In St. Vincent French
settlement did not prosper much after the French were defeated, together
with their Carib allies, in the last Carib war of 1794. But in Dominica,
St. Lucia, Grenada and Trinidad French and British planters settled
their differences peacefully under British administration (in spite of a
melodramatic 'duel' between the two nations in St. Lucia).

It is clear that the geographical situation of St. Lucia, in between and
close to both Guadeloupe and Martinique, is likely to have been a factor,
as also are the continuing ties of kinship between St. Lucians and
Martiniquans and between Dominicans and Guadeloupeans. It seems
likely that in addition to the demographic history we must take account
of the patterns of urbanization, of internal as well as external communications (the former very good in Grenada, very poor in Dominica and St.
Lucia), of labour migration within the Eastern Caribbean, and the
administrative history of the islands, in order to find factors associated with
the retention or loss of Creole French. The history of missionary activity
in the region is another factor to be considered, as Table 2 suggests.

We see that those islands which have remained French Patois-speaking
are also those which have remained overwhelmingly Roman Catholic.
Nevertheless, there is no straight correlation between religion and language.
Table 3 summarizes census information at the beginning of the century
about the place of birth of the various populations.

From Table 3 we see the extent of Barbadian and Vincentian emigration
to the Patois-speaking islands. In the case of Trinidad, immigration from
Barbados had been even more considerable in the nineteenth century. In
1831, out of a population recorded as '3,319 white, 16,285 coloured, 762

Table 2. *Population percentages according to religious allegiance claimed in censuses (nearest whole number)*

	Dominica		St. Lucia		St. Vincent		Grenada		Trinidad & Tobago	
	1871	1921	1871	1921	1871	1921	1871	1921	1871	1921
Roman Catholic	88	87	93	not	9	8	56	60	35	33
Anglican	3	5	6	available	43	48	34	33	24	26
Nonconformist	8	7	1		45	38			8	10
Hindu							} 10	} 7	33	24
Muslim										5
Other	1	1			3	6				2
	100	*100*	*100*		*100*	*100*	*100*	*100*	*100*	*100*
Total pop.	27,178	37,059	31,610		31,755	44,447	37,684	66,302	109,638	365,913

Note: Except for St. Lucia, whose historian in 1844, H. H. Breen, was himself the Registrar, census figures are hard to find before the middle of the nineteenth century. Table 2 summarizes the information that is available; it must be noted that most of the figures are unreliable, concealing conflicting (sometimes wildly discrepant) estimates, and that even the 1946 Census Report contains considerable internal discrepancies and obvious errors of tabulation.

Table 3. *Population percentages by place of birth, 1911*[a] *Census (nearest whole number)*

	Dominica	St. Lucia	St. Vincent	Grenada	Trinidad & Tobago[b]
Native	90	90	95	93	19 Native-born EI 45 Other native-born
Barbados		3	2	6	7
St. Vincent	1	1			3
Grenada		2	1		3
Other BWI					3
Leewards	6				
French WI	1	1			
Venezuela					1
India					16
China				1	
UK	2	3	2		3
Other					
	100	100	100	100	100
Total pop.	33,863	48,637	41,877	66,750	312,790

Note: [a] The year 1911 was chosen because 1901 was atypical for St. Lucia in that there was exceptionally heavy immigration of building labour at that time; 7 per cent of the population had been born in Barbados or St. Vincent.
[b] Where separate figures are available for Tobago, native-born percentages are approx. 90 per cent: 12,744 of 14,378 (87%), in 1851, 26,240 of 27,161 (97%) in 1946. The figures in the table, therefore, are more representative of Trinidad and Tobago.

Indian (i.e. Amerindian), 21,302 slaves and 7 Chinese', approximately half of the total were Barbadian-born. By 1946, however, Grenada had overtaken Barbados in this respect, and the Trinidad and Tobago Census records the place of birth of the population of 531,000 as approximately 88 per cent native, 5 per cent Grenadian, $2\frac{1}{2}$ per cent Barbadian and $2\frac{1}{2}$ per cent Vincentian, with 2 per cent from 'India, Burma and Ceylon'.

St. Vincent: a boundary case

The Island Caribs of St. Vincent were left in peace by the Anglo-French treaty reserving Dominica and St. Vincent to them, until a cargo of African slaves was wrecked on Bequia in the latter part of the seventeenth century and took wives from among the Caribs. The offspring of this mixture and their descendants are known as the Black Caribs or Garifuna, now living mostly on the southern coasts of Belize. At the beginning of the eighteenth century the French intervened in quarrels and wars between Island and Black Caribs, as a result of which, in 1719 a number of French planters and their slaves came over from Martinique to settle in St. Vincent. The treaty having been thus breached, the British from 1723 onwards began to try to gain a foothold in the island; but the French prevailed, building up their population to nearly 1,000 Whites and 3,000 slaves by the middle of the century. However, the British expedition of 1762 against Martinique also seized St. Vincent, which was ceded to the British in 1763. According to Shephard (1831) British planters then came from North America, from Barbados and from Antigua to take up land; their greed led them to try to appropriate Carib lands also, and Carib opposition to this was construed as an act of rebellion. The first Carib War in 1772 led to a treaty of 1773 which expropriated some of the Carib lands but reserved some to them, and prohibited 'undue intercourse with the French Islands'. Six years later however the French of Martinique managed once again to persuade the Vincentian Caribs to cooperate with them against the English, and re-possessed the island until 1784, when it was once more ceded to Britain. When, in the aftermath of the French Revolution, the French-settled Antilles adopted republican principles, the movement spread to the British islands. Shephard gives a detailed and graphic account of the various insurrections which followed, led by a coalition of Caribs and French, until they finally surrendered in 1797 and the Black Caribs were transported to Roatan, their lands expropriated by the English planters. The Caribs who remained on the island were pardoned by an Act of 1805 and were allotted 230 acres of land at Morne Ronde.

St. Vincent offers us a most interesting boundary, as the texts in Chapter 3 show, between Western and Eastern Caribbean usage. And if we consider the four Windward Islands of Dominica, St. Lucia, St. Vincent and Grenada, also Trinidad, each of them having had a Creole French-speaking past, and each being at some stage on the road to a creolized-English-speaking future, it is interesting to try to discover what social factors are associated with the particular linguistic outcome in each case.

St. Vincent has almost (but not quite) forgotten its French past. When Le Page first visited the island in the early 1950s he was told that there was an old lady who still spoke 'the Carib language', and he went up the coast to her village to spend an afternoon with her asking her the 'Carib' words for things. Those that he was able subsequently to identify turned out to be mostly Creole French – terms such as ['pã] 'bread' and ['ʃtã] 'dog'. The French occupation of part of St. Vincent, in intimate association with both the Island Caribs and Black Caribs, was short-lived (Shephard 1831). The Creole English of St. Vincent seems in a number of phonological, grammatical and lexical respects to occupy an intermediate position between the Jamaican-like, or Leewards-like Creole English dialects of the northern Caribbean, the Bajan-influenced dialects of the Eastern Caribbean and Guyana, and the dialects of the more clearly French-influenced islands such as Grenada (see, e.g., Le Page 1957/8).

The case of St. Lucia

We can now fill in some more details in respect of St. Lucia, since that is one of the territories we have included in our sociolinguistic survey. (A more detailed account of its socio-economic history will be found in the full report of the St. Lucian stage of the survey (Le Page and Tabouret-Keller 1977: Ch. 1).) Our chief authority is Breen (1844).

The French were more successful than the English in their seventeenth-century attempts to settle the island. English colonists of 1605 and 1639 (the latter numbering several thousand) were mostly slaughtered by Caribs. In 1651, however, a French expedition of 40 men led by de Rousselan (with a Carib wife), from the garrison of Fort Saint-Pierre in Martinique, made a settlement near the subsequent site of Castries. They cultivated ginger, cotton and tobacco. After de Rousselan's death, three of his successors were killed by Caribs, but the colony survived despite vicissitudes. Reinforcements were sent from Martinique in 1657; an attempt by the English from Barbados to capture the island was beaten off in 1659. In 1663 1,000 Barbadians sailed to claim the island by virtue of its 'purchase' from the Caribs and the French garrison surrendered. The English settlement was unsuccessful; sickness and Carib raids reduced its numbers to 89; they evacuated the island in 1666. The French attempted to return, and were driven out by the Governor of Barbados. From the 1670s on, shuttlecock claims to the island were made by Barbados and by the French Antilles; settlers continued to arrive in small numbers from both, but predominantly from Martinique. In 1713, French military and naval deserters arrived to increase the colonist population and take up land. In 1722, a disastrous expedition from England via Barbados under Nathaniel Uring landed at the Petit Carénage (on the northern side of Castries harbour). It was driven out of the island by the French, who had been reinforced by 1,400 men from Martinique (Breen says 2,000 from Martinique and Guadeloupe). The French and British jointly agreed to evacuate the island and so neutralize it, but French settlers in fact stayed on to work the estates which they had acquired. More joined them from Martinique. The harbour, La Carénage and its upland environs became the main area of settlement. In the 1730s, planting of coffee and cocoa was extended by settlers, predominantly French, and their slaves, from Martinique, St. Vincent and Grenada (cocoa and coffee are upland crops). By 1745 there were fairly well-established French settlements in the island

and it had been divided for administrative and parochial purposes into *quartiers*. As yet, however, there were no resident priests. By 1752 there were four. The island at this time was administered mostly from Martinique or by a local French civil or military commandant. Most of the Caribs seem to have withdrawn to the more northerly islands or into the interior of the island. We hear no more about them. In 1762, Admiral Rodney, having subdued Martinique, compelled St. Lucia to surrender. There was British administration until 1763, then the island reverted to France. Administered independently of Martinique until 1768, it then reverted to being administered from that island. There was a series of French administrators until 1778.

In 1765, the first sugar estate was established, at Vieux Fort. Now began the development of lowland riverine plantations, with the concomitant need for large numbers of Negro slaves. By 1769 the population was estimated at 'over twelve thousand', the vast majority imported slaves; by 1772 it was set at '2,018 white, 663 coloured and 12,795 blacks' a total of 15,476. By 1778, England and France were again at war. St. Lucia was now prized by the British for its commanding position, fine harbours and healthy upland locations for barracks, for example on the Morne Fortuné. Twelve transports and about 5,000 men were sent from New York and captured the island in spite of heavy counter-attacks by the French. Now it was placed under British administration, with a considerable garrison and Fleet base. Runaway slave or 'Maroon' settlements grew up in the interior, probably with Carib connivance and intermingling. Agriculture and trade suffered a bad setback in the devastating hurricane of 1780, and as a result a number of the planters abandoned their estates and left the island. The hurricane was estimated by Breen to have killed 6,000 people in St. Lucia alone.

In 1784, the island was once more ceded to France; Grenada at the same time was ceded to Britain, and de Laborie transferred as Governor from Grenada to St. Lucia. In 1785 Soufriere, with its hot sulphur springs, became a spa for French colonials and military both from St. Lucia and from neighbouring islands. By 1789 the population was estimated at '2,198 white, 1,588 coloured, 17,992 black', a total of 21,778, with a number of Maroon settlements whose population was unknown.

When revolution came in France in 1789, the Antilles Negroes took it up with alacrity. Planters and their families were driven out of Martinique, Guadeloupe and St. Lucia and took refuge in Trinidad. As we have said, slavery was abolished in the French Antilles in 1794. During this period all the towns and villages in St. Lucia were given Republican names. With the outbreak of war again between Britain and France (1794) Britain re-took the island, and Martinique, with an expedition from Barbados. The French garrisons of Martinique and St. Lucia were sent back to France. However, in St. Lucia insurgent slaves and runaway French troops took to the woods and carried on a guerilla war against the British, and by the middle of 1795 the British garrison, which had evacuated all the island except for Castries and Vieux Fort, was forced to leave and abandon the British colonists there. In 1796 it was re-taken by 12,000 British troops who forced the French, concentrated on the Morne Fortuné above Castries, to capitulate, but the formidable guerilla forces in the woods did not surrender until 1797, and then only on condition that they should not again be enslaved. Many of them were formed into a regiment and sent to serve on the West African coast. This was a turbulent period for the island, with Whites against Blacks, English against French, pro-slavery against anti-slavery factions; many settlements and plantations formerly prosperous were now abandoned. By 1799 the island was being pacified once more, and the colonists making progress under General Prevost. When he retired in 1802, of the names of those who signed a memorial addressed to him (Breen 1844: 110), 12 are obviously French, three probably British, one doubtful. In 1802 St. Lucia was briefly restored to France, but recaptured by the British in 1803 (who administered it from then until the transitional arrangements of the 1950s and 1960s which led to the settlement of 1967 when it became an independent territory in association with Great Britain). The island, however, was not formally ceded to Britain until the Treaty of Paris of 1814.

Factors shaping the identity of the nineteenth-century St. Lucian community. By 1803 we can discern certain factors shaping the identity of the nineteenth-century St. Lucian community:

(i) In spite of (to some extent because of) the terrible ravages of disease (notably malaria, yellow fever, tuberculosis, cholera, stomach disorders and venereal disease) and of snake bite; in spite of natural disasters such as hurricanes (six of which laid the island waste between 1756 and 1831 – the 1780 hurricane was estimated to have killed 22,000 people in Barbados, St. Lucia, St. Vincent and Martinique) and heavy rains; in spite of the changing fortunes of war both outside and within the island, one can discern a steady drift towards a sense of community within the island as its very heterogeneous population grows. The colonists, the white and coloured Creoles, made common cause under the leadership of good administration, whether French (as under de Laborie) or English (as under Prevost). We are told by Breen of great rivalry between French and British settlers coming to a head in an absurd 'duel' proposed in 1819, after which the rivalry subsided.

(ii) The centres of white and coloured settlement were the string of small ports which grew up around the coast, serving the riverine sugar estates, and the settlement around the major harbour and its dominating military position, Le Carénage and the Morne Fortuné respectively. The eleven administrative *quartiers* of the island established by 1745 were based on these riverine ports, each a *barquadière* for sugar and a stage in the coastal navigation and coastal road services of an island which had virtually no roads into the interior, and whose many small but sometimes torrential rivers made communication by sea easier than by land.

(iii) The mountainous nature of the island has been the main cause of its poverty in the past compared with rich sugar islands such as Barbados.

(iv) This mountainous terrain, however, which determined the nature of plantation settlement and concentrated it on riverine plains also, as in Jamaica, provided a haven for Maroon settlements in the interior and for subsistence farming up and down the central spine of the island by a black population which absorbed the remnants of the Caribs and multiplied much more rapidly than the white. Thus, as in Jamaica and in contrast to Barbados and Antigua, a black creole Patois, brought in this case mainly from Martinique, to a less extent from St. Vincent, Grenada and Guadeloupe, or taking shape locally on St. Lucian plantations, was retained in use as the vernacular of many conservative, remote, small mountain settlements. Moreover, although the connection between the anopheles mosquito, its lowland breeding pools and swamps, and the fatal malaria was not realized until much later, the mountainous settlements were at least often immune to malaria and comparatively free from yellow fever. They were, however, (this was not realized fully until very recently with the work of the Bilharzia Research Unit) peculiarly susceptible to bilharzia once the parasitic liver fluke which transmits it had been brought by African immigrants and unwittingly set to breed in the snails of St. Lucia's rivers.

(v) The white population had two external regional foci in the administrative centres of Martinique and Barbados, and two metropolitan influences in France and Britain. The black population had continuing cultural contact with Africa through its oral traditions, and through fresh arrivals of slaves. We have been able to discover very little about the direct slave-trade to St. Lucia. It is likely that it was mostly in French hands, and in that case that most of those slaves who were shipped through Martinique (Rawley 1981: 130) in the eighteenth century had come from

Table 4. *Slave re-exports to St. Lucia*

	1796	1797	1798	1799	1800	1801
From Grenada	—	—	—	80	—	—
St. Vincent	—	—	—	—	—	20
Martinique	—	—	—	99	10	29

Senegal or the Gambia or Guinea ports. There are some tables available for the British trade at the end of the eighteenth century (see *BPP* 61a, b) for the years 1796 to 1801 and for 1805, which show only one shipment of 175 slaves from an unspecified African port to St. Lucia in the former period, and only two ships, with 372 Negroes, in 1805. Re-exports from other islands to St. Lucia are shown in Table 4.

The numbers involved are small. The period to which the tables refer is part of that during which, according to Breen, the black population shrank from 21,778 to 17,485. But even during the period of St. Lucia's most rapid expansion, under de Laborie, the *rate of increase* does not seem to have been very great. This fact tells us little about the volume of slave importations since mortality was so high, but it seems likely that Martinique would have been able to supply St. Lucia's slave needs to a large extent and that established slave merchants in Martinique would have tried to keep the St. Lucian trade in their hands. In the latter part of the eighteenth century Martinique was the third largest slave exporter listed in the British returns, after Barbados and Jamaica; the six-year totals are: Barbados 8,789; Jamaica 5,294; Martinique 3,691. But during this period neither Barbados nor Jamaica exported to St. Lucia. We find ourselves still with no very satisfactory picture of the origins of St. Lucian slaves beyond this: the majority reached the island after spending some time in Martinique, and of these, a considerable proportion in the early years of settlement may have come from Senegambia and Guinea but the majority towards the end of the century possibly came from the Bight of Benin and Angola (see Rawley 1981: 129).

(vi) The whole population was subjected from time to time to external threats of natural disaster and war which had a centripetal influence; and to other factors such as the political ideas of the French Revolution and the tensions between Roman Catholicism and Anglicanism which were socially divisive, as were the tensions between the interests of a slave-owning plantocracy, those of a growing urban coloured mercantile class and those of the administrators. On the whole, however, Roman Catholicism and

French Creole Patois, contributing to a creole oral culture and a pantheon which could accommodate both African and French aspects, united most people in the island to the exclusion of the urban, Anglican and Barbadian-dominated administrators who had replaced their French opposite numbers for good by 1803. The fact that the Roman Catholic Church continued to recruit most of its priests from France contributed to the cultural history of St. Lucia in the nineteenth and twentieth centuries.

(vii) The population link with Martinique was to continue long after the administrative link had been severed, as a source of maintained family connections and influences, as a source of both open and surreptitious immigration, and as an entrepôt for slaves and trade. It is only within the comparatively recent years of the present century that family and linguistic connections and trade with France have dwindled together.

(viii) The administrative link with Barbados has been a continuing factor in shaping the nature of the urban Creole English of Castries which today serves as a model for rural dwellers who wish to identify with their urban fellow St. Lucians.

Nineteenth-century factors affecting the British Caribbean as a whole

Labour immigration after the end of slavery. From the 1840s until the end of the nineteenth century the tropical sugar plantations were looking for alternative sources of labour, since it was found that the freed slaves preferred, wherever possible, to be their own masters on smallholdings to working on the plantations. Recruiting agents were active with false promises in Scotland and Ireland. It should be noted that much of the immigration of so-called 'free' Africans and Asians, and indeed of the Europeans also, was under conditions very little different from slavery – they are graphically described in a pamphlet, *Emigration to the British West Indies* (Anon. 1842). A number of enslaved Nigerians, cargoes set free by the Royal Navy, came to the Caribbean as indentured labourers and were responsible for the introduction of Shango ritual (still found today, particularly in Grenada, Carriacou and Trinidad and also in Haiti, Puerto Rico etc.). Madeira and Hong Kong were both the scene of labour recruiting, but comparatively small numbers were involved. The really large-scale recruitment was from India, from the 1850s until the 1880s. The East Indians went to all parts of the Caribbean, but by far the largest numbers went to Trinidad and to Guyana. Table 5 gives the numbers of Indian-born inhabitants in 1891 in various territories.

The Madeiran Portuguese and the Chinese tended to leave plantation labour to become shopkeepers, but the East Indians tended to form their

Table 5. *Population recorded in 1891 Census as born in India*

Dominica	(not recorded, but 25 in 1881)
St. Lucia	1939 (+ St. Lucian-born East Indians, 580)
St. Vincent	332
Grenada and Carriacou	1,017
Trinidad	45,577 (+ Trinidadian-born East Indians, 24,621)
British Guiana (Guyana)	(not available, but 90,211 had reached the colony between 1871 and 1891 – see Sessional Papers 1892)

own plantation communities and to cohere as a labour force for several generations (see Rambissoon Sperl 1980 for Trinidad; W. F. Edwards 1977 for Guyana). Guyana and Trinidad are, however, sharply distinguished in the linguistic outcome of this immigration: in Guyana the East Indians had the outgoing Creoles as their tutors on the plantations and in due course inherited the most rural variety of Guyanese Creole as their *lingua franca* (W. F. Edwards 1977); whereas in Trinidad they seem to have mixed far less with black Trinidadians, who were in any case speaking a variety of English far less creolized than that of Guyana. In both countries there has tended to be racial friction between East Indians and Creoles. It was not until the 1950s that the rural East Indians began to break through in large numbers into the urban professions (teaching, medicine, the Civil Service, the law) which had been the jealously guarded preserve of the Creoles; but once the process began it proceeded at a rate which alarmed the latter and led to attempts to entrench their position in society by political means.

The case of Belize

The history of Belize differs quite considerably from that of any of the territories discussed so far, particularly in that it never was a plantation colony. It owed its existence initially to the convergence of two more-or-less piratical migrations, both of them hostile to Spanish claims of dominion over the whole of Central America; and one of them – the initiative of the Providence Company and of the various buccaneer groups discussed earlier – was responsible, at least in part, for initiating what are today Creole-English-speaking settlements around the Caribbean coasts of Central America from Panama to the Yucatan Peninsula (Holm 1982b). (There is a continuing underlying hostility in the region between 'Spanish' and 'Creole', reflected *inter alia* in the claim of Guatemala to the territory of Belize.)

The other migration came primarily from Jamaica. Both migrations have uncertain beginnings in the latter part of the seventeenth century; both made encampments on the coast partly as bases in which to shelter from Spanish attempts to clear them out, partly as bases from which to cut logwood on the coast and, later, mahogany in the interior. Entry to the interior was via the rivers, particularly the Belize river. The name Belize is supposed by some to derive from an Anglicization, [bə'liz], of a Hispanization, [bɛlis], of the name of a seventeenth-century Scottish buccaneer, Wallace (Young 1973: 58). It may, however, derive from a Maya word meaning 'muddy waters' (Dobson 1973: 52). Conditions in the tiny communities, partly on St. George's Cay, an island of the reef off Belize, partly among the mangrove swamps at the mouth of the river where Belize City has grown up, and partly in the logging camps formed in the interior for each winter logging season, led to very close relationships between Whites and Blacks and Indians. Their community of interests mitigated the institution of slavery and led to the emergence of a strong communal identity with its own language – the forerunner of today's Belize Creole. (For maps, see pp. 118, 119.)

The population has always been small, predominantly of African or Afro-European descent, closely-interactive, dependent (partly because of the conditions, partly because of Spanish prohibitions on plantation) on imported food and goods in exchange for exports of forest products. They have felt threatened not only by the Spanish but, to some extent also, by the Negro/Amerindian Black Carib settlements on the coast to the south, from Stann Creek to Punta Gorda, and by people whose ancestors were deported from St. Vincent by the British after the Carib Wars (Shephard 1831) at the end of the eighteenth century. Belize and Miskito Coast Creoles are in the minority among Caribbean Creole English settlements, as far as we know, in referring to themselves as Creoles and to their language as Creole or ['kriːa] rather than by the more common term, 'Patois' (see *DJE* s. 1980: CREOLE 4). (Hancock, in a personal communication, has however reminded us that scholarly work on creole languages has itself stimulated the popular and political use of the term 'Creole', or, as in St. Lucia, 'Kwéyol'.) The indigenous inhabitants before the arrival of the Spanish had been the Maya (including the Kekchi) whose monuments are dotted about the whole region but whose civilization collapsed, perhaps for economic reasons. Since the end of the nineteenth century, their descendants have re-entered Belize from Mexico and from Guatemala as refugees from political troubles. Their coming was recalled by one of our informants, Mr JW of Bullet Tree Falls, in conversation with us in 1978 (standard orthography has been used for what was in fact mixed local Creole and local English):

My grandfather was from England...My grandmother was a Indian from Guatemala...Juliana...My father come from Belize and he married to my mother...I grow up in Cayo [he claimed 90 descendants living in the District, he thought]...My mother used to talk in Spanish to we an' my father talk in English...My father never talk a half a half one word in...in Spanish...mia mada yes...my mother used to talk the Spanish and Maya...the majority of me children-dem talk Maya, Carib...Aye, they go amongst them an' they learn the language you see...they talk it, talk it, yes...right today...here in Bullet...the old set of Indian you see...not this young people...because...they got school and they brought the Spanish and the English. And they forget that [i.e. Maya]...When we come here the people...they nearly was naked...the Indians-them, yah. We have big revolution here with the Indians-them you know...That was 'bout – oh, nineteen eight [1908]...They was stealin'...there was some parts of Mexico people that...I will let you know it plain...The country use to be develop by the, by the Guatemantican and the Mexican-them you know, because 1910 Mexico got a revolution and by the thousand they used to come into the colony...By the thousand...I was a big boy already...They used to go to the States and buy arms to continue fighting. They used to steal money...Mm...We have a next revolution here that, they cramp...they cramp the colony. They tief-out the chicle-them, they tief out your mule-dem and kill you behind that...Yah, I work fifty years chiclero...

The Belize River is navigable during the rainy season up to within a few miles of the Guatemalan frontier, and until comparatively recently the river boats were the main means of contact with the western part of the colony, known as Cayo District. The small town, San Ignacio del Cayo, which is the capital of the District, stands at the upper limit of navigation, just above the village of Branch Mouth where the river branches to form the Cayo or island. A few miles beyond San Ignacio, where one branch of the river crosses the frontier, lies the even smaller town of Benque Viejo, founded by 'Spanish' refugees from Petén Province of Guatemala. The development of this region owes a great deal to the exploitation of chicle, the gummy sap of the sapodilla tree from which chewing gum used to be made. The chicle trade was organized to a large extent by Lebanese and Syrian traders, who established their depots in San Ignacio, brought trade goods up by river, advanced money and tinned provisions and flour to the chicle-tappers, and bought from them the slabs of congealed chicle which were the fruits of the tapping season. The descendants of those traders are today known as The Turks (*Los Turcos*). It is only since the exhaustion of the mahogany forests and the development of synthetic chicle that alternative agricultural industries have been attracted to the colony – mainly sugar, rice, citrus and cattle ranching. The Spanish and mestizo and Maya-Kekchi populations have practised subsistence farming on their *milpas*, or smallholdings. The Caribs from the coast, tending to be good linguists, have provided a high proportion of the schoolteachers for the out-Districts (outside Belize); the Creoles from Belize City have provided the urban teachers, policemen, professional people and government servants.

However, the building of a road from Belize City to run roughly parallel to the river as far as the frontier changed the situation. Since the 1950s people have moved in to populate villages along the road from each end and from each side, to take up land for farming or to work in the service industries along the road – shops, gas stations, small cafés, carpentry workshops, schools, the Government Agricultural Station at Central Farm, the hospitals in Belmopan and San Ignacio, the buses that run from Benque Viejo to Belize City. Into this region also has come an entirely new element from outside – German-speaking Mennonites from Mexico, from Canada and from the USA, who have formed farming settlements. These people have made several large settlements, one being at Spanish Lookout in Cayo District. They have made their own schools, workshops and hospitals and try to be self-sufficient, but they come into town from time to time on their carts to sell their produce and buy goods, and have been known to adopt children from Belizean parents. They still use their German dialect among themselves.

Two final factors affecting the mixture of population that has taken place in Cayo District must be mentioned. The devastating hurricane 'Hattie' of 1961 resulted in a grant from the British Government to build a new capital, Belmopan, 50 miles inland, close to the village of Roaring Creek in Cayo District but near also to the junction of the Orange Walk, Stann Creek and Belize Districts and only a little way from the new Belize-Cayo road. A good deal of the capital has now been completed, and although it is on a Lilliputian scale it has certainly brought the people of the out-Districts much closer to the seat of government, and also to a new hospital. The second factor is the animosity of the Guatemalan Government towards the notion of an independent Belize. Their case is that they have never recognized the legitimacy of the country and have always claimed it as part of Guatemalan territory. The Belizean government has attained full independence while asking Britain to continue to guarantee its frontiers. Whereas in the early 1960s the Government of Belize was inclined to flirt with a Guatemalan alliance, today recurring threats from Guatemala have led to vigorous rejections of their claim and the more rapid evolution of a sense of Belizean nationhood. This fact is particularly relevant to Cayo District, through which the road runs to the Guatemalan frontier.

The population drawn into the new lands opened up by the road, therefore, was in the 1950s highly diffuse ethnically, linguistically, in religion, in education, in economic status and way of life, and in cultural loyalties. Focussing agencies have been at work however in the growth of mobility and interaction among disparate sections of the population; the movement towards a common and more secular education, the common need to find work in the new agricultural and urban industries to replace logging and chicle-tapping, and the need to make common cause against the Guatemalans. The development of insecticides, the provision of electric power in the District, and the development of bus services, have played their part in making life in the roadside villages more tolerable than previously for the families who have spread out from the urban centres at each end of the road.

The population of Belize today (1983 estimate) is only approximately 150,000. The English-born population is unlikely ever to have numbered more than a few hundred, and the total population of the colony in the last few years of slavery, including slaves, was less than 4,000. Emancipation did not lead to any great demand for fresh sources of labour for the logging camps, in which, as we have already noted, a degree of egalitarianism had long been established; and the sparse population of the country has often been a matter of concern. The Caste War in Yucatan led to an influx of several thousand refugees from Mexico in the middle of the nineteenth century, and there have been sporadic surges of immigration from Guatemala, especially at the end of the nineteenth century. Mr JW's narrative, above, refers to the influx from Mexico in the first decade of the twentieth century. This immigration from Spanish-speaking countries has provided the northern and western Spanish, Mestizo and Maya 'fringe' around the Creole colony. There has also been sporadic very small-scale immigration from the southern United States since the mid-nineteenth century, to grow sugar or commence ranching. There have been small but steady numbers of immigrants from other British West Indian colonies, by far the largest number from Jamaica, coming to develop the banana and citrus plantations in Stann Creek District, or as recruits into the police or public services. Belize has received only a very small share of the Chinese and East Indian labour imported by the other colonies. The Black Caribs along the coast to the south of Stann Creek have been augmented by others coming in from Honduras and Guatemala; they tend to be regarded, along

Table 6. *Linguistic affiliations of the population according to the 1960 Census of British Honduras*

Languages claimed as spoken[a]:	Men	Women	Total
English only	22,072	24,018	46,090
Spanish only	4,190	4,697	8,887
Maya only	1,258	1,552	2,810
Carib only	605	790	1,395
English and Spanish	9,627	8,197	17,824
English and Maya	480	359	839
English and Carib	2,233	2,792	5,025
Spanish and Maya	1,629	1,486	3,115
Spanish and Carib	24	17	41
Maya and Carib	nil	nil	nil
Unrecorded[b]	2,541	1,938	4,479
Total	44,659	45,846	90,505

Note: [a] 'English' here, the term used by the Census taker, must be understood to mean, primarily, Creole. Maya must be understood to include Kekchi and cognate languages.
[b] This in fact is a balancing figure, the amount by which the official census tables do not add up.

with the Miskito Indians, with some suspicion and dislike even by the Creoles, and certainly by the Spanish and Mestizos, as we show later in Chapter 6.

Table 6 illustrates the linguistic affiliations claimed by the Belizean population at the 1960 Census. Within the past few years Spanish-speaking refugee immigration has again increased because of the civil-war-like conditions in a number of Central American countries such as El Salvador. In December 1981 (*New Belize* 1981: 4) immigration statistics showed approximately 6,000 such refugees, but most of these moved on again; a site to the north-west of Belmopan was earmarked for the resettlement of the remainder.

4. More recent aspects of political and cultural development in the Anglophone Caribbean

Education in the nineteenth and twentieth centuries in Jamaica and the Eastern Caribbean

The Vincentian historian Charles Shephard comments:

The want of education has been a sore evil in the Colonies, but a decided improvement has taken place, under the auspices of the Bishop, and in a few years the parochial schools will manifest their utility. There is a laudable institution by a few coloured persons in Kingstown, for the education of the coloured poor...   (Shephard 1831: 209)

In the eighteenth century there were a few small endowed schools scattered about the British West Indies, for example, Harrison College in Barbados, but most of the white planters sent their children back to Europe to be educated and most of the slave population received no education at all except from the pulpit, either through the agency of missions like those of the Moravians or through the parsons of the Established Church. After Emancipation the emerging free elementary school system of Britain began to be paralleled in the West Indies, the Churches organizing most of the schools with the help of government grants. The Mico Charity Training Colleges were set up in Antigua and in Jamaica, and Codrington College in Barbados, by 1840. The language of education was uniformly supposed to be Standard British English; both Creole English ('bad English') and Creole French were supposed to be 'eradicated', and a high proportion of Headmasters and Principals were expatriate Englishmen. The curriculum was preoccupied with British subjects and directed eventually towards secondary school examinations set and marked in England. Self-help was a major hallmark of the system, producing some remarkable black scholars, such as the Trinidadian Creole grammarian J. J. Thomas (1869). To this day people work on their own or through correspondence courses for the external degrees and diplomas of overseas institutions. The will to do so, however, has often had to be strong in the face of severe obstacles: large and grossly overcrowded primary school classes, lack of books for those learning to read, lack of any quiet place or even lamplit place free from mosquitoes in which to study in the evening, and so on. The Island Scholarships and Rhodes Scholarships and other endowments that became available to take West Indians to universities and colleges overseas were won mostly by middle-class urban boys; St. Lucia had to divide the competition in two to overcome this bias. Primary school teachers were recruited mainly through the pupil-teacher system, taking bright adolescents out of the sixth grade of the primary school and setting them to work simultaneously teaching and learning to teach under the Headteacher's supervision. Such teachers had themselves very little direct access, except in books, to the Standard British English they were supposed both to teach and to teach in. Nevertheless, a pass in the English language examinations for many years acted as the entry-ticket to higher education and to a salaried job of any kind (Le Page 1968a); and approximately 70 per cent of the entrants failed.

What emerged from this system in the second half of the nineteenth and the first half of the twentieth centuries was an urban coloured middle class, bilingual in a fairly standard educated local variety of English and in the creole vernacular of their territory. To this class belonged the headteachers and senior school teachers, the local West Indian recruits to the Civil Service, office workers and shop workers. Unconsciously, or perhaps partly consciously, they provided an alternative linguistic model to the expatriate model (Le Page 1977a).

Changes came with the approach of independence in the middle of the twentieth century. The University (College) of the West Indies was established as a federal West Indian institution in Jamaica in 1948 to work for degrees in medicine, science and the arts under the general supervision of the University of London. At first staffed very largely by expatriate British teachers, it is now staffed in the main by the West Indians they trained; it is now wholly independent of London; further faculties have been added to campuses established in Barbados and Trinidad and extra-mural centres have been set up in other territories. Guyana has opted out of the system and set up its own university in Georgetown. A local Caribbean Examinations Council has to a large extent taken over the functions of the Cambridge and London examining bodies. (Unhappily, today the dismemberment of the University between the main participating territories is in progress.)

One of the major results of these activities from a linguistic point of view is that the University of the West Indies, as the apex of the educational system, has had to try to define and standardize an acceptable educated standard language for the region. This has been a large part of the task of the Caribbean Lexicography Project in Barbados. Another result is that expectations have been aroused of mass access to higher education and these expectations cannot always be fulfilled. A third is the demand in some quarters that Creole English and Creole French be treated with due respect and that provision be made for their use in the educational system, at least in initial reading and writing classes. One cannot forecast the linguistic outcome of all these educational processes, since there are many political and economic variables involved, some working directly on linguistic behaviour, others through the educational system and the media. What is certain is that they have to be taken into account when trying to understand the acts of identity made by West Indians in the past, and those being made today by older and by younger generations both in the West Indies and in Britain.

As in every country, teachers in the West Indies have in the past had a strong interest in the continuance of a system in which they themselves have invested so much of their professional training. However, a system in which the vernacular is not the medium of education inevitably leads to educational elitism and the linguistic marking of a social hierarchy; it can be a self-perpetuating system. Today, however, quite apart from considerations of egalitarianism, local pride, and also local chauvinism, sheer demographic considerations have made change in the direction of the vernacularization of education inevitable (see Craig 1977).

Education in Belize

The educational system in Belize has undergone fairly radical change in recent years. It had always been left to the religious denominations to provide most of the secondary schooling available and much of the primary schooling also. The Spanish-speaking township of Benque Viejo was very largely Roman Catholic, and the main school there, Mount Carmel School, was a Catholic school at which, in the early 1950s, nuns of a German teaching order were to be found teaching Maya- and Spanish-speaking children to try to pass English-language examinations. The main secondary school in San Ignacio was the Roman Catholic Sacred Heart College. There were missions from other Christian sects, even in Benque Viejo where, for example, the Seventh Day Adventists had for a long time run a clinic and a school. Among the people of Belize City and in Belize District non-Roman Catholic sects, in particular the Anglican and Methodist churches, had been strongest and had provided most schools. In the colony as a whole, of course, the Church of England was the established church, but the Roman Catholics had always tried to maintain a strong presence there, and the American Jesuits in particular had done a great deal to develop good secondary education at St. John's College in Belize City.

Since the Second World War moves towards independence throughout the Caribbean have been accompanied by greater state provision of education, either directly or through the agency of the various religious denominations. Thus – not without sectional friction – Government schools and a Government Teacher Training College have been established in Belize, and the expatriate teachers of old have gradually been replaced by local people, just as other Civil Service posts have been filled by local people in the Education Department as elsewhere. There are still, however, expatriate Canadian and American teachers in the country. The old pupil-teacher system, whereby bright students were recruited as assistants without any college training while they studied under the Headteacher's supervision for various preparatory examinations, is today buttressed for more and more teachers by a year at the Training College. In the past, however, there had been a tendency for the majority of teacher-trainees at College to be either Creoles from Belize City or Caribs; only in recent years has the number of 'Spanish' and 'Maya' trainees become appreciable.

Independence movements, political and cultural

Colonial processes always involve struggles for local autonomy as against dependence on, and government by, the colonizing power. Two main streams of colonizing migrants were involved in the Caribbean up to the middle of the nineteenth century: European and African. The Africans and those of African descent always tried to maintain their cultural independence of the Europeans, both by preserving aspects of traditional African culture within slavery and also by running away to form Maroon settlements which established alternative societies along traditional African lines. Within these Maroon settlements the influence of dominant groups can be discerned, in the form of their language and the nature of their oral literature, and each of them has provided a centre of cultural and linguistic conservatism, or even of 're-Africanization'. The latter term seems a reasonable one to describe the influence of fairly large numbers of Yoruba speakers arriving in the Eastern Caribbean in the middle of the nineteenth century as indentured labourers. Perhaps it also describes the influence of newly-arrived runaway slaves on the usage of those Saramaccan Maroon settlements they joined in seventeenth- and eighteenth-century Surinam. (However, whether the tone contrasts of Saramaccan represent conservation of an old creole feature lost in Sranan and Jamaican, as argued by Alleyne 1980, or are examples of 're-Africanization' as we suggest here, is debatable.)

African struggles for cultural and political independence have taken other courses and provided other models. Most prominent among these have been the various 'back-to-Africa' movements. Sometimes these were sponsored by European abolitionists, and resulted among other things in the establishment of settlements for freed slaves in, for example, Liberia and Sierra Leone. The subsequent history of these settlements is outside our scope, but the Krio language of Sierra Leone preserves today some features that link it with Jamaican ex-slaves taken there at the beginning of the nineteenth century (Hancock 1971, 1980c; Fyle and Jones 1980). Krio culture in turn spread an influence across West Africa in the former British colonies of The Gold Coast (Ghana), Nigeria and The Cameroons (Cameroun) which is reflected in the various forms of West African Pidgin.

The back-to-Africa movement of the black Jamaican/American Marcus Garvey in the 1920s was intended to be a large-scale 'repatriation' movement, a kind of Black Zionism. One problem was, where was the Promised Land? In the late 1930s the colonial wars of Italy in Ethiopia brought into prominence the defender of Ethiopia, the Emperor Haile Selassie, and the Ras Tafari movement was born in Jamaica. The Emperor,

Ras Tafari (= King of Kings) was identified as a black man and as a spiritual leader, and Ethiopia took shape as The Promised Land. The movement has been far more important, however, as a movement of total cultural and economic independence (see Smith, Augier and Nettleford 1960), an alternative society first within Jamaica (specifically, within Kingston) and later within other Caribbean territories and today within the black communities of Britain. Linguistic aspects of this cultural independence include the refusal to use *me* as a pronominal form since the oblique case is felt to be 'subordinate' and dialectal; it is replaced by strongly-stressed *I*; and the plural *we* by *I-and-I* (*DJE* 1980, Supplement). In other respects, however, Rastafarians seem to cultivate many Creole forms (Pollard 1983).

Movements for political and cultural independence among West Indians of European or mixed descent have been more ambivalent. Although the white plantocracy always struggled to be free of British control, they also struggled to keep British protection and British citizenship, and commonly repatriated their fortunes and their children to Britain. Most white labourers and artisans have tended to be birds of passage. Free people of colour, on the other hand, have been those whose allegiance to the various West Indian territories has been strongest; they have tended to form an urban elite; their descendants are known in Jamaica (see *DJE*) and elsewhere as 'Brown' men, and the term has implications of wealth; an abusive term for them has been 'Red Ibo'. Their children have attended the fee-paying secondary schools set up in each of the colonies, schools such as Queen's Royal College in Trinidad and Harrison College in Barbados; they have provided the core of the non-expatriate Civil Service in the region, and won the various scholarships to study abroad. They have, until recently, almost monopolized professional and managerial jobs, and it was they in the first instance who provided the political leadership which led each territory to independence. They have also provided the artists and writers, in particular those who contributed to the remarkable flowering of West Indian prose and poetry in the period after the Second World War, men like Edgar Mittelholzer of Guyana, Samuel Selvon of Trinidad, George Lamming of Barbados – although by mentioning Samuel Selvon we are now having to recognize the eruption into this coloured middle class of descendants of the East Indians who replaced Blacks as an estate labour force in the second half of the nineteenth century (see pp. 61–2).

The emphatic political assertion of an Afro-Caribbean identity has frequently provoked political reaction among West Indians of East Indian descent, many of them today distinguished, sometimes wealthy, people.

There are many attempts in both Guyana and Trinidad (Rambissoon Sperl 1980) to keep Hindu culture and the Hindi language alive and officially recognized, and politics in these two countries has regularly divided people along ethnic lines, sometimes violently.

One of the most distinguished poets in English today is Derek Walcott, son of a St. Lucian schoolteacher of Barbadian descent. Linguistically the coloured middle class has always bridged the gulf between Creole-speaking workers and expatriates. As in so many other countries, the managerial classes have had to be bilingual, in this case in Creole and educated West Indian English. They have provided the model for what the education ladder could lead to. The Rastafarians have provided an alternative model, and the political activism of the labourers a third model, by-passing the educational system. Each of these models has its own linguistic norms, replacing the old single norm of expatriate Southern British Standard English and written English. The West Indian writers have struggled for a long time to achieve cultural independence, with varying success. There was a time when Creole could be used only for either oral literature such as Anansi or Brer Rabbit or Old Witch (Ole Higue) stories, or for humorous verse or prose. Serious West Indian writers modelled themselves on English writers, so that Derek Walcott's early poems are a pastiche of Eliot and Auden.

In *New Day*, one of the first of the post-war Jamaican novels, Vic Reid felt constrained to invent a language that was neither Standard English nor Creole. Of course, West Indian writers, just like West African writers, have had to face the dilemma that if they use too strange a language their audience and market will shrink, whereas if they use too standard a language they may lose their authenticity. Some West Indian writers have stayed in the Caribbean to work out an answer to this dilemma, one common to many post-colonial societies. Derek Walcott is the outstanding example. Others have emigrated to London or New York, to become cultural exiles. It is difficult for post-colonial writers of any region or period to feel free of the colonial past until they also feel free to use their vernacular, if they wish to, in all its registers to reflect many-faceted daily life and the interaction of characters. Meanwhile, the writers have yet to assert that focussing influence in the multidimensional sociolinguistic space of the post-colonial Caribbean that Chaucer had in post-colonial England (cf. Traugott 1981); the Rastafarian movement may be providing an alternative focussing agency.

The Anglophone Caribbean as a cultural region

In 1954 James J. Parsons in his Presidential Address to the Association of Pacific Coast Geographers claimed that 'There is a feeling of kinship relationship and a community of interest which still stretches from Belize and Kingston to Bocas del Toro and Colon.' We would extend that claim to include the Eastern Caribbean, Trinidad and Guyana. Carnival has spread northwards from Trinidad (and is now a major feature of Notting Hill, London also); Rastafarianism has spread all over from Jamaica. The Black Caribs keep alive the John Canoe dances (and, the Creoles claim, *obeah*; see Chapter 6) in Belize; *Tunkanoo* is also the great festival of the Bahamas (see Holm and Shilling 1982).

It is also true that the Spanishness of the region tends to reassert itself. In the southern United States, in Florida and Texas, as well as in New Mexico and California, the linguistic frontier between Spanish and English is today being pushed northwards again. Miami is a Spanish-speaking city. The Spanish refugee population in Florida is financially well established and exploitative, able to assimilate Cuban refugees to some extent; but black refugees from Haiti are in a much more precarious situation. Our suggestion is that one important dimension of ethnic and linguistic acts of identity in the Caribbean is an underlying mutual ambivalence or hostility between 'Creole' and 'Spanish', these groups being to some extent marked by colour and hair-texture and cultural traits. In this situation the straight-haired but dark-skinned Amerindian and East Indian can form alliances in either direction, and in our detailed study of Belize we can observe the process closely (see Chapter 6).

Another aspect of the region is on the surface negative but at a deeper level positive: that is, the apparent cultural rootlessness of the Anglophone West Indians, of which Rastafarianism is the most recent symptom. What it is to be a Francophone Creole is well marked in the highly stratified and focussed societies of Haiti, Guadeloupe, and Martinique and, formerly, in Dominica, St. Lucia and Grenada. What it is to be an Anglophone West Indian is far more difficult to describe, and a number of West Indians have looked outside their own societies for some more clearly marked cultural claims, in an imagined 'Africa' or in revivalist religion or, more recently, in Marxism. These searches are reflected in Rastafarianism, in West Indian literature and in West Indian political movements. And yet, in spite of all the factors distinguishing each territory, the Creoleness of Belize, of Antigua, of St. Vincent, of Jamaica, of Tobago and of Guyana is strongly similar, and shared also in Limón, in Bluefields, in San Andrés and

Providencia and Panama. This cultural identity was based originally on the maritime and coastal activities of an Anglo-African-American-Amerindian community of Protestant or atheistic, anti-Spanish and anti-Catholic, persuasion of the seventeenth century – the world described so vividly in Dampier's various voyages (Dampier 1697). Speaking, for example, of Rio la Hacha he says (p. 39): 'The *Jamaica* Sloops used often to come over to Trade here'; and of the pearl fisheries off Rancho-Reys: 'the old Men, Women and Children of the *Indians* open the Oysters, there being a *Spanish* Overseer to look after the Pearl. Yet these *Indians* do very often secure the best Pearl for themselves, as many *Jamaica*-men can testifie who daily trade with them.'

Subsequent links between the Anglophone territories were provided by inter-territorial migrations, by common features of colonial government and a certain interchange of government servants, by common missionary and educational activities such as those of the Mico schools and training college and, more recently, of the University (College) of the West Indies, and by common recruitment for labour in various parts of the region (e.g. for the Panama Canal, banana planting, railway building, cane and tobacco cropping, defence works etc.). Links were fostered in North America and Britain also, where, for example, Brooklyn and Brixton respectively are 'West Indian' rather than 'Jamaican', although culturally dominated by Jamaicans. To a certain extent West Indians made common cause against slavery, and, in the 1920s to 1940s, against the colonial system, only to break up the consequent Federation of the West Indies into local units when the common 'oppressor', Britain, had withdrawn. Today we must distinguish local, regional and pan-Caribbean cultural identities, and it is with the linguistic symptoms of these that our studies have been concerned. At the local level, each territory has its own particular history, contacts, ambitions, and political and economic and ethnic pressures. At the regional level we must certainly distinguish, at least historically, between Jamaican and Barbadian spheres of influence, between mainland and island communities, between the Western Caribbean and the Eastern Caribbean, and between the formerly-French and the continuously-British settlements. At the pan-Caribbean level the Afro-Creole identity is to be seen in relation to the Amerindian, the Hispanic, the East Indian and the North American.

The demographic background to the linguistic history of all the Creole English-speaking Caribbean is dealt with in some detail in John Holm's *A survey of pidgin and creole languages* (forthcoming).

Table 7. *Numbers of West Indian-born residents in 1971 in some London boroughs*

Brent	18,320
Hackney	14,325
Haringey	13,170
Lambeth	18,320
Lewisham	10,260
Wandsworth	12,505

Source: CRC (1975)

West Indian immigration into Britain

It is necessary finally, as a background to our discussion of language and identity among West Indians in Britain, to give some details of the large-scale migration which took place in the 1950s and 1960s. This migration stemmed from a variety of causes, such as the recruitment of Barbadians for work on the London Transport system, the 1952 McCarran Act which put a severe curb on West Indian immigration into the United States, and the operations of a particular shipping line whose agents were particularly active in Jamaica persuading Jamaican workers of ways by which they could raise the fare to the UK to make their fortunes. Basically the movement reflected the old problem of underemployment in the postwar Caribbean and a need for labour in British industries and transport. In the early 1950s the migrants numbered between two and three thousand annually, of whom approximately 70 per cent were men; in 1955 they totalled more than 25,000 and their numbers reached a peak with the announcement of legislation partially to exclude them in 1962, the last year of net inward migration being 1963. The proportion of women rose steeply after 1959. As a result of this mass movement of labour, the 1971 Census gave a total of approximately 300,000 West Indian-born residents in Britain; of these, 15.2 per cent lived in the West Midlands (mainly in the Birmingham area) and 65.3 per cent in the south-east, mainly in the Greater London area. Their chief concentrations within London in 1971, as estimated by the Community Relations Commission (1975) are given in Table 7. Of the immigrants, approximately two-thirds came from Jamaica, and 8 per cent from Barbados. All the other British West Indian territories sent some immigrants. Thus every variety of Creole English and Creole French dialect was represented among the immigrants, but the dominant linguistic influence among them has been Jamaican Creole.

Since 1971 a good deal of dispersal has taken place, reducing the 'black ghetto' effect of a number of areas. A number of our young black informants in schools in outer boroughs of London – for example, at Eltham Green and at Crown Woods schools in Eltham, in the Borough of Greenwich – have told us that their parents deliberately chose to live in such an area and to send their children to such schools where there were very few black children 'in order to give us a better chance'. At the University of York, English specialists among the undergraduates in the Language Department are sent to work in various schools during their second year, sometimes with children of immigrant parents, to study their situation; we have, during the past fifteen years, observed some quite remarkable shifts in the ethnic make-up of some schools, as the one-time 'immigrant' community becomes a 'black British' community and is absorbed, at least in certain respects, into the English social class structure (Sebba and Le Page 1984).

Today, a great many of the young British people of West Indian parentage were born in Britain and have grown up here; most of them speak the dialects of London or the other urban centres in which they were born – Birmingham, Nottingham, Derby, Manchester, Leeds, Liverpool, Sheffield, Bristol and so on – virtually indistinguishably from other natives of those cities. Nevertheless, as an identifiable ethnic group they seem on average to have greater difficulty in achieving well within the British educational system, and among the many complex factors to which this difficulty has been attributed is that of language. Educational failure appears to be linked with unemployment, and with the emergence of something resembling an alternative culture among young West Indians, accompanied by the use of an argot referred to as 'Jamaican' as a sign of group identity. It is the relationship of language to these other phenomena with which we shall be concerned in the case of Britain.

3 Sample West Indian texts

1. Introduction: general presentation

From Chapter 4 on we shall be concerned to illustrate acts of identity (a) through their linguistic symptoms, using the model of a multidimensional universe set out in Chapter 5, and (b) from what our informants in Belize, in St. Lucia and in London have actually said about their linguistic and social identities, and the stereotypes these statements reflect.

In this chapter we present texts which are a sample (from a huge range of material we have collected, more of which may be published as a separate volume for lack of space here) chosen to reflect certain cultural and linguistic properties of the so-called Anglophone Caribbean, some of whose basic cultural unities we drew attention to at the end of the previous chapter. We have tried to illustrate, in a compact way, various strands and layers of usage which are parts of the cultural nets which link regional and local communities with each other and with external cultures; we have provided some of the data, also, on which Chapters 4 to 6 are based. The translations which have been added to each narrative keep as close as possible to the style of the Creole.

The range and raison d'être *of the sample*

The grammar questionnaire sample is taken from the first section ('Substantives') of an instrument devised as part of Le Page's Linguistic Survey of the British Caribbean in the mid-1950s. (The team for this survey consisted of Le Page, Beryl Loftman Bailey, Louise McLoskey and David DeCamp. Great care and a long time was taken in each island to find, train and work with a comparable informant; in Jamaica Le Page worked alongside each of his colleagues, in the other islands he worked on his own with a local informant, but the method remained the same. The data collected in Jamaica was used by Beryl Loftman Bailey as a check on her own intuitions for her 1966 *Jamaican Creole syntax*.) Here we have chosen to give comparable sentences for Jamaica, St. Vincent and Grenada.

We chose these three because the languages used reflect three important facets of the cultural history of the Caribbean, as described in Chapter 2.

Jamaica (like the Leewards, Barbados and Belize) has a continuous history of more than 300 years of Anglophone Creole culture. Grenada, on the other hand, was until two generations ago (and to some extent remains) strongly affected by its Creole French past, as St. Lucia and Dominica still are today. St. Vincent, as we shall see, falls between these two, having had a very short period of Creole French settlement in the eighteenth century, and showing today not only its historical links with the northern Creole English culture of the Leeward Islands and Jamaica, but also its close proximity to the most English of all the islands, Barbados. The Grenadian texts illustrate the usage of an island population of Creole French speakers who were supposed to learn English as a new language at school. That school English, however, has been to some extent re-creolized according to a pattern partly due to Barbados, and partly to interference from Creole French itself, and which is found in the vernacular English also of Dominica, St. Lucia and Trinidad.

The short excerpt from an old newspaper column illustrates the Nevis-Leeward Islands usage, and also how one journalist at least resolved the problem of how to relate the pronunciation of that dialect to the spelling of Standard English. The result is clearly a compromise, both in pronunciation and grammar – the kind of compromise usually referred to as 'mesolectal' or 'mixed-lect' usage. From Barbados we give a short illustrative excerpt from a raconteur's account of a court case in which a man sued the owner of a dog which bit him; from Trinidad, a schoolboy's story illustrating the French Patois of his grandparents mixed with his own English. To help complete the Eastern Caribbean picture we include a short excerpt from a Guyanese conversation about an old witch, collected by John Rickford. The final text, before we come to the Belize stories, is from the code-switching of London teenagers of West Indian descent, recorded by Mark Sebba.

When these texts are scrutinized it is apparent that if we think about the English-speaking Caribbean as in some respects one cultural region, the linguistic behaviour of its inhabitants varies along many dimensions; there are, however, identifiable common strands in their pronunciation, their grammar and their vocabularies.

As there is no room here to print in full any of the long stories from Cayo District which form part of the results of our fieldwork there, we have given excerpts from the beginning, middle and end of three, illustrating at least five of the cultural relationships through which and with which our speakers may identify themselves: those of their age group, their level of education, their degrees of Spanishness and of Creoleness, and their command of the oral story-telling culture. The tellers are linked also to the Maya, Carib, Miskito Indian and Lebanese of their own country. But their 'educated' links reach out beyond the Caribbean to Britain and America of today and of previous centuries, their Creoleness to Belize City and to the rest of the Miskito Coast and to the Caribbean islands, their Spanishness to Petén Province of Guatemala, to Yucatan Province of Mexico, and beyond these, beyond Guatemala City and Mexico City, to Spain. Their age groups link them with the local conditions of their childhood and their status within their families; their story-telling prowess makes them each part, in a different way, of a dying but still quite strong oral culture with its roots in Africa, in Europe and also in Spanish Central America. Each of our informants formed part of a self-identifying community in Santa Elena; they were culturally related to one another along many networks, distinct from each other along many social parameters, different mixtures of the same ingredients that make up Cayo District 'Creoles'.

Our informants' links with the Creole world of the rest of the Caribbean can be illustrated from common strands in pronunciation, in grammar, and in their lexicon; so also can their more local and personal particularities. One brief illustration must here suffice of the pan-Caribbean Creole and more educated regional English elements (we give further illustrations in Chapter 5): that of the form which the infinitive of the verb takes in sentences where it forms a complement to the main verb. In the stories we find first a form similar to Standard English:

> evribadi *staat tu baal*
> 'Everybody started to bawl (cry)'

We also find just one example of another construction common in Standard English after *come* and *go*, that is, *go and see* alongside *go to see*, although it is difficult to distinguish this usage semantically from verb phrases in which *and* is a conjunction between successive actions: *wait and see*, *wait and meet her*, etc. (ð = th as in *then*):

> shii *kom aut ang* i *fees* ði gyal
> 'She came out and she faced the girl'

In addition, three constructions are common which do not occur in Standard English. One of these possibly reflects an archaic English still in use in America, as in 'Go get yourself a cup of tea'; as in Marlowe's 'Come live with me and be my love' or Donne's 'Go chide...sour prentices' – a construction in fact common much earlier, in Old English:

brada taida and brada anansi *mi gwoing go chap* planteej
'Brother Tiger and Brother Anansi were going to chop plantage'
(i.e. clear the bush)

a waang *go go stan* fo ði beebi
'I want to go to stand for the baby' (i.e. stand godfather for...)

The next is unknown in Standard English, though it uses *fu*, a derivative of the English word *for*, to give a purposive meaning to the first of two verbs; *for* in this context is to be understood as a reduced form of *for to*, and both *for* and *for to* are still used in this way in a number of British Isles dialects:

a weng *trai fu ron* we
'I'm going to try to run away'

ðat a hau ði geet...*kaal*...*fu oupn*
'That was how the gate...called...to be opened'

ði prinses *sen* ðis shuuz *fu go araung* wid am
'The princess sent this shoe to go around with it' (i.e. for me to go around with it)

Finally, a construction common in Standard English with the auxiliaries *shall* and *will* and the modals *may, might, would* etc. is extended to other verbs and overlaps with what are sometimes regarded as serial verbs; the two verbs follow one another, in the first two cases the first verb being auxiliary to the second, in the last form the second verb phrase being adverbial to the first:

ef nat a *weng biit* yu
'If you don't I'm going to beat you'

a *weng trai*
'I'm going to try'

ðeng *gyalan go* aal rait raung ði dansing haal
'They gallanted went all right round the dancing hall' (i.e. went in a dashing manner...)

ði gyal *fansi se* da i sista
'the girl thought (fancied, but was not sure) that it was her sister'

i no *waan go go chap* planteej
'He did not want to go and chop plantage' (i.e. clear the bush)

Comparison with Jamaican and Vincentian forms may be made by turning to p. 89. (An outline of other pan-Caribbean comparisons will be found in Le Page 1957/8, and some lexical comparisons in Le Page 1978b; but a great deal of further pan-Caribbean work is in progress – see, for example, Alleyne 1980; Hancock 1983.)

The writing system

There is of course no standard system for writing West Indian Creole languages. In popular literary use a number of conventions have developed for using a modified form of the metropolitan written language – English or French or Dutch or Portuguese or Spanish – to represent Creole usage. This is illustrated in our extract from the Nevis newspaper column. It gives us a good deal of information about how far the writer felt able to identify the Creole words as English words, and where he felt defeated by the attempt. Many of the literary citations in the *DJE* were written in similar adaptations, and some of the conventions that have developed have become almost universal, for example, *-h* as a final consonant indicating a pronunciation of words which in RP have a final vowel in an open syllable, words like *so*, *go*, *sir*, and so on. In RP these vowels tend to be long and often to be diphthongs or glides, whereas in creole or black English they remain short and not diphthongs; hence popular spellings which represent them as if they were in closed syllables: *soh*, *goh*, *sah* etc. At the other extreme, we have the option of a phonetic representation of what people actually are heard to say on particular occasions, or what segmental phones they are thought to be using – these will, when they are needed for illustration or clarity be put between square brackets [ ]. But it is possible to use a broad phonetic transcription which, when interpreted in the light of the given key, will give some indication of the variation in pronunciation of the same words within a speech sample without providing a regular orthographic representation of each word. We can if we wish go beyond that and concentrate on the phonemic structure of speech in terms of the systematic phonological units we discover in each dialect. This was the procedure followed by F. G. Cassidy in *Jamaica talk* and subsequently by Cassidy and Le Page in the *DJE* for those words recorded in Jamaica only from oral sources. This phonemic writing system for Jamaican Creole has been used for the grammar questionnaire, and in modified forms – to suit the particular characteristics of the dialect of each territory – it has formed the basis of the representation of the other speech samples also; the particular modifications have been specified in each case.

There is thus no over-all total consistency in the representations that follow; and some of the subsequent examples embedded in the discussion in Chapters 4–6 are at different levels of abstraction. The extracts from the four versions of the 'Three little pigs' stories in Chapter 5 are necessarily in a broad phonetic notation; most of the other examples are cited either in the form in which they appear in these texts, or in a phonemic or standard spelling representation. To avoid a profusion of brackets, slashes and other conventions we have adopted the general convention that phonemic or broad phonetic representations cited as examples in the main text will be printed in italic, with any subsequent gloss in standard roman type.

It must be remembered that to date the only writing system taught in West Indian schools is standard orthography; the only written language is the standard literary language, the only grammar taught and the only usage regarded as correct is that of the standard variety, and the complex systematic relationship of this to the various vernacular languages or dialects, which we have tried to illustrate in our extracts, is rarely recognized other than by linguists.

2. The grammar questionnaire for Jamaica, St. Vincent and Grenada

The fieldwork here was done in the 1950s. In each island an informant was selected after Le Page (and, in the case of Jamaica, his colleagues) had spent some weeks getting known in the vicinity (in St. Vincent, with the help of Mr Fandolph Cottle, and in Grenada, of Mr Claude Francis), and getting to know various possible local informants. In each case the informant was a young locally-born person with not more than primary school education, but with intelligence and the ability to understand that what we wished to record was a possible and likely way of expressing in the broad local vernacular what was expressed in the Standard English sentence. Plenty of time was given to each informant to consider the 'most likely' version in each case (sometimes several versions were offered), with at least a week being taken over each questionnaire. The complete questionnaire covered most aspects of the grammar; here we have room only for a sample from the section on 'Substantives'. The values of the letters used are shown in Table 8.

Substantives: a section from the questionnaire

It must be emphasized that both the syntactic structure and the vocabulary selected by each informant as the most appropriate way of expressing the concept in the vernacular will be idiosyncratic, and we

Table 8. *Consonants in Jamaican Creole* (*based on F. G. Cassidy's phonemicization*)

Jamaican Creole	Approximate pronunciation at initial, middle and final position illustrated from British English RP		
	Initial	Middle	Final
b	bed	rubber	web
bw[a]			
ch	church	reaching	church
d	dead	ladder	dead
f	fed	coffin	roof
g	gag	ragged	gag
gy[b]			
h	head (as occasional voiceless aspiration in final position also)		
j	jag	reject	ple*dge*
k	king	lo*ck*er	ro*ck*
ky[b]			
l	lead	polly	sell
m	mad	coming	came
n	ned	neddy	pan
ng[a]			
p	pad	copper	tap
pw[a]			
r	red	carrot	As in the '*r*-coloured' or 'burred' West of England pronunciation of words like *dear*. But for *r* after *e*, see *er* in Table 9
s	set	passage	puss
sh	shut	pusher	push
t	top	patter	pat
v	van	cover	cave
w	wed	wedding	—
w after b, p[a]			
y	yes	lawyer	—
y after k, g[b]			
z	zeppelin	razor	seize

[a] After *b* and *p*, w is used for a labial glide as in 'bwai' *boy*, 'ripwuot' *report*. -*ng* after a vowel may have any value from simply the nasalization of the vowel itself to the nasal consonant as in RP *singing*.
[b] After initial *k* and *g*, y is used for the palatal glide heard in *queue* and in some very old-fashioned British pronunciations such as 'gyel' for *girl*.

cannot therefore always compare one informant's syntax exactly with another's. Nor, once again, do we make any claim that forms not elicited and therefore not recorded here are not used in any of the islands.

Table 9. *Vowels in Jamaican Creole (based on F. G. Cassidy's phonemicization)*

Jamaican Creole	Approximate pronunciation illustrated from British English RP
ii	speak
i	pig
ee	paid (monophthongal pronunciation)
e	peg
er	third, work etc. (i.e. *r*-less long vowel), but sometimes the same vowel with some *r*-colouration
a	*Northern English* pad
aa	*a lengthened variety of* a
o	Tom
oo	*a monophthongal pronunciation of* home, those
u	put
uu	food
Diphthongs	
ie	fierce
ei	chase
ai	ride
au	house
ou	goat
uo	poor

Note: When the letter is doubled it indicates that the vowel tends to be longer than where there is a single vowel letter, and also to be higher in quality – as in the difference between RP *leave* and *live*. However, this distinction is not true in quite the same way for those communities which are, or which have been, in close touch with speakers of Spanish or of French Patois (e.g. Belize, or Grenada, or to some extent St. Vincent) as it is of Jamaica; in those communities it is possible for the short vowel to have the same high quality as the long one, without lengthening; and in some varieties of Jamaican Creole it seems as if any of the short vowels may become more like their long counterpart: for example, the fish *bream* may be /briim/ or /brim/. We have done our best to reflect these variations in our orthography for the texts.

(1) J   di pikini dem gaan huom
     StV di pikni an dem gan hoom
     G   di childrin go hom aalredi
          'The children have gone home'

(2) J   di kyat } wash im fies wid im fut
              pus }
     StV di kyat da wosh i fes wid i fut
     G   di kyat doz wosh is fes wid i fut
          'The cat washes its face with its paw'

(3)   J   mi nyam wan harinj dis maanin
         StV   mi bina iit won arinj dis maanin
         G   ai iit arinj dis mounin
                'I ate an orange this morning'

(4)   J   gud pikni ga-a hebm
         StV   gud pikni doz gu a hevn
         G   gud childrin go-in tu hevn
                'Good children go to heaven'

(5)   J   mi waak trii mail ga-a ⎰ maakit
                                go-a ⎱
         StV   mi waak trii mail fu gu a maakit
         G   a waak tri mailz tu di maakit
                'I walked three miles to market'

(6)   J   hag a mash op mi yam   ⎰ grong
                              nyaams ⎱
         StV   hag a ruut op mi yam
         G   pig iitin op oul mi yam in mi gyadin
                'Pigs are destroying my yam field'

(7)   J   him waan fi bai haas an kou
         StV   i waan fu bai won haas an won kyatl
         G   hi waan tu bai a haas an a kau
                'He wants to buy a horse and a cow'

(8)   J   him ha arinj an chuocho an banana an tandariin ina him
                bangkra
         StV   i bin got arinj, tanya, tanjariin an bunaana in i baaskit
         G   in i baaskit hi hav arinj, tandariin, kristofin an banaanaz
                'In his basket were oranges, chocho, bananas and
                tangerines'

(9)   J   jan an de hada wan bena hit manggo anda wan trii
         StV   jan an dem bina iit manggu anda won trii
         G   jan an dem di iitin manggo onda a trii
                'John and some others were eating mangoes under a tree'

(10)   J   him gi him tiicha di besis ⎰ pier
                                   bes ⎱
         StV   i gii i tiicha i bes pe i ben got
         G   i di av pez an i giv ii tiicha di bes wonz
                'He gave the best pears to his teacher'

(11)   J   jien mada get sik fram laas mont ⎫
               jien mada ben sik wan mont abak ⎭
        StV   jen muma tek sik laas mont
        G   jen muma get sik laas mont
             (note also: jen muma on dai-in, shii il tu ded)
             'Jane's mother fell ill last month'

(12)   J   di daangki hiez kech di haas anda him nuoz [lit. 'the
             donkey's ears catch the horse under his nose']
        StV   dongki iaz longga dan haas iaz
        G   dongki ez mo langga dan haas ez
             'The ears of the donkey are longer than those of the horse'

(13)   J   wi hep ⎰ di puo
                  ⎱ di puo piipl dem
        StV   aawi doz hep di pu
        G   wi doz giv moni tu di po piipl
             'We give help to the poor'

Similarities and differences illustrated from the grammar questionnaire

Table 10 illustrates, by setting out the forms actually used by our Jamaican, Vincentian and Grenadian informants, something of the patterns of similarity and difference between these three islands. We do not claim that what follows is in any sense exhaustive or complete; nor that a form not shown, e.g. for Jamaica, cannot be used there – merely that our informant did not use it.

It is evident that the St. Vincent informant reflects a dialectal boundary between North-Western (e.g. Jamaican), Bajan, and Eastern Caribbean usage – sharing, for example, plurals with Jamaica and Belize, the habitual marker *doz* with Bajan, some progressive *-ing* forms with Grenada. Interestingly, he also shares with some of our Belizean informants an unstressed *am* ~ *om* form for the oblique case of the third person singular pronoun.

By examining the comparable forms, we can see that sometimes Jamaica and St. Vincent are close, sometimes St. Vincent and Grenada; sometimes all three yield the same form, sometimes all have different forms. There is certainly enough general similarity to support our claim that the 'Anglophone Caribbean' constitutes a single cultural region in respect of language, but that each territory also has its own idiosyncratic cultural and linguistic identity and links.

Table 10. *Comparable forms used by Jamaican, Vincentian and Grenadian informants*

	Jamaica	St. Vincent	Grenada
Definite article	di	di, i	di
Indefinite article	wan, ∅	won	∅, a
Demonstratives			
these	dem ya, demaya	demya de...ya	diiz
this	disaya, disya	dat...de, dat...a	dis
that	da...de	dat...oba de	dat...wa de
those	dem, dem...de	dem, dem...de	dooz, ing wa de
Plurals and generic terms			
The children	di pikini dem	di pikni an dem	di childrin
Good children	gud pikni	gud pikni	gud childrin
Three miles	trii mail	trii mail	tri mailz
Pigs	hag	hag	pig
Oranges and bananas	arinj an bunaana	arinj an bunaana	arinj an banaanaz
The ears of the donkey	di daangki hiez	dongki iaz	dongki ez
The poor	di puo, di puo piipl dem	di pu	di po piipl
The two cats	di tuu pus dem	tu kat	di tu kyats
Quantifiers			
Many chickens	hiip a chikin, nof chikin	plenti faul	plenti faulz
A whole pudding	wan huol pudn, wan huol a pudn	won hool dukuna	a hol hol pudin
Half of the children	haaf a di pikni	haaf a dem	haaf av dooz childrin
A bunch of flowers (or roses)	wan bonch a ruoziz	won bonch a flauaz	a bonch a flauaz
Possessives			
My mother	mi muma (fi mi muma emphasizes *my*)	mi moda	mi muma
My mother's	(not in corpus)	fu mi moda	(not in corpus)
Jane's mother	jien mada	jen muma	jen muma
Pronouns : singular			
I	mi	mi, a	ai, a
me (dir. obj.)	mi	mi	mi
me (ind. obj.)	mi	mi	mi
my	mi	mi	mi
mine	fi mi	fu mi, fu mi oon	mainz
you (subject)	yu	yu	yu
you (dir. obj.)	yu	yu	yu
you (ind. obj.)	yu	yu	yu
your	yu	yu	yo
yours	fi yu	fu yu, yuoz	youz
he	him, im	i, hii (emphatic)	hi, i, hii
she	him	i	shi
it	it, i	i	it
him (dir. obj./ind. obj.)	im, hi, iim	am, om	im
her (dir. obj./ind. obj.)	im	am, om	a
it (dir. obj./ind. obj.)	im, it	it, a	it
his (hat etc.)	him, im	i	i
her	im	shi, i	shi
its	him, im	i	i
(it is) his	fi him	fu hi oon	hiz oun
hers	fi ar	fu shi oon	heez
(its)	fi im	(not in corpus)	(not in corpus)

Table 10. (cont.)

	Jamaica	St. Vincent	Grenada
Pronouns : plural			
we	wi	wi	wi
us	wi	aawi	os
our	wi	wi, aua	wi
ours	fi wi	wi oon	au-az
you	unu	aayu, yu	amongs-yu
you (dir. obj./ind. obj.)	yu	yu	yu
your	unu, hunu, fuunu	aayu	amongs yu, oul-yu
yours	fi yu	yuoz, fu yu oon	youz
you all, all of you (subject)	di huol a unu	aal yu	oul av amongs-yu, oul amongs yu
they	dem, de	di, dem	de
them	dem	de	de
their	dem	de, dea	de
theirs	fi dem	fu dem oon	deez
Reflexives			
myself	misef	mi won	ai miself
yourself	yusef	yusel	yu self
himself	himsef, im sef	i self	iself
herself	him wan	shi won	shi along
yourselves	unu sef	(not in corpus)	(not in corpus)
Verb forms in context, illustrated from 'go': *Unmarked for tense: habitual* (Good children) go (to heaven)	ga	doz gu	go-in
Continuative or progressive aspect			
(I) am going	a gwoen	a gu	a go-ing
(she) was going	ena gou	ben gwoing	di go
(where) were (they) going?	bena go, de go	bina gu	di go-in
(They) will be going	a go go	a gu	hav tu go
Future tense or volitional			
(I) will go	wi go	gu gu	go go
Past punctual			
he went	him gaa	i di bin, i bin	hi go
she went	him in (~ en) go	i gu	shi di go
Past completive			
(They) have gone	waak...gaan, gaan	gan, gaa	gan, go aalredi, gon
(She) has not been (to church)	neba go	nuba bin	dong go
Complements			
(No intention) of going	fi go	tu gu	tu go
(When did she) leave here to go?	lef hya gaan?, lef go?	lef...fu gu?	di liiv...tu go?
(We plan) to go	fi go, a go go	fu guin	tu go
(She is willing) to go	fi go	fu gu	tu go
(I cannot) ask him to go	aks him fi go	tel om fu gu	aks im tu go
He refused to go	him no waan fi go	i nu waan fu gu	i rifyuuz tu go
Imperative			
Go (to the shop)!	ga lang...!	gu...!	go...!

3. A short Anansi story from St. Vincent

(*er* here represents a vowel without *r*-colouration, [ɜ] or [ɜ:])

won de, nansi wen dong tukuma gu tel aal dem gyel hau hi doz raid bru lai-an. wel bru lai-an didn fiil su veri pliiz abaut dat su neks taim wen i sii brer nansi i aks brer nansi hau i kud gu aut tukuma gu tel aal dem gyel hau i doz raid om.

mi? mi gu tel gyel hau mi doz raid yu bru lai-an? dem gyel mos bi kreezi, hau dem gu se a ting laik dat? yes, bra nansi, yu tel dem su...enghau bra nansi (se) yu waan mi gu dong gu pruuv it? yes kom nau gu nau, le wi gu pruuv tu dem gyel dat yu se su.

oo god bot brer nansi (se) mi sik, mi kyaan waak an mi en got nu dongki. i se kom mi goin tu hav tu kyeri yu pon mi bak – yu got tu gu gu pruuv tu dem gyel we yu doz raid mi. su brer nansi get on on brer lai-an bak an daun tu tukuma de staat tu gu. wel wen brer nansi si aal dem gyel daun tukuma an hi on brer lai-an bak hi staat tu sing:

> si mi nansi komin daun
> si mi nansi komin daun
> si mi nansi komin daun
> kom si dem gyel a kooram –
> wips! wops! wips! wops!

dats hau i staat tu draiv an lash on brer lai-an an wen i riich de i se gyel aal yu si au mi stoori a truu? a aks yu doz ai riali raid brer lai-an in truut?

an dats di en ov mi stoori.

'One day, Anansi went down to Tukuma to go and tell all those girls how he was accustomed to ride Brother Lion. Well, Brother Lion didn't feel so very pleased about that so next time when he saw Brother Anansi he asked Brother Anansi how he could go out to Tukuma and tell all those girls how he was accustomed to ride him.

"Me? Me go and tell the girls how I ride you, Brother Lion? Those girls must be crazy, how did they say a thing like that?"

"Yes, Brother Anansi, you told them so..."

"Anyhow" Brother Anansi (said) "you want me to go down to prove it?"

"Yes, come now let's go now, let us go and prove to these girls that you said so."

"O God but" Brother Anansi said "I'm sick, I can't walk and I haven't got a donkey". He (Lion) said "Come, I'm going to have to carry you on my back – you've got to go and prove to those girls how you ride me." So Brother Anansi got on Brother Lion's back and they set off down to Tukuma.

Well, when Brother Anansi saw all those girls down at Tukuma and he on Brother Lion's back he started to sing:

"See me, Anansi, coming down" etc.

That's how (i.e. wips! wops! etc.) he started to drive and lash on Brother Lion, and when he got there he said "Girls, you all see that my story is true? I ask you, do I really ride Brother Lion in truth?"

And that's the end of my story.'

4. The Nevis newspaper column

This extract is from the *Nevis Recorder* for 26 November 1955. Two stereotype local women gossips Chatty and Papsy (i.e. Popsy) were created by the columnist to comment on topical issues in a humorous way. A good deal of adjustment in the direction of the standard language has taken place. The extract illustrates some of the problems confronting a publisher wishing to render the vernacular with a writing system which can be read by those familiar only with writing the standard language, so that there are many inconsistencies from a phonological point of view.

Chatty: Papsy lay arbee tark bote de Haspitul this week.

Papsy: Man no! Arbee chat enough to get de Haspitul finish, so now up day finish arbee can check arf.

Chatty: Who tell you up day done? When ting warntin a Nevis dem stap lang foo do, an when dem do, dem stap langer foo done.

Papsy: Well, well! Chatty me hear people a arks if me an you no weary chat.

Chatty: Tarl! Becars arbee a get wonderful result.

Papsy: Arbee carn chat foo-ever.

Chatty: Nevis carn backwud foo ever.

Papsy: You a wan de kine dat can wait lang. But you no meekly, an you murmur plenty.

Chatty: You is right. You ever noartice moars a de head people a Nevis an study way dem come fram?

Papsy: Yes dardy but me no say nutten becars me no warnt to start no ill-feelin.

Chatty: You carn start wha done begin. But dese days you gat to be brard mindid. Diffrunt islun people mus mix in Feda-rear-shun.

Papsy: Chatty me a hear plenty bote Feda-rear-shun af dese isluns. Wha dat mean?

Chatty: To tell de troot me no know wat e mean, but as Ah hear everybady a use de wud me use um too.

Papsy: Ah see how mean. You better goo lang go Federate.

Chatty: Dat's a good idea foo you too!

Translation

'Chatty: Popsy, let us talk about the Hospital this week.

Popsy: Gracious no! We've talked enough in order to get the Hospital finished, so now it is finished up there we can stop.

Chatty: Who told you it's finished up there? When something's needed in Nevis they take a long time to get started, and when they do it they take even longer to get it done.

Popsy: Well, well! Chatty, I hear that people are asking if you and I aren't tired of chatting.

Chatty: Not at all, because we get wonderful results.

Popsy: We can't chat for ever.

Chatty: Nevis can't always be backward.

Popsy: You are one of the patient ones. But you are not meek, and you complain a lot.

Chatty: You are right. Have you ever noticed most of the top people in Nevis and considered where they come from?

Popsy: Yes man! (*or* Yes, certainly!) but I didn't say anything because I didn't want to start any ill-feeling.

Chatty: You can't start what has already begun. But these days you've got to be broad-minded. People from different islands must mix in Federation.

Popsy: Chatty, I hear a lot about Federation of these islands. What does it mean?

Chatty: To tell the truth, I don't know what it means, but as I hear everybody using the word I use it too.

Popsy: I see the meaning. You had better go and Federate!

Chatty: That's a good idea for you too!'

5. The Bajan story

This was told by a raconteur, Mr Joseph Tudor, an amateur broadcaster and native of Barbados. It purports to be the evidence given by a man who tried to sue Mr Tudor in the magistrates' court in Barbados because Mr Tudor's dog had bitten him. Mr Tudor recorded the story for us in 1955. The values of the letters used are shown in Table 11.

Table 11. *The values of the letters used in the Bajan story*

з	a central vowel as in RP *shirt*; it can be long or short (зз, з)
a	a somewhat lower front-central vowel
œ	a mid front rounded vowel
b	in final position (e.g. in *gib*) is a bilabial fricative
ng	in postvocalic position indicates velar nasalization of the previous vowel
r	in postvocalic position indicates that the previous vowel has some *r*-colouration
ll	a long 'dark' *l*
ʔ	a glottal stop or glottalized consonant

Otherwise as in Tables 8, 9

Mr Tudor's account of a court case

wel sɜ ai waz waakin gwoing langap gavʔmɜnʔ hil an je-ez ai geʔ in franʔɜ
mistɜ tyudɜ pleas hi dag rashœut an hi boiʔ mi pan mi fuit...no sɜ hi di
boiʔ mi pan mi fuʔ sɜr...aaz a geʔ inʔ frangʔ di pleas di dag bang œuʔ pang
mi... wel di ting riiali puʔ mi œuta kamooshn fɜ a kapɜlɜ wiiks veri...wel
ai kɜan wɜɜk ɜtaal ɜtaal...ai daz sel swiidiz a...a di skuul...yes sɜr...ai
daz meʔ ɜbœuʔ trii or for dallz ɜ dea...wel aaz puʔ trii or for dallz ing i
trea an sel trii or for dallz an mek trii or for dallz sɜr...da iz a prafit yes
daiz wɜ aaz sel...

'Well sir, I was walking along up Government Hill, and just as I got in front
of Mr Tudor's place his dog rushed out and it bit me on my foot. No sir, it bit
me on my foot sir...As soon as I got in front of the house the dog bounded out
on me. Well the thing really put me out of commotion (*sic*) for a couple of weeks
certainly, I couldn't work one bit...I sell sweets at...at the school...yes sir,
I make about three or four dollars a day...Well, I put three or four dollars' worth
in the tray and sell three or four dollars' worth and make three or four dollars,
sir. That is a profit, yes, that is what I sell.'

eni we sɜ an ai haʔtɜ staing houm ai did biin tu i daktɜ tuu...an i daktɜ
se mai fuʔ waz teribli infleeɜmid...baʔ aʔ...noo i didn gib mi natʔn sɜr
i wudn gib mi nathn ɜtaal sɜ...iiz tel mi tɜ bring ii tɜ di kuuorʔ...pudi
ing kuuorʔ...duu wa ai laiʔ wid i...da ɜ wɜ i tel mi tɜ duu so ai haʔtu pudi
in kuorʔ koo hi laik hiiz ɜ vagyɜbɜn...yes sɜr...an ai...no ai diʔn aten
hoospiʔll sɜr...ai...ai...ai did riiɜli wenʔ tiiʔ daktɜ ɜn i gib mi dresing
...an i puʔ dresing pan di fuʔ...an di...di fuʔ...luʔ di fuʔ diʔ aaktyɜli
tɜɜrn œuʔ aaftɜ liʔll taim sɜ ɜm tɜɜrn œuʔ di wɜɜrs weɜ...

'Anyway sir, I had to stay at home. I went to the doctor, too, and the doctor
said my foot was terribly inflamed, but I...No, he didn't give me anything sir,
he wouldn't give me anything at all sir...he told me to bring him to the court,
put him in court, do what I liked with him – that is what he told me to do so
I had to bring him to court because he...well, see, he is a braggart...yes sir,
and I...No, I didn't attend hospital sir, I...I...I actually went to the doctor
and he gave me a dressing, and he put the dressing on my foot, and the...the
foot...well, see, my foot actually swelled up after a little time sir it swelled up
in a bad way...'

yes sɜr an aaftɜ daʔ den sɜʔ wel ʔai diʔ hooum tuu wiiks an ai diʔ biin
baʔ tu mistɜ tyudɜ an mistɜ tyudɜ wang duu naʔn ataal fɜ mi...bikaa mistɜ
tyudɜ...wel ai wu laiʔ sam sardɜ kampangseeshn sɜr koɜz aaftɜr aal ai diʔn
wɜɜʔ fɜ ɜ tɜim an ii...ii k...i shɜʔ gib mi sam sorɜ kampangseeshn ai waang
ten paung fram i.

'Yes sir, and after that then sir, well I was at home for two weeks and I went
back to Mr Tudor and Mr Tudor wouldn't do anything at all for me...because

Mr Tudor...Well I would like some sort of compensation sir, because after all I didn't work for a time and he...he c...he should give me some sort of compensation – I want ten pounds from him.'

6. Creole French and English code-switching in Trinidad

Le Page recorded this Trinidad story in 1966 from a boy in his 'teens living in the Maraval Valley, a cocoa-growing district in the Northern Range where Creole French used to be the common language. It was the language of the boy's grandparents and, to a less extent, of his parents. His story derives from a Creole French version and he used many of the terms of 'broken French' (as he called it) and explained them as he went along. The values of the vowel letters used are shown in Table 12. The consonant symbols have approximately the same values as in Jamaican (see p. 84), except that lengthened and syllabic consonants are marked thus: *dvang*, *schok*.

Table 12. *The values of the vowels used in the Trinidad story*
(*transcribed by Dr Pauline Christie*)

Vowels			
ii	[i], as in	*liiv* 'leave'	
i	[ɪ]	*liv* 'live' (verb)	
e	[e]	*gem* 'game', *get* 'get', *den* 'then'	possibly allophones
ɛ	[ɛ]	*wɛl* 'well', *wɛt* 'wet'	of one phoneme
a	[a]	*dat* 'that'	
aa	(a:]	*smaat* 'smart'	
aw	['ɒᵘ]–['ɔᵘ]	*dawg* 'dog'	
o	[ɔ]–[o]	*along* 'along', *bot* 'but'	
oo	[o:]	*rood* 'road'	
u	[u]	*yu* 'you'	
uu	[u:]	*huu* 'who'	
ɜ	[ɜ]	*wɜ* 'were'	
Diphthongs			
eə	['eə]	*weə* 'where'	
ai	['aɪ]	*mai* 'my'	
ou	['oʊ]	*nou* 'now'	
uo	['uɔ]–['ua]	*guot* 'goat'	

The story of Lion, Rabbit, Dog and Goat

mai nem iz m....g....ai liv at opa mont koko rood maraval. goin tu tɛl yu a stori about a rabit huu klem tu bi veri smaat an a la-yon huu chaid evritin tu kech him an iit him.

wɛl it staatid awf weə di la-yon gev a gyamblin sɛshan an invaitid di rabit along. rabit disaided tu go. nou di gem staatid an de wɜ ple-in dais la-yon tuk hiz fɜrs chaans an hiz dais red bon vyan ki ve ni pa ka ale miinin gud miit dat komz dont go bak. den deə woz kabrit wich iz guot in brokn frɛnch

hi tuk hiz chaans an sɛd ki ven isi kompwon miinin huu heə ondəstan. den
deə woz dawg shyang brokn french hi tuk hiz chaans an hi sɛd ki muun ki
pa teni byang pye pwang ɖvang miinin huu havn got gud lɛgz tek in front.

'My name is M....G.... I live at Upper Mount Cocoa Road, Maraval. (I
am) going to tell you a story about a rabbit who claimed to be very smart and
a lion who tried everything to catch him and eat him.

Well it started off when the lion gave a gambling session and invited the rabbit
along. Rabbit decided to go. Now, the game started and they were playing dice.
Lion took his first chance and his dice read "Bonne viande qui vient ne s'en
va pas", meaning "Good meat that comes does not go back." Then there was
"Cabrit", which is "Goat" in broken French. He took his chance and it said
"Qui vient ici comprend", meaning "Those who are here understand." Then
there was Dog – "Chien" in broken French. He took his chance and it said
"Ceux qui n'ont pas bons pieds prennent le devant", meaning "Those who
haven't got good legs go in front."'

oke, dɛn rabit fɛlt hi woz winin dawg fɛlt hi woz winin guot nyuu hi
woz winin bot guot wawntid tu liiv so hi sed dat hi woz jos goin tu paas
waata an hi lɛft nou wid di intɛnshan tu go stret huom but in goin hi had
tu kraws a riva an hi woz afrɛd dat hiz kluoz mait get wɛt so hi disaidid
hi woz tingkin about a weə tu get uova widout getin wɛt den a tawt ʂchok
him hi dogd a huol an lɛft hiz hawnz out kova op hizsɛlf. den dawg tɜrn
an sɛd kompe tiig dat iz la-yon o pa ko net se ale ale kabrit ale miinin iz
go guot gawn hi gawn stret huom so hi sɛd oke ail go an luk fo him an hi
lɛft wid di intɛnshan tu luk fo guot bot hi ryeli wawntid dat chaans tu go
huom tu bikawz hi had a lot of pokit moni in hiz pokit so hi lɛft. nou wɛn
hi kem tu di riva swam akraws kawz az yu nuo dawgz kyan swim an hi wɛnt
huom.

'OK? Then Rabbit felt he was winning, Dog felt he was winning, Goat knew
he was winning, but Goat wanted to leave; so he said he was just going to pass
water and he left, now, with the intention of going straight home, but in going
he had to cross a river and he was afraid that his clothes might get wet, so he
decided – he was thinking about a way to get over without getting wet. Then a
thought struck him; he dug a hole and left his horns out, covered up himself.
Then Dog turned and said "Compère Tigre", that is Lion, "vous ne savez
pas (que) Cabrit s'en est allé, allé", meaning "Goat has gone, he has gone
straight home." So he said "OK, I'll go and look for him" and he left with
the intention of looking for Goat, but he really wanted that chance to go home
too because he had a lot of (pocket)money in his pocket. So he left. Now, when
he came to the river (he) swam across because, as you know, dogs can swim, and
he went home.'

den deə woz rabit an la-yon aluon at huom so la-yon tuk dat chaans tu
chai tu kech him an iit him so hi sɛd kompal i ka fe fwet miinin its mɛkin

kuol ma ke shen shamla miinin hiil kluoz di hous staatid kluozin di duoz an windoz an so awn bot ryeli wawntid tu hav rabit kyej in.

so afta a wail la-yon wich iz tiig kem bak tu di tyebl an sɛd kompal oswa ma tinyu miinin tunait ai hav yu an hi hɛld awn tu hiz lɛg. so rabit tɜrn an sɛd u tu ku nu se pa mwe u ka chombe se pye taabla miinin yu tuu ṣchupid iz not mi yu huolin iz di tyebl fut. so la-yon ṣchupid az hi woz lɛt go rabits lɛgz an snach di tyebl fut instɛd dis taim so dats di chaans rabit had to uopn di duo an den ran out.

'Then there was Rabbit and Lion alone at home so Lion took that chance to try to catch him and eat him; so he said "Compère, il fait froid", meaning "it's cold"; "Je vais fermer la chambre" meaning he'll close the house; started closing the doors and windows and so on but really wanted to have Rabbit caged in.

So after a while Lion, which is 'Tigre', came back to the table and said "Compère, ce soir je vous tiens", meaning "Tonight I have you", and he held on to his leg. So Rabbit turned and said "Vous (êtes trop) stupide, ce n'est pas moi que vous tenez, c'est le pied de la table", meaning "You (are) too stupid, (it) is not me (that) you (are) holding, (it) is the table-leg." So Lion, stupid as he was, let go (of) Rabbit's legs and snatched the table-leg instead this time. So that's the chance Rabbit had to open the door and then ran out.'

wɛn hi kem tu di riva rabit az yu nuo a gud jompa doz jomp stret uova di riva. nou la-yon outrɛjos yu nuo hou hi kudn kech awn tu rabit hi stud op deə an sing if ai kud hav get somting aid pɛlt it afta yu so deə it woz guot hawnz stikin out of di ɜrt hi sɛd gaadi de u u ke we keshoy miinin luk bihain yu yuul si somtin tu pɛlt at mi so hi luk bihain la-yon yu nuo iz a strong animal doz snach huol of di hawnz an chuu it stret uova di riva den yu saw guot fawlin uova di riva on hiz fuo lɛgz an buot of dɛm join in an laaft at la-yon.

'When he came to the river, Rabbit as you know (is) a good jumper, jumps straight over the river. Now Lion outrageous (outraged), you know (at) how he couldn't catch Rabbit, he stood up there and sang: "If I could get something I'd pelt it at you." So there it was, Goat's horns sticking out of the earth. He said "Regardez derrière vous; vous verrez quelquechose", meaning "Look behind you, you'll see something to pelt at me." So he looked behind. Lion, you know, is a strong animal and he snatched hold of the horns and threw it straight over the river. Then you saw Goat falling over the river on his four legs and both of them joined in and laughed at Lion.'

7. The Guyanese text

The Guyanese text has been supplied by John R. Rickford, from those he has collected for *The Guyanese creole continuum* (forthcoming). 'Granny' (G), a retired sugar estate weeder, was 58 when interviewed by Rickford

(J) in 1974. The word *higue* ['haɪg] derives from the English word *hag*, here meaning a 'witch' (see *DJE*: HIGE). As in the Bajan text, *ʔ* here stands for a glottal stop or glottalized consonant. In Rickford's collection of texts this account occupies lines 490–555.

The Ole Higue who sucked her brother's neck

J: wo bo ting laik ool haig an so, yu biliiv in dem ting? yu evo heer bo dem tingz?

G: wel ye-es. mi biliiv in am, bikaas--mi brodo wo--am--bina chrobl o--a ool aig wuman. mi brodo bi smaal, ii bin de bou ten yeer....hii bina chrobl o--a--o--a ool leedii, an shi bin shi tel am se ii gu sok am. an ii bigin fu sok dis bai, an dis bai ge sik, an den kyarii tin aaspital in esteet. mi fado kyarii tu aaspital. an wel, a di nait wen--wen di--wen dis ool aig kom an ii a sok dis bai, sok om bihain ii nek hee, bak o ii nek.

J: yu sii o mark?

G: ye-es. ii sok am bak a ii nek so. dis bai a sii ii an ii a halo fu--mi fado bina sliip wid ii in di aaspital, pon di bed. an ii se--am--am-- "paa! paa! luk! luk! luk wo--luk ou dis wuman a sok mi nek!" an wen ii oo--wen ii wach so, ii sii pyoo blod, a ron out ii nek. an aal di bed in pyoo blod, mes op id blod. bot noo skrach an noo kot, wen dem luk di plees.

J: iz jos di blod kom out?

G: jos di blod poor out, an mes op a...

J: bo di blod bin de, doo? soo o--it reelii hapn?!

G: mi teʔ uʔ evribadi sii di blod, an sii di ee o ii poor out bak ii nek.

J: soo wo hapn den? dee di tek ii tu aspitol, an wo--di dohkto di noo wi tu duu?

G: yes. wel dem chrai wid ii--an ii--an ii get oova. ii na ded. so das wai mi biliiv dat ii ga hool aig.

'J: What about things like Ole Higue and so? Do you believe in those things? Have you ever heard about those things?

G: Well, yes. I believe in it, because my brother who--am--he used to tease an Ole Higue woman. My brother was small, he was about ten years old...he used to trouble a--an old lady and she was--she told him she would suck his blood. And she began to suck this boy, and the boy got sick, and they carried him to the hospital on the estate. My father carried him to the hospital. And well, in the night when--when the--when this Ole Higue came and was sucking this boy, she sucked him behind his neck here, at the back of his neck.

J: Did you see a mark?

G: Yes. She sucked him at the back of his neck here. This boy is seeing and he's hollering for--my father was sleeping with him in the hospital on the bed. And he said--am--am "Pa, Pa! Look! Look! Look at this woman sucking my neck." And when he--when he looked, he saw a lot of blood running out of his neck, and all the bed drenched in blood, messed up with blood. But there was no scratch and no cut, when they looked at the place.

J: It's just that the blood came out?

G: Just the blood poured out, and messed up a...

J: But the blood was there though? So it--it really happened?!

G: I tell you everybody saw the blood, and saw the way it poured out of his neck.

J: So what happened then? Did they take him to hospital, and what--did the doctor know what to do?

G: Yes. Well they tried with him--and he--and he got over(it). He did not die. So that is why I believe in Ole Higue.'

J: so dis leedii hee, so wo shii yuustu duu? shii yuustu wok ool aig? yuaal di noo shi wuz o ool aig leedii?

G: yes, e--evriibadii no shiiz a ool aig in di esteet.

J: wee wuz dis? in--am--at mohnchrooz?

G: noo--da--ai in liv in vraiz los--di ool leedii.

J: da in vraid los. yuu wuz bout hou ool den?...

G: mii bin mosii--a--mii bin big. mi mosi bo--de bou--footiin, fivtiin yeer i di taim.

J: ˙ oo, bo hii di smaalo?

G: hii bin smaal.

J: oo, obout hou ool? siks? sevn?

G: bo ten yeer.... ii a kaal shii hool aig an faiya raas, an di leedi ton bak an sok i.

J: hou ool shii wuz?

G: do leedi bin hool! mi no noo hou ho--bot ii bin ool-- iina ben an waak, hou ii ool.

J: so afto dis ting hapm ee, so nobadii in tel shi noting ar so?

G: no, noobodii in tel shi notn.

J: di fraikn?

G: na tel shi notn. dee na kech--de na kech ii a di spat, yu noo. de beeri--di--oo--n di bai sii ii wid ii--ee--ii ai.

J: ii sii shii?

G: ii sii shi, bot mi no noo ou ii disapeer. bot ou ii waak dong from di aaspital--from til o opsteez, bin tuu stoori aaspital--hou ii waak dong fron oopsteez kom til a dongsteez, a so dii blod lii--iik til ii ton out, an gaan a di rood! di blod a wash a kom dong! shi--ii a-- vamit out di blod, rait chru di aaspital.

J: afto ii kom out?

G: afto ii kom out, di blod--ii a chro ou di blod a kom out. laik ii kyaan
     stomik di blod. aal i step, di aaspital step, aal o--fu waak in di gya--am--a
     di--a di--di gyalorii--aal in blod! fu kom dong di step a dongsteez
     aal!...dee falo di blod, di blod an hii aal. hou--dee a chrees dii blod
     an sii hou shi gaan. so ii vamit di blud fu kom out til a di rood.

'J: So this lady here, what did she do? She used to do the work of an Ole Higue?
     Did guys know that she was the Ole Higue lady?

G: Yes. E--Everybody knows she is an Ole Higue on the estate.

J: Where was this? In--am--at Montrose?

G: No. That--I lived in Vryheid's Lust--the old lady.

J: That was in Vryheid's Lust. About how old were you then?

G: I was, I must have been--am--I was big. I must have been about--about
     fourteen–fifteen years old at the time.

J: Oh, but he was smaller?

G: He was small.

J: Oh, about how old? Six? Seven?

G: About ten years old. He was calling her Ole Higue and Fire-Rass, and the
     lady turned around and sucked his blood.

J: How old was she?

G: That lady was old! I don't know how old--but she was old. She would bend
     over walking, she was so old.

J: So after this thing happened here, didn't anybody tell her anything or so?

G: No, nobody told her anything.

J: Were they frightened?

G: They didn't tell her anything. They didn't catch--they didn't catch her at
     the spot, you know. They barely--the--only the boy saw her with his--his
     eyes.

J: He saw her?

G: He saw her, but I don't know how she disappeared. But along the route that
     she walked down from the hospital--from till upstairs, it was a two-storey
     hospital--along the route that she walked down from upstairs to come
     downstairs, all along there the blood had lea--leaked, until the point at which
     she had turned out and went down the road! The blood was coming down
     in a wash! She--she was--she vomited the blood, throughout the hospital.

J: After she came out?

G: After she came out, the blood--she was throwing up the blood as she came
     out. Like she couldn't stomach the blood. All the steps, the hospital steps,
     the place to walk in the--ga--am--at the--at the--the gallery--all in blood!
     Coming down the steps leading downstairs and all!...They followed the
     blood, the blood and her too. The way--they traced the blood and saw the
     way that she left. She had vomited the blood all the way to the road.'

8. The London Jamaican text

This conversation was recorded by the two girls C (aged 15) and J (aged 16), when Mark Sebba left them on their own with the tape-recorder at a school at Catford, South-east London, in May 1982. C's parents had both come to England from Kingston, Jamaica; J's were both from the parish of St. Ann, on the North Coast of Jamaica. It must be emphasized that Sebba was not here concerned to record speakers of Jamaican Creole in London; his concern was to use the techniques of conversational analysis to study code-switching between London Jamaican and London English, and we return to his conclusions, and their relevance to our own study, in Chapter 5.

The orthography Sebba has used reflects as far as he can the code-switching of the two girls between their London dialect and their London Jamaican. He uses conventional orthography to a large extent for the former – using, that is, conventions already well-established for the representation of 'dialect'. Thus *Edit* for 'Edith' reflects the characteristic [t] for [θ] of Jamaican; *hæv* indicates that the vowel is the raised Southern English, rather than lowered Jamaican, vowel in *have*; we have put slashes around those sections where he uses the conventions of Cassidy's phonemic representation for 'Jamaican', as in /biebi/ *baby*; and the item in square brackets, [ʃɪmɪəsɪn], is a phonetic transcription of an unidentifiable word. In the phonemic transcription, we have for ease of representation used /a/ for Sebba's ʌ in /snabop/, /mada/, /ada/, /alo/, /nating/ and we have subsumed his distinction between [i] and [ɪ] under the graph /i/. As in most London varieties of English, intervocalic or final [t] is liable to be a glottal stop.

It will be seen that the incidence of 'Jamaican' forms increases steadily as the conversation proceeds, but that the mixing of elements is quite intimate.

J: [*piano*] start...talk about party...about blues you've been to...you start

C: you goin' to Edi's christening (though)...it's on Sunday...did you know she had a baby?

J: Who?

C: Edit'

J: Edit' hæv /biebi/?

C: Yeah man...she's 'avin' a christening /dis saturdi/

J: is it?!

C: No [*snaps fingers*]...Sonday night...Sonday the day

J: [ʃɪmɪəsɪn] she never did invite me...are you goin'?

C: No she never invite me neider

J: 's not fair!

C: no, she invite...erm...you know Johnny?

J: yeh

C: him tel mi...and my mum went to her house and she said she's o – she just told her she's avin' a christenin' /mi no nuo if mi a go/

J: so how old is the /biebi/ then?

C: about...let me see now...when di she ave it /tink shi av it/ last year November some time

J: is it?!

C: * * December, yeh man!

J: She keep her secrets to herself...innit?

C: mhm

J: 'cos Ja – I 'aven't seen Janny for ages an' he isn't told me anyfing

C: him and Maureen split(op) too you noh

J: is it?!

C: yeh man!

J: No lyin' to me Carol

C: /mi na a lai/...he's move – /im muuv bak in wid di mada/

J: ah ha ha [*laughs*]

C: dem splitop!

J: so did 'e tell you why dem split up?

C: no.../mi neva aks im/ a question

J: well de last time (mi) didn't /nuo/, right, Johnny turn off de gas /mienz/, so de /biebi/ couldn't get no food and M(w)aureen couldn't cook no food eiver [iːvɐ]' cause them did have one big argument... Maureen's too moany...oh my God

C: /mi no rieli nuo har/ [mi nɒ ɹɪəlɪ nəʊ hɐr]/mi no sii a fi long taim nou mi sii ha sista dem bot mi no sii shi/

J: oh dear [ɒ dɪəɹ]...so...no, you think she'll turn the christenin' out into a blues or what?

C: yeh, I feel say dat yeh, you know Scatney 'oe

C: feel say (dey're) holdin' it over dere y'know

C: christenin' in de mornin'

J: yeh

C: My mum /mi ma/ – my mum said I must go...bu

C: /mi no laik piipl-dem we goin bi de/

  ['I don't like the people who are going to be there']

J: I ge' what you mean.../em aalwez wid dem snabop piipl innit, wen dem tink dem nais...a si a/ down Deptford /di ada die (n) shi se alo ta mi shi neva did se nating about har biebi/

['they're always with those snobby people, aren't they, when they think they're nice?...I saw her down at Deptford the other day and she said Hullo to me, she didn't say anything about her baby']

C: is it?

J: so what she have?

C: /a likl gyal...mi si ar aaredi...shi aarait/

['a little girl...I've seen her already...she's OK']

J: what's 'er name?

C: /mi no riali/...I don' remember wha' she /kaal har/.../mi na iivn nuo/

J: oh dear [o: dɪəɹ]

9. Three stories from Cayo District, Belize

In the course of the 1970 survey of Cayo District, Belize, described in the next chapter, each of the 280 or so children in our sample was asked to record an Anansi story or an old witch story, and a great many did so.

Le Page had used this technique for many years in the Caribbean, as a way of eliciting Creole language data. The texts published by David DeCamp in the first volume of *Creole language studies* (Le Page 1960) were examples. It had been found that characteristically the informant would begin the story in a more standard English, and then, as the story took hold, would slip into the more vernacular (and sometimes archaic) mode of the oral tradition to which these stories belong. Frequently, magic formulae were embedded in the stories, often sung; they were repeated as remembered, even if not understood at all. Thus the technique of collecting traditional stories allowed a study of the language with some historical as well as synchronic dimensions to it.

In 1966, when making a pilot study for the survey, Le Page had visited a primary school in Santa Elena, a suburb of San Ignacio del Cayo, and asked the nuns if they would lend him their cheekiest girl pupil for an hour, to record some stories. They sent for GM, who was 12 years old at the time, and whom they had often heard telling stories to the other children in the playground. A room was placed at our disposal. The girl was of course both nervous and excited. Both these factors came out in the telling, since at times both the narrative and the characters were muddled. She told her stories first in ['kri·a], as she called Creole, and then in Spanish. She had been born in and had grown up in Cayo District, daughter of a

Table 13. *Values of letters used in the transcription of the stories from Cayo District*

er	a vowel close to the *r*-coloured [ɜːɹ] vowel in some English dialects in e.g. *work*
ch	as in the initial consonant in *choke* [tʃ]
sh	as in the initial consonant in *shake* [ʃ]
th	[tʰ] or [θ]
j	[dʒ] or [ʒ], in final position sometimes [ʃ]
vowel + ng	a nasalized vowel or a nasalized vowel followed by a palatal or velar nasal consonant (Ṽ, Ṽn or Ṽŋ]
ð	as in the initial consonant in *then* [ðen], or some partial friction of [d]
ʔ	glottal stop
ang	standardized version of 3rd person objective pronoun, to avoid confusion with *an* 'and'
weng	standardized version of the unstressed form of the future verb marker, which can vary between [ã] and [wɛ̃ŋ], to avoid confusion with *wen* 'when'

Note: It is quite possible that the copula when it occurs after a final dental should really be *da*; compare ð*is da we yu mi di du* 'this is what you were doing' and *dat a we yu di du nau* 'that is what you are doing now'. But see *DJE*: DA⁴ and A⁶.

'Bay-born' (i.e. Belizean Creole) father and a Mexican mother. We returned to record her again in 1970 and again in 1978, and we tell part of her story in Chapters 5 and 6. We give here extracts from the beginning, the middle and the end of a long story she told Le Page in 1966.

The second set of extracts is from a story told by the matriarchal 'nana' of one of our 1970 informants. She also lived in Santa Elena; she also claimed to be half Creole, half Spanish. But she was 83 years old and had been born in Orange Walk, a more 'Spanish' district, to the north of Cayo. Her Spanish was more fluent than GM's; she was in fact apparently translating a 'Spanish' Cinderella story (the story of Mariquita Plata and the mermaid) into Creole for our benefit. Again, we give only extracts here, from the beginning, the middle and the end.

Each of these story-tellers began by adjusting their language to Le Page as a member of the audience. Each became much less self-conscious as her story progressed; GM became positively excited, TA more of an actress, acting the various roles.

The third set of extracts is from a story told by DW to Pauline Christie in 1970. The girl was 13, and in Standard VI of Sacred Heart Primary School in San Ignacio. Her early conversation with Dr Christie was in fairly standard English; but this was the second of two Anansi stories that she told, and it is in most respects her most Creole usage.

The transcription is a broad phonetic transcription in which, although the form of many morphemes has been standardized throughout, some attempt has been made to reflect the inherent variability of the informant's phonology and morphology. Thus, for example, the first vowel in the word for *brother* varies between more [a]-like and more [ɛ]-like qualities (the latter here represented by *e*); the stressed form of the verb *know* tends to be [noꞏa], the unstressed [noꞏu], and so on. Some minor modifications have therefore been made to the Jamaican system, as shown in Table 13.

(1) *An Anansi story told by GM, aged 12*

GM told this story in 1966 when she was a pupil in the primary school in Santa Elena.

Brother Tiger and Brother Anansi
The beginning

mai neem iz g...m..., ai am twelv yiiarz oul ai liv in trapiich kaiya distrik and aim nau goin tu tel yu an anansi stuori...in kria...

wans apana taim brada taiga an brada anansi mi gwoing-go chap planteej...an braða taiga woz werkabl an braða ana...an braða anansi mi leezi...an so ðeng...ðeng gaan gan chap ði planteej...brada anansi fiil so leezi nau i no waan go chap planteej...so nau...ði...brada...i tel brada taiga ges wat...wan leedi waant mi fo komaadre...nau a waang go go stan fo ði beebi...sou brada hanansi (*sic*) tel ang oke ðen...yu go...bot...nat stee tuu lang...so brada hanansi...wen...braða anansi gaan an wen i gaan i gaan op an get di bota fam afa ði shelf...an wen i get ði bota afa ði shelf hi bigin tu iit an...i se...bra...i se wel ai weng iit bota nau an wen braða taiga ask mi wo di beebi neem a weng tel ang wan paung gaan...so...braða anansi bigin tu iit bota an i iit tel i get inof...wen i get inof i ss...bra...i gaan bak da braða taiga...braða taiga w...tel ang wa di beebi neem...wan paung gaan so i se bot wan ada leedi waant mi fu komaadre an i se a haftu go ðis iivnin...tuutherti...i se so ðat a kud get ðeh jost in taim fu di faada...so...i gaan agen an...wen i kom bak agen i iit tuu paungz a di bota...so nau brada taiga ask ang wa di beebi neem...i tel ang tuu paung gaan...i se bot ges wat a haftu go bak agen i se a no noa kompa i se a no no wai ðe laik mi fu komaadre...

'My name is G...M... I am twelve years old. I live in Tropeche, Cayo District and I'm now going to tell you an Anansi story...in Creole. Once upon a time, Brother Tiger and Brother Anansi were setting out to clear some scrub, and Brother Tiger was a good worker and Brother Ana...and Brother Anansi was lazy; and so they...they went to go and clear the scrub. Then, Brother Anansi felt so lazy that he did not want to go and clear the scrub. So then...the Brother...he told Brother Tiger "What do you think? A lady wants me as (godmother *sic* for) godfather...Now I want to go and be a godfather to the baby!" So Brother Anansi (*sic*) said to him "OK then – you go – but don't stay too long." So Brother Anansi...when Brother Anansi went and when he left he went up and got the butter from off the shelf...And when he got the butter off the shelf he began to eat it and he said..."Bro..." he said "Well, I will eat butter now and when Brother Tiger asks me what the baby's name is I will tell him 'One-pound-gone'". So Brother Anansi began to eat butter and he ate till he had had enough. When he had had enough he...ss...Bro...he gone back to Brother Tiger. Brother Tiger w...asked him "What's the baby called?" "'One-pound-gone' – so", he said "but another lady wants me as godparent and", he said, "I have to go this afternoon at two-thirty", he said, "so that I can be there just in time for the priest". So...he went again and...when he came back again he had eaten two pounds of the butter. So now Brother Tiger asked him "What's the baby called?" He told him "' two-pounds-gone'", he said, "but guess what – I have to go back again", he said, "I don't know, friend", he said, "I don't know why they like to have me as godfather"...'

The middle

...den...den a jos wan nyuusans ina piipl kin...piipl kin...da we dat brada taiga...ask ang...i se...piipl sskin...piipl sskin i se...oke...laas chaans a di gi yu i se laast laas laas chaans...oke...braða taiga ga...brada hanansi gaan an i liiv brada tai...i lef breða taiga...di chap planteej...wen breða taiga gaan gan chap plan...e...planteej nau wail brada hanansi di iit bota...wa di beebi neem...i se wel haha brada da wan neeng aal gaan aal aal gaan...i se aalawe aalawe aalawe gaan...i se bot we yo miin bai aalawe aalawe gaan...i se wel hhaiii i se kompa kyaan tel yu ða wan ataal no ða wan a kyaan tel...

'"They...they are just an annoyance in somebody's (s)kin." "Somebody's kin...what's that?" Brother Tiger...asked him. He said "Somebody's *skin*, somebody's *skin*" he said. "OK – I am giving you one last chance", he said, "the very last chance...OK." Brother Tiger wen...Brother Anansi went and he left Brother Tiger...he left Brother Tiger clearing the scrub. When Brother Tiger had gone to clear scru...em...scrub now while Brother Anansi was eating butter. "What's the baby called?" He said "Well, ha ha brother, that one's called 'All-gone, all-all-gone'", he said, "all-away-all-away-all-away-gone." He said "But what do you mean by 'all-away-all-away gone?" He said "Well, hahai" he said, "friend, I can't tell you that, certainly, that's one I can't answer"...'

The end

...nau...an...ii se...a no weng mek breda hikitii kong ya nau bikaz ii freed...an...ii noa ðat ii weng ded...so em plan fu troa brada taiga iina waata az ðe hiie em...braða hikitii se...laad...nau a weng troa iina waata...breða taiga ga [cough, cough] an...ii se...aha unu piipl aha unu

piipl a tel unu a tel unu se breda taiga no ded brada taiga no ded ataal...ii
se...an if braða taiga kik op iina ða kaafn wi weng noo an braða taiga staat
tu kik op iina ði kaafn an...i get aut a di kaafn an i jomp pan wan trii an
wen i jomp i jomp pan wan pin an if ði pin neva ben ði nansi stori neva en

'"now...and" he said, "I won't get Brother Hicatee to come now because
he is afraid and...he knows that he will be killed." So they planned to throw
Brother Tiger into water as they heard...em...Brother Hicatee say "Lord
...now I will be thrown into water." Brother Tiger went "ahem, ahem" and
said "Aha you people, aha you people, I tell you, I tell you Brother Tiger is
not dead, Brother Tiger is not dead at all", he said, "and if Brother Tiger kicks
up inside the coffin we will know." And Brother Tiger started to kick up inside
the coffin and...he got out of the coffin and jumped on a tree, and when he
jumped he jumped on a pin, and if the pin never bends the Anansi story will
never end.'

(2) *A Cinderella story told by TA aged 83*

TA told this story in Santa Elena, Cayo District, Belize, in 1970, to VS
(her niece) and members of her family and to Le Page and Andrée
Tabouret-Keller. (We are indebted to Diana Woollard for transcribing
the 'Spanish', with help also from John Green, and from Ava
Belisle-Chatterjee.)

Mariquita Plata and the Mermaid

The beginning

LeP: Can you tell me a story – an Anansi story? – Alligator and Tiger?
TA: o ai no no da wan...haligeta an taiga...no...marikiite plaata...yu
mos eskyuuz mi bikaz ai smook...ðis iz a leedi nong?...eskyuuz mi...yu
set it aredi? i had tuu...wan...tuu daata...wan iz hiz an ði neks wan iz
nat hiz...so di wan dat hav mada i kyier dat wan mo shiiz a...siimtris an
ði aða wan we no hav mada shi iz a...laik a kichin gyal...wel aalrait...
ði...de weng hav a daans laik tunait...fraidih...ðem gaan aal roung an
invait...aal ði leediz hu de pan di plees an jentilman hu had waif ðem keri
it an hu no hav waif ðem kyeri dem seem...seem wee...wel yes i se em
marikiita...i se yu gwoin...yu nat goin tu ðis dans i se aii mama i se ai
waan go tu dat daans...nau iz i prinses...i prinses yongis son hia aal abau?
ði daartar we had ðis staar tu i farid...i se mama yu no weng kyer mi i se
no yu nat going so i se hau...mi aða sista gwoin...se shii gwoin bot yuuv
gat tu ste fo niid a baril a flaua...an tek op wan baril a rais bifoo
deelait...aii mama i se yu shuda ponish mi wan difran kain a wee...pali
de tu di do...wan yelo hed...i no se nothin bot i had it in main...aarait...

'Le P: Can you tell me a story – an Anansi story? – Alligator and Tiger?
TA: Oh I don't know that one... Alligator and Tiger... no... Mariquita Plata...
you must excuse me because I smoke... This is about a lady – OK?... excuse
me, have you set it (the tape-recorder)? She had two... one... two daughters...
one was her own and the other was not her own... so that the one that had her as
mother, she cared more for that one... she's a seamstress and the other one that
did not have a mother she was a... like a kitchen girl. Well, all right... the... they
were going to have a dance as it might be tonight... Friday... they went all round
and invited... all the ladies who were there on the property and the gentlemen
who had wives, they took (the invitation to them) and they took it in the same
way to those who had no wives... Well, yes... she said em "Mariquita"... she
said, "you're going... you're not going to this dance." She said "Oh! mama",
she said, "I want to go to that dance."... Now it was the princess's... the
princess's youngest son who heard all about the daughter who had this star on
her forehead... She said "Mama, you're not going to take me?" She said "No,
you're not going." So she said "How is that! My other sister is going!" She
said "she's going!! but you've got to stay here to knead a barrel of dough... and
winnow a barrel of rice before daylight."... "Oh mama!" she said "you should
have punished me in a different way."... Polly (the parrot) was there at the
door... a yellowhead... he didn't say anything but he remembered it. OK...'

ðis satadeh ði daans koming i erm kil... i kil wan hag... an i kaung nain
piis a gots an i gii tu di gyal... di wan we no hav mada... i se nau yu
goa tu di waatasaid... an auta dis nain piis a gots wot a goin tu giv tu yuu
an if yu laas wan i se ail morda yu tude... gyal tek op ði bokit han i put
am pan i hed an i gaan tu di waatasaid... i di wash i di wash di gots i wash
ði gots... miiameed kong... an i grab a piis a di gots fan ang... miiameed
gan wid piis a di gots... nau i se mi ma gweng biit mi tel i kil mi an i bigin
tu krai... i krai i krai tel miameed kom...

ih getta wan plees... laik fam ia sa wi aalweez menshan a faar plees yu
sii... laik rak donda... miiameed ton bak... wid ði gots... i se mai
daata... i se yes ma... i se wat yu kraiing fa?... i se mi mama kil wang hag
dis maanin an i kaung nain piis a gots an i sei ðat... if ði bilam ðem tek
awee wan... im gwointu kil mi... wið biitn... i se neva main pet... i se sii
yo gots ia... wel ði... ði rood av ði waatasaid... ða tuu... laik wan strenj
yu no? wen yu goin op... i sez em... wen yu gwoin op ðis hil... i se yes
ma... i se yu gwoin tu hia ði ruusta... kroo... i se yu heng doung yo hed
gens ðis bengksaid... i se yes ma... i se wen yu hia ði jakaas baal... i sed
yu lif yu hed... ih kom... ih gwoin nuuntaim...

an i weet pan ðat jakaas i weet pan am tel ði ovakom ði jakaas baal i kom
(wið wan stari... *mistake*) faar di staar... niar antu i nooz brij... komin op
wi dis bokit... ði seem gyal... we... ðem gat ði... ðe lov hing mo bikaz da

i daarta...yu sii?...ðat a i daarta bot ðis nekst wan a no i daahta...iz a stepdaahta...aii mama i sed if...lo pan sista mama bot yu fu taak it in spanish bot ai di trai brok ang iina krioul no?

LeP: But tell me in Spanish.

TA: i se mama i se ya biene ermana mama i se beya lo ke tyene ermana...ermana tyene e...la...el luusero diise...en na frente...komo ba ser diise komo ba se...da...ung beks oul leedi yu no...kraas...se komo ba ser...wel shii kom aut ang i fees ði gyal an wen i fees ði gyal...i se aidios meeyu...onde kontsegites esso lo ke tienes...i se mama ke tenggo? i se tienes alwo en tu fa...en tu frente se no se behate la kobetah...e baya ensenyaselo a tu papa

'This Saturday when the dance was coming she em killed...she killed a pig...and she counted out nine pieces of the tripe and gave them to the girl...the one who had no mother...She said "Now you go to the riverside...and...from...these nine pieces of tripe that I'm giving to you and...if you lose one!" she said "I'll murder you today." The girl took up the bucket and she put it on her head and she went to the waterside...she was washing, washing the tripe...she washed the tripe. A mermaid came...and it grabbed a piece of the tripe from her...the mermaid went with a piece of the tripe..."now", she said, "my mother will beat me till she kills me" and she began to cry...she cried and cried until the mermaid came...

It reached a place...You see, from where we are now sir we always mention a far place you see, like Rock Dunder...The mermaid turned back...with the tripe...she said "My daughter." She said "Yes ma?" She said "what are you crying for?" She said "my mama killed a pig this morning and she counted out nine pieces of tripe and she said that if the fish took one away (from me) she was going to kill me...with beating."...She said "never mind, pet"...she said "here is your tripe." Well, the...the road from the riverside...had two...(like one [gesticulating with her hands] you know?) when you're going up...she says em..."When you're going up this hill"...She said "Yes ma?"...She said "you will hear the cock crow"...She said "You must put your head down against this bank of the river"...She said "Yes ma"...She said "and when you hear the donkey neigh"...she said "you must lift up your head"...She went...she was going at noon.

And she waited for that donkey, she waited for it until it passed the time that the donkey neighed...she came for the star...near to the bridge of her nose...Coming up (the hill) with this bucket...the same girl...who...they had the...they loved her more because she was her daughter – you see? That one was her daughter but this other one was not her daughter...she was a step-daughter..."Oh mama" she said "if...look at my sister, mama", but you should say it in Spanish, but I am trying to translate it into Creole, OK?

LeP: But tell me in Spanish.

TA: She said "mama" she said "here comes sister mama" she said "look what sister has got...sister has got the...the...the morning star" she said "on her forehead"..."What's up?" she said "What's up?"...that was a vexed old lady, you know...cross...she said "What's up?" Well, she came out and she faced the girl and when she faced the girl she said "My God! wherever did you come by that thing you've got?" She said "Mama what have I got?" She said "You've got something on your fo...on your forehead." She said "I don't know." "Lift the bucket down from your head and go and show it to your father."

so di lii gyal tek dong ði bokit...an...i gaan tu i pupa...aii maadre hesuuth diise...no se ira...d...a...a morir?...komo draahola lestreeya de la manyaana en la frente...nau ðis...ði neks stepdaata...shi...i... [*laughs*]...ði gyal neem marikiite plaata ya no...i se beyalo mama i se beya ke tiene la marikiite plaata mama i se mama maate un chancho mama maate...nau da grojful yu no...maate un chancho mama...baiya... kiitase di akii...i gan tu i papa...maate un chancha papa i se pa ke yo kongsiya ke tiene mi ermana...maatelo papa por dyos maatel...i pa get op beks...i se bais a be (i) gaan an i kil ðii hag i se unu ponggang awa kaliente...pa ke yo rasp el maraano i ke yo le saake la tripa...wel...ðe haal dobl bengk ðis ting ðem se...di auaz di paas...di gyal nau weng get ði siem ting...

'So the little girl lifted the bucket down and...she went to her father..."Holy Mary!" he said "does it mean that we are all going to die? Where did you get the morning star from on your forehead?" Now this...the other stepdaughter she...she [*laughs*]...the girl's name was Mariquita Plata you know...she said "Look at it mama", she said, "look what Mariquita Plata has got mama", she said, "Mama, kill a pig, mama, slaughter...' now that one is mean you know..."Kill a pig mama." "Go on, get out of here." She went to her father. "Kill a pig, papa" she said "so that I can get what my sister's got...kill one, papa for God's sake, kill one." Her pa got up, vexed, he said "You'll see." He went and he killed the pig, he said "You make the water hot so that I can shave the pig and take out its tripe." Well, they did all this at great speed. They said – time was passing – that the girl would now get the same thing...'

The middle

...an ði jakaas baal hi hib daung (donkey noises) hi hib daung ði bokit da graung deso buf...ang az hi hib daung ði bokit ang du so...i tink i gat ði staar...i se nau a gwoing wið him...i se kwando oigas ke relinche el gayo...i se...agacha to kabesa...i gi am ði rivors wee nau...kwando relinche el gayo...agacha tu kabesa...i sez yes ma...i gwoing i gwoing i gwoing wang...ruusta gi ang di feeva...a kroo...uui i hib daung ði hed agen...wen ih...wen i di lif op ði hed i gat tuu haan...tuu haan kom aut...bot dem smaala... an so hau i gwoing...di waak gwoing...deng di haan di groo...bigar an biga...di shoo aut a litl muo...shoo aut a litl

muo tel wen i get tu ði doo...ramm i kudn kom iin...ði haan iz tuu big
yu sii?...aarait...

'...and the donkey neighed, she lifted down...she lifted down the bucket to
the ground right there – boof! And as she lifted down the bucket and did so...she
thought she had got the star...She said "Now I will be going with him." She
said "When you hear the cock crow", she said, "put down your head!" She
said it the reverse way round now..."When the cock crows put down your
head." She said "Yes ma", she was going on and on when a...cock did her
the favour of crowing...Gee! She thrust down her head again...When
she...when she was lifting up her head she had two horns...two horns came
out...but they were not very big at first and so it was as she was going...she
was walking along...then the horns were growing bigger and bigger...becoming
more and more visible...until when she got to the door...Crash!...she couldn't
get in...the horns were too big, you see?...All right...'

The end
...nau ðe had ang neks bwoi going raungd...wi dis shuuz...
[*aside to children playing in room*: lisn a tel yo fu stap it...ef nat a weng
biit yu an go tu yo mashiin go go so]
...i se ai nou dat a sista...i se nombadi diia feeva mi sista so laik dat...dat
a moss mi sista...man gaan i gaan aal raung wi dat priti shuuz pyuar
gould...bot i fut dis abaut dat [*indicating short length between her
hands*]...an di gyal fut abaut mail an a haaf...ði man kom tu ði geet...ring
ring ring i se hu iz ðat? i se da mii sah...i se wat yu waant yu waang kom
iin ar nat? i se a waang kom iin sah...i se ði prinses sen ðis shuuz fu go
raung wid am...an if i fit...eni wan we i fit iiða oogli ar priti if i fit eni
wan i se ðat a ði prinses waif...i kom iin...nau da gyal di de en haid...da
paarat gwoing tel pan am yu no...ðis wan kom aut wid di big ould haan...i
gat di haan pan i hed...aii i se muma ða shuuz priti ma ða shuuz...ða shuuz
kud fit mii...i se go an waip yo fut...i gaan an i waip i fut an i gat ða shuuz
di fuus am di fuus am i se...hau...hau ði shuuz stan? maind yo tear ði...ði
ouna av ðat shuuz...i se ði ouna av ðat shuuz iz intu ðat oovm haid...i
se an yu ask fu ðat gyal kom aut...i se misiz i se yu no had am a...neks
daata? ooa nou a no gat nan...i nou...wai i gat am haid...bika i si di gyal
fut liil...an az ði gyal kom aut ðis pali se ðats ði ouna av ði shuuz...an
ði gyal tek ði shuuz an ðem waip i fut an i...az i du am so plups...ðer
iz ði kyerij kom bak an tek ði gyal an gaan wið am...tu ði prinses...son
an marid ang...ðat ði end av di stoori.

'...now they had another boy going round...with this shoe...
[*Aside to the children in the room*: "Listen, I told you to stop it...If you don't
I will beat you – and go to your machine – go on, away with you!")]
...She said "I know that is my sister" she said, "nobody could possibly look

so like my sister as that...that must be my sister." The man went, he went all round with that pretty shoe...pure gold...but its foot was just about that long and the girl's foot was about a mile and a half...The man came to the gate...ring, ring, ring. He said "Who is that?" He said "It's me, sir." He said "What do you want? Do you want to come in or not?" He said "I want to come in, sir." He said "The Princess sent this shoe (for me) to go round with it...and if it fits...anybody that it fits, whether ugly or pretty, if it fits anybody," he said "that is the princess' (for prince's) wife." Now the girl was there hidden...The parrot was going to tell about her, you know. This (other) girl came out with the big old horns...she had the horns on her head..."Aha!" she said, "Mama, the shoe is pretty ma, the shoe...the shoe could fit me." She said "Go and wipe your foot." She went and she wiped her foot and she got the shoe and was forcing it and forcing it...She said "Well – how does the shoe look?" "Mind you don't tear the...the owner of that shoe," he said, "the owner of that shoe is hidden inside that oven"...he said "and you should ask for that girl to come out." He said "Missus", he said, "didn't you have em...another daughter?" "Oh, no, I haven't any." He knew...why she had hidden her...because he saw the girl's foot was small...and as the girl came out this parrot said "That's the owner of the shoe"...and the girl took the shoe and they wiped her foot and she...as she put it on so – there! There the carriage came back and took the girl and went with her...to the princess's son and married him...that is the end of the story.'

(3) *A short Anansi story told by DW, aged 13, from San Ignacio*
Anansi and his children

The beginning

a taim bra nansi mi ga ang plantieshan...i mi ga fiftiin children...wan mi neeng chiki wan mi neeng joo wan mi neeng piinots...so i mi kyaang fiid aal di chilren deng ka i yustu liezi so wan de i tel i waif waif a gwoing a bush a plantieshan den i tel ang ookee den so wen i gaan i sii di em plaantin we deng yong feva banaana so i put it iina i duori wen i mi di go i miit rong di em rong di remoliino an di duori ton ova den di plaantin jrap an i sii i an daiv fur it...di terd taim i fain wan pat den i se jos dis uol pat a fain den di pat se no no no ai neeng as lo ke pwedes deng i se as lo ke pwedes an di pat uopm and i bigin tu iit...

'(Once upon) a time Brother Anansi had a plantation...he had fifteen children, one called Chicky, one called Jo, one called Peanuts...so he couldn't feed all the children because he was lazy. So one day he told his wife, "Wife, I'm going to the bush, to the plantation." Then she said "OK then!" So when he went he saw the plantain which, when young, looks like a banana, so he put it into his canoe. When he was going he ran into the...into the whirlpool and the canoe turned over, then the plantain fell out and he saw it and dived for it...the third time he found a pot, then he said "All I've found is this old pot", then the pot said "No, no, no, I'm called 'Do what you can'!" Then he said "Do what you can!" and the pot opened and he began to eat...'

The end

di lii bwai chiki se mama mama evri die ai si papa di go op da laaf i ma
tel ang go go si wat de wat papa hav op de...di lii bwai se bot chruu da
jos wang lii uol wip di wip se no no no ai neeng as lo ke pwedes...an az
i ma se as lo ke pwedes di wip lash ang i lash ang az chiki mi ang
rong...rong di wip lash ang an wen bra anansi mi di kom rong di bush
i hea i si i hea dem di krai so i se seek a intafearing di wip di lash unu no...

'The little boy Chicky said "Mama, mama, every day I see papa going up
in the loft." His mother told him "Go to see what's there, what papa has up
there." The little boy said "Well, there is just a little old whip." The whip said
'No, no, no, I'm called 'Do what you can!'"' and as his mother said "Do what
you can!" the whip lashed them; it lashed them, as Chicky went and ran the
whip lashed him and when Brother Anansi was coming round the forest he
heard...he saw...he heard them crying so he said "The whip is beating you
now because of interfering."'

4 The sociolinguistic surveys in the West Indies and of immigrants in Britain

1. Linguistic symptoms of social structure: the individual as locus

The grammar questionnaire answers and the conversations and stories in Chapter 3 are designed to show something of the range of vernacular language in the former British West Indian territories. Of course, the sample is very incomplete and biassed. Nevertheless, it seems clear that there are marked similarities as well as differences between the different territories. Moreover, there are groupings within those similarities and differences; for example, St. Vincent seems to be a half-way house in some respects between northern Caribbean usage and Barbadian usage – using, e.g., for habitual aspect sometimes the Bajan *doz* constructions and sometimes the unmarked Jamaican constructions. It also shows signs of being affected by the vernacular characteristic of islands once Creole French-speaking, like Grenada and Trinidad, where habitual constructions use the *-ing* of the present participle without the verb BE: *ai selin in di maakit* 'I sell (things) in the market.' There are therefore both island-by-island and regional variations within any general concept of 'West Indian vernacular'. Within each island there are regional variations too.

Moreover, migration from territory to territory – for example, immigration into Guyana from both Barbados and Jamaica, or into Trinidad, St. Lucia or St. Vincent from Barbados – has meant that the social value (prestige or stigma) originally attached to the immigrants themselves becomes transferred to their linguistic usage as that becomes a new variant or model available within the territorial repertoire. Thus, *doz* verbal auxiliary forms brought in originally by Bajan-speaking immigrants have prestige within the system of variables available in both Guyana and St. Lucia, but are today marked as 'rural' (Escure 1984) among the Black Caribs of Belize, who originally went there from St. Vincent but whose younger generation now look to the urban Creole of Belize City for a model.

There are also social and idiosyncratic variables of indigenous origin, as in any community. Among the social groups we find such distinctions as those of age, sex, level of education, religion, economic standing and aspirations apparently making a difference to the kind of language used (although it is not possible to publish data-analyses for all of these). The old people tend naturally to be more conservative than the young, but young people in any case try to distance themselves from older people by their language. The effect of a more educated milieu (that of her home) and the effect of the school playground can be contrasted in the very first sentence of GM's Anansi story (p. 104):

> wans apana taim...braða taiga woz werkabl an...braða anansi mi leezi.

Here, *woz* 'was' belongs to her more educated repertoire, *mi* to Creole.

The long and arduous undertaking since 1952 of transcribing phonetically all the tape-recordings of these and a great many more West Indian conversations and stories had led to our endeavour to discover systems in the observable facts about the many parameters of variation, within the behaviour of individuals and from one individual to another. It became increasingly difficult to reconcile these facts with the monosystemic concepts formerly accepted by most linguists as their major concern, summed up by De Saussure's *langue* on the one hand and Chomsky's (not by any means the same) competence of an 'ideal speaker–listener, in a completely homogeneous speech-community' (1965: 3) on the other. 'Problems of description in multilingual communities' (Le Page 1968b) was a fairly early formulation of the difficulties. Labov had already published his *The social stratification of English in New York City* (1966), but his approach to the problem of variation did not seem adequate to deal with that encountered in the West Indies, and for at least two reasons. Firstly, he assumed that he was dealing with variation within 'English' whereas we had been working within a context in which it was difficult to know, or put a boundary round or a name to a distinct, discrete language system – a point we shall have to explore again later. Secondly, he started with certain known groups in his community, divided according to the socio-economic class status assigned to them by a social welfare study already carried out, whereas we had no such prior definition of groups, nor did we feel competent at the outset to know just how creole societies were structured. This indeed was one of the things we wished to discover (see Le Page 1980b and Labov's reply in the same book).

'Problems of description in multilingual communities' outlined the first tentative formulation of a hypothesis which tried to subsume in one general statement the factors which constrained the way people spoke to one another. It owed a good deal to W. J. H. Sprott's account of the way human groups form and evolve their rules of social behaviour (Sprott 1958); a good deal to Roger Brown's general social-psychological approach to language in *Words and things* (1958); but above all, it had evolved as a response to a mass of West Indian data collected over the years, and to the great amount of painstaking analytical work which had preceded the publication of Beryl Loftman Bailey's *Jamaican Creole syntax* (1966) and Cassidy and Le Page's *Dictionary of Jamaican English* (1967), including the historical phonology which forms an introduction to that work. In its revised form, the hypothesis and the constraints within which it is supposed to work are set out in detail in Chapter 5. In its original form it was very much a response to Labov's survey of the incidence of certain phonological variables among a sample of Lower East Side New Yorkers (Labov 1966) and the conclusions he drew as to common, shared targets among speakers of 'the same language', in the light of the rather different conclusions forced on Le Page during his search for a general hypothesis about language which would allow him to account for the observations he had made of Caribbean communities during his work on Creoles since 1951. The original version of the hypothesis and its four riders ran as follows:

The individual creates his systems of verbal behaviour so as to resemble those common to the group or groups with which he wishes from time to time to be identified, to the extent that

(*a*) he is able to identify these groups
(*b*) his motives are sufficiently clear-cut and powerful
(*c*) his *opportunities* for learning are adequate
(*d*) his *ability* to learn – that is, to change his habits where necessary – is
       unimpaired.   (Le Page 1968b: 192)

   It is essential to consider this hypothesis and its riders in connection with the metaphor used for verbal activity in Le Page 1978a (p. 80), 'Projection, focussing, diffusion...', a metaphor drawn, not from the technical vocabulary of psychology (where the word 'projection' has a similar but not identical meaning) but from cinema projection and focussing on a screen. As the individual speaks he is seen as always using language with reference to the inner models of the universe he has constructed for himself; he projects in words images of that universe (or, of those universes) on to the social screen, and these images may be more or less sharply focussed, or more or less diffuse, in relation to each other or in relation to those projected by others in their interaction with him. As he speaks, he is inviting others to share his view of the universe (even if that means agreeing to keep out of it!), and the feedback he gets may lead him to focus his own images more sharply, and may also lead him to bring his own universes more into focus with those projected by others. A fresh contact, a fresh point of view, may on the other hand for a time at least make his projection more diffuse. The individual is thus seen as the locus of his language, envisaged as a repertoire of socially-marked systems. Each system is a property with which he has endowed a group which he himself perceives; neither systems nor groups, in the way in which we are talking of them here, are objective properties of 'the real world' but percepts of each individual. Such systems are all more or less fragmentary and overlapping. A group is any perceived cluster of two or more individuals. Language, however, in use by individuals, is the instrument through which, by means of individual adjustments in response to feedback, both 'languages' and 'groups' may become more highly focussed in the sense that the behaviour of members of a group may become more alike. The concepts are intended to apply to all language acquisition; no distinction is made (and it is evident from long study of multilingual societies that no sharp distinction can be made) between 'first' and 'other' language acquisition.

'Focussing' will imply greater regularity in the linguistic code, less variability; 'diffusion' the converse.

Since we carried out our own surveys, other work has been done: in Leeds (by Rama Kant Agnihotri), in Belfast (by Lesley Milroy), in Brazil (by Stella Maris Bortoni-Ricardo) and in Australia (by Annette Schmidt) which has made use of these concepts. The Belfast and Brazilian surveys have in particular related them to the behaviour of *social networks*, those structural complexes within communities made up of chains and criss-crossings of friendship, relationship and acquaintanceship to which each of us belongs. Networks are a means of defining social units with which to correlate kinds of linguistic behaviour. They are a more satisfactory alternative to the social or economic or other groups taken as given by Labov and those whose work followed his, and possibly more satisfactory also than the clusters of many socio-economic variables against which we ourselves tested membership of linguistic groups. Had we been familiar with the concept of networks when we planned our survey, we might well have used it ourselves. It is not surprising that the density and multiplexity of social networks have been found to correlate with the degree of focussing around a set of linguistic norms, since joining and maintaining membership of such networks is itself an act of identity which our hypothesis supposes to have linguistic concomitants. The networks are the groups which the individual has actually joined; their isomorphism with the 'group or groups with which from time to time he wishes to be identified', which he has created in his mind and endowed with linguistic characteristics, will of course be constrained by factors subsumed under our four riders. (The hypothesis and its riders were in fact tested against the behaviour of British pop groups by Peter Trudgill – see Trudgill 1980.)

Testing the hypothesis. In order to test the adequacy of the earlier formulation of this hypothesis and constraints it was decided to undertake a survey of a number of communities in turn. Since social, psychological and linguistic factors are all involved, the ideal would have been for a team from these three disciplines to work together. The research programme indeed envisaged this, and a ten-year scheme was drawn up to study three or four multilingual communities in turn, both in the West Indies and among immigrants from the former West Indian colonies in Britain and France. (Andrée Tabouret-Keller has been the psychologist member of the team from the outset, Robert Le Page the linguist. The late Douglas Taylor was the original social anthropologist. The other members of the team have been recruited as needed: Anthony J. Weekes as statistical adviser; Pauline Christie and Baudouin Jurdant as fieldworkers and analysts for Belize, Ghislaine Maury and Marcel Diki-Kidiri for St. Lucia; Jean Thomson, and subsequently Damian McEntegart, as statistical data analysts.) The work among immigrant West Indians in London, however, has had to be on a different basis, as will be described on page 153.

2. The chosen territories

Belize : collecting information

The first choice of territory to test our hypothesis was Cayo District, in what was then British Honduras and is now Belize (see Maps 1 and 2). There were many good reasons for this. It was *par excellence* a multilingual community in a state of post-colonial flux, in which those who had formerly had an identity as 'Spanish' or 'Carib' or 'Maya' or 'Kekchi' or 'Waika' (a somewhat denigratory term in common use for the Miskito Indians) or 'Lebanese' or 'Creole', and as British colonial subjects, would now, if they chose to stay in the country, have to find an identity within the new state. Cayo District itself lay as a kind of rather empty buffer zone between the coastal Creoles of Belize District and the Spanish, Maya and Mestizos of Guatemala who had spilled across the frontier as political refugees to establish the small town of Benque Viejo. Until the 1940s, access to Cayo District was mainly by shallow-draught steamer up the Belize River past a number of riverside landings to the District capital of

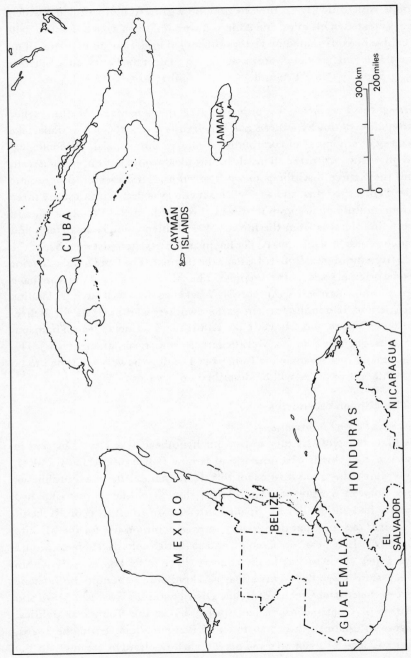

Map 1. Belize and the Western Caribbean

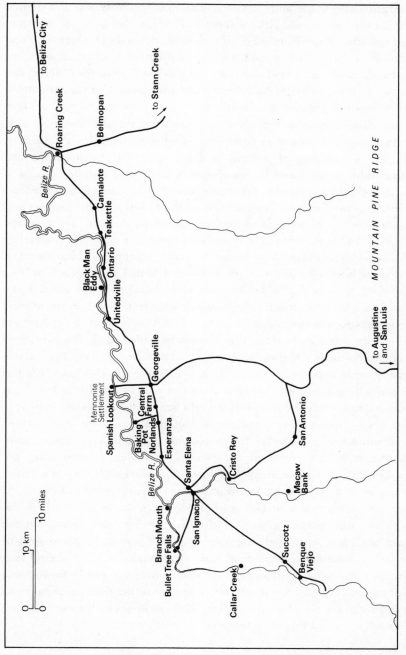

Map 2. Cayo District, Belize

San Ignacio del Cayo, and the chief function of this town was as a trading post for the lumber and chicle-tapping industries, bringing up imported food and other goods from the coast and taking down the chicle (the natural resin of the sapodilla tree, and the basic ingredient of chewing gum). In the 1940s, however, a road was built from Belize City to the Guatemalan frontier at Benque Viejo. As a result, land was opened up for agriculture into which the population spread from either end and from the Maya Indian villages on either side. Not only, therefore, was the identity of each ethnic group of the country to be reassessed in a new political situation, but the new degree of mixing of the populations taking place had considerable implications for the choice of identity by individuals and, if our hypothesis was correct, for the linguistic symptoms of those choices.

In 1969/70, therefore, the team established itself in Cayo District and began the long process of collecting information about the linguistic behaviour of the children in relation to the various groups with which they might conceivably identify (or be constrained by circumstances to identify). One quite basic idea in this work, borrowed from Labov's work in New York City, was the shift in behaviour that might take place as the children relaxed and became more informal in their speech; if therefore one of their model groups was associated with more formal aspects of life and others with more intimate aspects, this should be reflected in the way their language changed. Another, intersecting, idea was taken from the analysis already made over the previous twenty years (see e.g. DeCamp 1960) of people telling traditional Anansi stories. In these studies it had been observed that while the story-teller might start with an outsider in a fairly formal way and a more standard kind of English, as the story gained momentum the language tended to become more and more conservative and non-standard, frequently – especially in dialogue – recovering the language in which the story had been heard originally by the teller. Examples of this are to be found in all the stories printed in Chapter 3; they are frequent also in DeCamp (1960), even to the point where the narrator sings 'magic' gibberish of which he is unable to explain the meaning. Thus, even with the intersection of just these parameters of formal vs. informal conversation, and conversation vs. story-telling and, as we mention below, vs. reading, the speaker moves into a multidimensional sociolinguistic space; he can exhibit symptoms of the position he takes up in that space *vis-à-vis* his interlocutors of the moment by the use he makes of socially-marked linguistic features.

Sampling: social and linguistic. One child in four between the ages of 10 and 16+ was selected (by simply taking every fourth name on the registers) from the primary school population of Cayo District, and a number also from the one secondary school in the district, Sacred Heart College in San Ignacio; 280 children were chosen in this way. The team then established themselves in a house in Benque Viejo and proceeded to track down each child and the family with which it was living. While Pauline Christie recorded the child's conversation with her, one of the other members of the team visited its home, trying to collect information about all those demographic, geographical, socio-economic and ethnic variables which might conceivably affect the child's linguistic behaviour. The conversation with Pauline Christie was designed to range over more formal topics (like school) to begin with; then the child was asked to tell a story – if possible both a traditional 'Old witch' or Anansi story and also one it had read or heard read at school, such as the 'Three little pigs'; then there was more conversation, this time about homely topics such as cooking and ghosts, and a reading test. Finally, each child was asked questions about what language or languages it used at home for talking with various members of the household (grandparents, parents, older brothers and sisters and younger brothers and sisters), for telling jokes on the one hand and for talking about serious subjects on the other (the full range of information collected is described in Le Page 1978a).

The linguistic variables. Subsequently, a small number of the tapes were transcribed in a pilot study to decide on the linguistic features which seemed to be most clearly of likely social significance, and to work out other details of the full analytical programme. Five features were finally decided upon.

1. The nasalization of vowels before a nasal consonant, frequently with the complete loss of the consonant itself or its velarization. This is a very common feature of relaxed Creole speech, so that for example *town* is represented by [tõŋ], *them* by [dɛ̃], *and* by [ã]. It is not, however, so common in educated Belizean English, and that is the variety supposed to be taught in schools, the variety therefore which native speakers of Spanish, Maya, Kekchi and Carib are supposed to learn.

2. The *r*-colouration of vowels in words which have an *r* in the spelling after a vowel. (This feature was also among the variables used by Labov in his 1966 New York study.) Historically there has been gradual disappearance of the pronunciation of *l*, of *r* and of *h* after vowels in some dialects, with the concomitant lengthening, and in some cases diphthongization, of the preceding vowel where Chaucer's English, for example, had a short vowel before one of these consonants. (Each of the consonants

is in fact a continuant, overlapping with the vowel-category in that respect, and the process is an assimilatory one.) The process has gone on at a different pace in different parts of the English-speaking community, and in different parts of each person's lexicon also, depending to some extent upon what followed the *l*, *r* or *h*, to some extent upon the commonness or rarity of any particular word in the speaker's usage, to some extent on an avoidance of awkward homophones and to some extent on the degree to which any individual speaker has felt constrained by the spelling or by the usage of a more literate model group.

The *r*-consonant is completely absent in this position both in RP and in some broad Creole dialects of English in the Caribbean, where *work*, *church* and so on are pronounced ['wɒk] or ['wɒʔ], ['čɒč] etc. It tends to be used in more educated varieties of West Indian English, and especially among those educated in schools with American teachers. Its use is to some extent influenced by the spelling, as is seen from the fact that our children tended to make much more use of it when reading than when conversing.

3. The devoicing of final sibilants. This is a feature associated with the 'Spanish' pronunciation of English in the region. Where English has voiced [z] at the end of a word when preceded by a vowel or voiced consonant, but voiceless [s] after a voiceless consonant, Spanish has only final [s]. Thus the Spanish tend to pronounce English final /-z/ as [-s]. In contact situations such as that in Cayo District, some people are more and some less 'Spanish-like' in this respect.

4. The inflection or lack of inflection of nouns for plural, or the use of the Creole plural suffix -*dem*. Normally the Creole plural is either unmarked other than by numerals or marked by a plural demonstrative or by -*dem*, or a combination of these, as in the Jamaican usage:

di tu breda dem 'the two brothers'

So that when GM, in her Anansi story, says *i iit tuu paungz a di bota* 'he ate two pounds of the butter', this is a variation in the direction of Standard English from her more normal story-telling mode as in *tuu-paung-gaan* 'two-pounds-gone' or as in *i tel aal di ada animal-dem* 'he told all the other animals'. Thus the use of an unmarked plural or of the suffix -*dem* tends to be associated with Creole speakers; and the use of the standard forms of inflection for plural is associated with those who speak a more standard variety of English, either as their native language or as learned in school.

5. The inflection or lack of inflection for past tense in verbs, or use of the Creole past marker *mi*. In the regular or 'focussed' Creole of Belize City, past tense is never marked by verb inflection as in Standard English;

it is either inferred from the context or marked by the auxiliary *mi*, which derives from the unstressed form of English *been* (see *DJE*: bin). Thus in GM's story *braða taiga staat tu kik op iina ði kaafn an i get aut a di kaafn an i jomp pan wan trii* means 'Brother Tiger started to kick up in the coffin and he got out of the coffin and he jumped on a tree'; but if it is necessary to mark progressive aspect in the verb (by using *di*) as well as putting it in the past tense, then it is essential to use *mi*, as in *brada hikatii neva mi di kom* 'Brother Hicatee was not coming'. Elsewhere *mi* is optional.

Speakers of more standard varieties of English, whether learned as their native language or at school, will tend to use standard past tense inflections, although of course these will, in the case of weak verbs, be subject to the usual phonological rules which lead to their assimilation to a following dental consonant and thus frequently to their loss in rapid or relaxed speech, as in *he walk(ed) through the park*.

The quantification of variants and preparation of profiles for cluster-analysis. This last point illustrates one of the fallible assumptions we were forced to make. In order to avoid the very large amount of work which would have been involved in distinguishing in our analysis those contexts in which the lack of inflection might be due to phonological assimilation, we decided to try to find a size of sample of discourse for which we could say, 'all speakers will on average in such a sample use verbs in roughly the same proportion of phonological contexts'. By counting at 100 words, 200 words, 300 words and so on in our pilot analysis we concluded that a 400-word sample was one in which we could reasonably ignore the effect of different phonological and grammatical contexts. The analyses made subsequently by McEntegart (1980; McEntegart and Le Page 1981) showed up some weaknesses in this conclusion. It was, however, one of a number of somewhat arbitrary decisions which had to be taken to keep our rather ambitious study feasible within our limited means. (Other problems associated with the quantification of the variants are discussed on pp. 131ff.)

Eventually, each child in our sample was represented by a profile consisting of up to 25 quantified linguistic attributes – that is, the extent to which they used each of the five linguistic features listed above in each of the five modes of behaviour into which we divided the interview: early conversation, telling a story read to them or by them at school (e.g. 'The three little pigs'), telling a traditional story of the oral tradition (an Anansi-type story), later conversation, and reading (we give below sample data sheets for three of the children). These linguistic profiles then formed

Data sheet 1.

Informant: SM, No. 84; Age: 12; Sex: F; School: Norland, Standard: V; Home town or village: Esperanza

Feature	Anansi story: No. of words (A): 400			Non-Anansi story: No. of words (A): 400			Conversation: early sample No. of words (A): 400			Conversation: late sample No. of words (A): 400			Reading and word list No. of words (A): 200		
	No. of cases (B)	No. of loci (C)	(B) as % of (C)	No. of cases (B)	No. of loci (C)	(B) as % of (C)	No. of cases (B)	No. of loci (C)	(B) as % of (C)	No. of cases (B)	No. of loci (C)	(B) as % of (C)	No. of cases (B)	No. of loci (C)	(B) as % of (C)
Nasalization > [ṽ] or [ṽŋ]	77	144	53	70	132	53	30	112	27	95	152	63	3	34	9
r-colouration or postvocalic r	2	41	5	3	14	21	17	42	40	4	26	15	36	36	100
devoicing of /-z/ in syllable-final position	0	4*	—	0	2*	—	4	15	27	0	5	0	0	13	0
past tense ∅ or mi	35	40	88	44	44	100	0	0*	—	26	26	100	5	28	18
plural ∅ or -dem	7	11	64	3	5	60	9	16	56	13	16	81	0	1*	—

Note:
* too low for calculation

Data sheet 2.

Informant : FB, No. 136 ; Age : 12 ; Sex : M ; School : Blessed Edmund Campion, Standard : V ; Home town/village : Teakettle

Feature	Anansi story No. of words (A): 333			Non-Anansi story No. of words (A): 141			Conversation: early sample No. of words (A): 402			Conversation: late sample No. of words (A): 356			Reading & word list No. of words (A): 315		
	No. of cases (B)	No. of loci (C)	(B) as % of (C)	No. of cases (B)	No. of loci (C)	(B) as % of (C)	No. of cases (B)	No. of loci (C)	(B) as % of (C)	No. of cases (B)	No. of loci (C)	(B) as % of (C)	No. of cases (B)	No. of loci (C)	(B) as % of (C)
Nasalization > [ṽ] or [ṽ̞]	64	119	54	8	36	22	26	100	26	30	119	25	12	58	21
r-colouration or postvocalic r	3	38	8	7	12	58	18	42	43	4	34	12	35	38	92
devoicing of /-z/ in syllable-final position	2	2*	—	1	3*	—	10	23	43	12	28	43	4	19	21
past tense ø or mi	42	45	93	7	17	41	5	9	56	1	1*	—	7	38	18
plural ø or -dem	4	5	80	1	3*	—	0	10	0	10	31	32	2	3*	—

Note:
* too low for calculation

Data sheet 3.

Informant: AM, No. 163; Age: 13; Sex: F; School: San Jose, Succotz, Standard: V; Home town/village: Succotz

Feature	Anansi story No. of words (A):			Non-Anansi story No. of words (A): 237			Conversation: early sample No. of words (A): 400			Conversation: late sample No. of words (A): 333			Reading & word list No. of words (A): 300		
	No. of cases (B)	No. of loci (C)	(B) as % of (C)	No. of cases (B)	No. of loci (C)	(B) as % of (C)	No. of cases (B)	No. of loci (C)	(B) as % of (C)	No. of cases (B)	No. of loci (C)	(B) as % of (C)	No. of cases (B)	No. of loci (C)	(B) as % of (C)
Nasalization > [ṽ] or [ṽŋ]		DID NOT		6	75	8	0	90	0	2	80	3	0	32	0
r-colouration or postvocalic r		TELL		3	3*	—	47	57	82	29	33	88	35	35	100
devoicing of /-z/ in syllable-final position		AN		12	14	86	20	28	71	13	26	50	13	14	93
past tense ∅ or *mi*		ANANSI		12	34	35	0	2*	—	0	3*	—	2	29	7
plural ∅ or *-dem*		STORY		0	1*	—	3	15	20	4	19	21	0	1*	—

Note:
* too low for calculation

the basis of a computer cluster-analysis program. Such programs are designed to calculate – according to set constraints – which profiles, made up of sets of quantities, are closest to one another and so form groups or clusters in a multidimensional space.

The process of cluster-analysis itself seemed to provide a reasonable analogue for what we were supposing the children themselves to be doing in their linguistic behaviour: positioning themselves in a multidimensional social space so as to reflect the extent of their identity with, or distance from, all others in their community, but being constrained by the factors listed under our four riders (see Chapter 5). We then hoped to be able to establish a hierarchy in the degrees of association which might be discovered between membership of clusters and each of the possible constraining factors, tested in turn.

Possibilities of the method. The preliminary results of our clustering for Belize, and the tests made for the degree of association between membership of a linguistically-defined cluster and each of the social variables (age, sex, home area, father's occupation etc.) were promising, and we reproduce here, as Table 14, Table 1 from Le Page, Christie *et al.* (1974). We were at that time in possession of reasonably full data for 16 groups, of which 11 were very small indeed. Table 14 deals only with the five main clusters – Nos 1, 2, 3, 15 and 16 – covering 164 of our original 280 children; the symbols used in the table to denote language use are shown in Figure 1. Table 14 thus visually relates 'bilingualism', as revealed by the analysis of the linguistic data, to 'bilingualism' in a more orthodox, stereotypical sense as reported (a) by the children (the five left-hand sub-columns) and (b) by their parents or family elders (the three right-hand sub-columns).

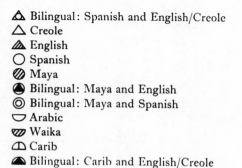

Figure 1. Symbols in Table 14 denoting claimed language use for Belize children.

Table 14. *The five main clusters of Cayo District children (from Le Page, Christie et al. 1974)*

(cont. overleaf)

Table 14 (*cont.*)

Cluster 1 (N: 59)	Cluster 2 (N: 15)	Cluster 3 (N: 47)	Cluster 15 (N: 17)	Cluster 16 (N: 26)

Key to Table 14 (*overleaf*)

KEY TO TABLE 14

N = 164.

The clusters analysed in Table 14 are those optimal in relation to internal verbal behaviour characterized by three linguistic features in each of three modes, giving nine dimensions:

Features	*Modes*
(1) nasalization	(1) early conversation
(2) *r*-colouration	(2) late conversation
(3) devoicing	(3) reading

The clusters analysed in Table 14 are those optimal in relation to internal consistency and distance between clusters.

Table 14 relates these clusters to the verbal behaviour claimed by each child in answer to the linguistic questionnaire.

Each cluster-column has nine sub-columns. Each of the first five sub-columns denotes a member of the child's intimate circle, from left to right as follows:

(1) mother
(2) father
(3) older siblings
(4) younger siblings
(5) best friend

Sub-columns 1–5 inclusive are further divided into two lines for each informant or group of similar informants. The top line of these two specifies the claim made in respect of school topics, the bottom in respect of jokes. Each number specifies a child and each suit its place of living, as follows:

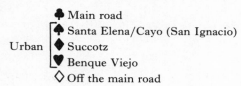

Urban
♣ Main road
♠ Santa Elena/Cayo (San Ignacio)
♦ Succotz
♥ Benque Viejo
♦ Off the main road

Sub-columns 7, 8 and 9 refer to the answers given by the parents of the child (usually the mother) to questions on language use in the family, as follows:

(7) first language of mother
(8) first language of father
(9) language claimed to be used at home

Commentary on the clusters and degree of association tests ; their limitations, and an alternative method. We comment in detail later on the revealing relationships between the linguistic behaviour within its family claimed by each child and shown in Table 14 by the symbols in the five left-hand columns, and those claimed by its family elders as shown by the symbols in the right-hand column (see Chapter 5).

Here we give, first, the results of the 'degree of association' tests carried out with a series of non-linguistic variables, showing the extent to which each variable could be associated with membership of a cluster. If, for example, we had had just two clusters, and Cluster 1 had consisted entirely of boys and Cluster 2 entirely of girls, the degree of association here between the sex of the child and membership of a cluster would have been 1.0. In fact, of course, none of the degrees of association approaches that level. (The test used is described in Le Page, Christie *et al.* 1974. Those interested in pursuing the method should refer to Theil 1972.)

The strongest calculated association was that between the linguistic clusters and place of living (EMI, or Theil's Expected Mutual Information co-efficient = 0.3452). This means that the social factor 'place of living' subsumed only about one-third of the information needed to explain the clustering; two-thirds of the information remained beyond our reach here – some of it of course was subsumed in the other social factors investigated.

Most of the children in Cluster 1 lived in the urban area of Santa Elena/Cayo. Among the 21 living along the main road, one-third lived in Esperanza which is very close to Santa Elena. Surprisingly, another third of these 21 lived at the further east end of the road in the direction of Belize. In Cluster 2, most children lived in Cayo. In Cluster 3, the majority lived along the main road excluding Esperanza. Cluster 15 reveals a majority of children living off the main road, especially in the Maya-Indian villages such as Bullet Tree Falls (a few miles away to the east of Cayo), San Antonio (in the bush) and Santa Familia (in Cayo neighbourhood). Cluster 16 shows a majority of children coming from Benque Viejo, Succotz and San Antonio.

The second strongest degree of association was between the linguistic clusters and the occupation of the father of the family (EMI = 0.2584). Cluster 2, for example, contains no child whose father was in an agricultural or seasonal occupation, whereas these comprise the majority of Cluster 16, which contains no children from the homes of skilled workers.

The third strongest degree of association was between the linguistic clusters and a socio-economic profile for each family, made up by assessing a number of factors culled from answers to the family questionnaire, to which a cluster analysis program had been applied (EMI = 0.1367). It cannot be pretended that this is by any measure a strong degree of association; those established for age, and for religious affiliation, were even weaker.

The limitations inherent in our data, and in our methods of analysis, have been described in detail in McEntegart (1980) and McEntegart and Le Page (1981). The weakness of the degrees of association is, however, mainly due to a general diffuseness of 'the language of Cayo district' and of its systematic features in a society in a high and rapid state of flux.

The use of cluster-analysis, best suited to finding real typologies in data, threw this state of flux into relief. Real typologies would only have existed had we had something resembling a ghetto situation (whether physical or psychological) in which no mixing was taking place between communities, whereas a major attraction of Cayo District for us was that what used to be more like a ghetto situation ('Spanish' Benque Viejo, 'Maya' Succotz, 'Creole' Roaring Creek etc.) was dissolving into a new, mixed kind of community. Factor analysis might well have served our purposes better, although not providing such a powerful analogue for our hypothesis. As it was, we had to content ourselves with administrative rather than truly discrete clusters – that is, a clustering which could not be justified by saying that these and these only were the groups into which the children fell on the basis of their linguistic behaviour, but which represented areas of greater density within the data, which could form the basis of further tests. We were epidemiologists in a multidimensional universe. We ourselves feel that the picture presented by the cluster-analysis accurately reflects important aspects of the society whose language we were investigating; the children were trying out models of behaviour in a society in which there were no clear-cut, highly focussed models.

It was the telling of Anansi stories in particular which most sharply divided the children. These belong to a 'Creole' oral tradition and children who told them were therefore trying out a mode of behaviour which might well be strongly marked for ethnic association (although it should be noted that two of our story-tellers excerpted in Chapter 3, GM and TA, were both able to tell them in either 'Spanish' or 'Creole', and, further, that today the Caribs are among the main conservers of another 'Creole' cultural tradition in Belize, the John Canoe dances). One objection made to the Anansi stories as a source of data for nasalization (a Creole-associated feature) was that they tended to be full of connectives – *and*, regularly reduced to [ãŋ] or [ã] – which distorted the statistics.

McEntegart therefore re-worked our data using only two modes – the early and late conversation – and the phonological data. He used three different tests of association, and his results were summarized as follows:

Bearing these complications in mind it would appear that the location of a child's home, the religious affiliations of the family, the language claimed to be spoken at home, the claimed race of the family and the child's claimed most natural language are the best predictors of linguistic performance in an interview situation. Less strong but significant associations include school standard, family's wealth, newspaper reading of child, radio listening of child, child's consciousness of speech stigma as measured by his response to the question on speech ridicule and the child's desired occupation. The low values of the coefficients are no cause for concern. We cannot construct a model containing all the variables to arrive at some overall predictive figure. The fact that the maximum uncertainty is 0.135 does not mean that this is the expected reduction in uncertainty for any prediction we make given the full set of socioeconomic data for a child.   (McEntegart and Le Page 1981: 118–9)

St. Lucia

Importance of its geographical position. It was decided to undertake the second stage of our survey in the island of St. Lucia, one of the Windward Islands of the Eastern Caribbean, lying roughly in the centre of the left side of the triangle formed by Martinique, St. Vincent and Barbados (see Map 3).

This geographical position was important for our purposes. Barbados, as we have seen in Chapter 2, was one of the earliest English-speaking plantation colonies in the Caribbean, being settled from 1627 onwards. Its language was affected by large-scale immigration from the West of England and from Ireland, by the high proportion of Whites to Blacks in the formative years, and by that great prosperity at the height of its sugar fortunes which led to the early establishment of schools and colleges. The Windward Islands, on the other hand, were not really settled by Europeans until the following century, and then in the first instance by the French and their slaves, on whose plantations was used the Creole French which had originated earlier in Martinique and Haiti. As we have already noted, Dominica, St. Lucia, Grenada and St. Vincent experienced varying fortunes in the struggles between England and France in the latter part of the eighteenth century. The French dominance in St. Vincent was on a small scale and short-lived, but the other three islands remained culturally Creole French until the present century in spite of the gradually growing influence of an English-speaking administration and English as the medium of education in the schools. Grenada is today the most

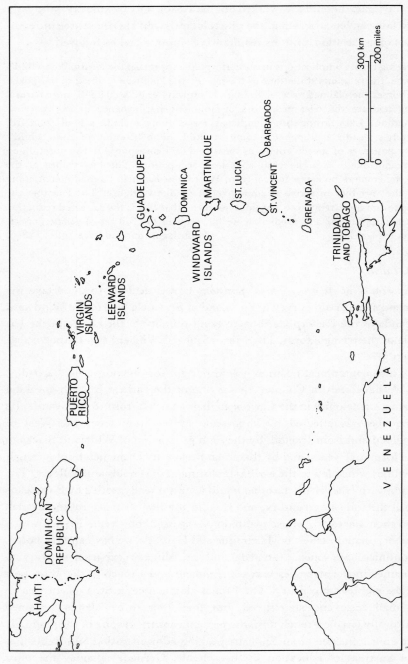

Map 3. St. Lucia and the Eastern Caribbean

completely Anglicized (and Anglo-creolized) of the Windward Islands; St. Lucia and Dominica the least so. St. Lucia is affected by the neighbouring presence (a) of Martinique, a Creole French-speaking island; (b) of St. Vincent, a Creole English-speaking island; (c) of Barbados, an Anglophone island whose creole phase, if it ever had one, has left comparatively little trace on modern vernacular Barbadian speech ('Bajan'). The vernacular of St. Lucia is still predominantly Creole French ('Patois' or 'Kwéyol'). The schools are supposed to teach in the medium of Standard English; and in the capital and port of Castries, and in the tourist developments both there and around the main international airport of Vieux Fort in the south, a good deal of English vernacular is heard. Our study of the English spoken in the northern half of the island by a sample of 100 children, between the ages of ten and 16, was designed to explore the effect of these various cultural influences on the younger generation of the newly-independent island. The report and tables which follow are drawn from Le Page 1980d.

Fieldwork and sample. After an initial training period in York the team established itself in a house on the outskirts of Castries, and spent one month on a pilot study. This time the sample of children was not random, but only randomly selected from what were felt to be representative schools: rural primary, main road primary, urban primary, middle and secondary schools. Because of our experience with transcribing in careful phonetic detail very large quantities of recorded conversation from Belize, it was decided to keep our sample of children to a more manageable size (roughly one in seven instead of one in four) and to concentrate on morphological rather than phonological features in their speech. The collection of the children's recorded conversations was entrusted to Ghislaine Maury and of the details of their circumstances to Marcel Diki-Kidiri. The practical difficulties each encountered in their field work were far greater than those encountered in Belize, and the use of exclusively morphological features for quantification, coupled with defects in the planning of the fieldwork, contributed to making the statistical results of the St. Lucia survey of more doubtful value. Nevertheless, as in Belize, we were able to learn a great deal about social and linguistic change in the island from our work, particularly from detailed study of individual interviews.

The linguistic variables. Once again, after an intensive study of a small sample of the tapes, we selected for quantification linguistic features which seemed to be associated with particular social groups. As we have mentioned, they were all features which would be expressed in Standard English through morphological modification: pronominal forms, forms for the plural of count nouns, for the marking of tense and aspect in verbs:

(a)   Features associated with Standard English and the written language:

SE1   Correct past inflection of verbs, either strong (e.g. *took*) or weak (e.g. *cooked*).
        Correct 3rd person singular inflection of verbs.

SE2   Correct use of plural inflection on count nouns.

SE3   Correct use of *-ing* forms (nominal/verbal *-ing* or verbal continuative aspect in BE...*-ing* constructions).

(b)   Features associated with Creole English/Bajan speakers:

C1   *does* as an aspectual marker, as used by informant 1 below.
        did as a general past marker with verbs, as in *I did go* for *I went*.

(c)   Features associated with Patois-speaking groups:

P4   Use of a 3rd person pronoun [i], singular and plural.

P5   Use of *have* instead of *be* in such sentences as 'I am ten years old' or 'there is..., there are...' which are parallel to Patois 'mwɛ̃ *ni* diz ã', 'i *ni*...' and to French 'j'*ai* dix ans', 'il y *a*...'

(d)   Features shared by Patois and Creole English speakers:

C2P1   Invariability of verb forms in 3rd person present singular and all persons past tense.

C3P2   Invariability of count nouns as to number.

C4P3   Use of *-ing* alone as an aspectual marker; as used in the speech-sample below, this is common today in the creolized English of the formerly Francophone islands, and may therefore in St. Lucian speech derive either directly from the influence of Patois or from e.g. Grenadian or Trinidadian use.

A number of these features are exemplified in the following short extracts in conventionalized spelling, from the narratives of three of our informants:

First informant (speaking of an evil spirit)

'They say he taking your hair and go with it...they [spirits] does go with you...they say they does take you and kill you and take your blood for the devil...they giving theyself to the devil and they does give them money...'

'The people be in the roads and the people come, they coming, they making something and when they reach they seeing a man paying in front of them and they asking him what he want and he telling them what they want...'

[Later, talking about the games people play]

'In the shop they play for sweets they drinking rum.'

Second informant

'You put water in there...you put all your things in it...curry poivre [kari 'pwev] you putting in and you boil...and you put vegetable, carrots...My sister have eighteen. I have fifteen and my little brother have five [years].'

Third informant

'I just hear the lady speaking about that...a girl that staying by our house she not afraid ['gaze] (witches) no she going all in the darkness but she no ['gaze'in] ('witching')...sometimes they have (there are) ['gaze] staying in the bush when you passing i prick you and then sometimes you dying.'

Linguistic analysis and clustering. Each child had two conversations with the fieldworker, which were tape-recorded. The first, more formal one, concerned topics such as school work; the second, more informal topics

Table 15. *Mean scores of nine linguistic features in each of four clusters, in Formal (A) and Informal (B) Modes*

Linguistic clusters	Mode A: Formal interview Linguistic features								
	SE1	SE2	SE3	C1	C3P2	C4P3	C2P1	P4	P5
A I (N = 49)	96.54	90.67	86.40	3.45	9.32	13.59	·18.03	0.73	25.87
A II (N = 21)	97.83	94.43	36.88	2.16	5.56	63.11	35.70	0.30	34.44
A III (N = 10)	95.85	60.08	35.83	4.14	39.91	64.16	58.04	12.85	40.00
A IV (N = 20)	70.39	88.61	47.07	29.61	11.38	52.92	34.33	4.06	22.83

	Mode B: Informal interview Linguistic features								
	SE1	SE2	SE3	C1	C3P2	C4P3	C2P1	P4	P5
B I (N = 24)	96.50	92.57	63.95	3.49	7.40	36.04	19.97	2.83	36.80
B II (N = 44)	89.59	93.05	18.83	10.40	6.94	81.16	44.27	4.44	68.18
B III (N = 14)	98.34	58.83	33.79	1.65	41.16	66.20	46.56	19.67	57.14
B IV (N = 18)	41.68	79.44	19.95	58.35	20.55	68.93	42.93	5.17	66.66

Note: Italic and roman type faces have been used to bring out similarities in patterns of usage.

Table 15a. *Membership of clusters for Mode A: Formal interview*

Cluster I		Cluster II		Cluster III		Cluster IV	
A	B	A	B	A	B	A	B
3	(I)	35	(I)	56	(II)	2	(II)
4	(I)	37	(I)	59	(II)	14	(II)
9	(I)	41	(I)	15	(III)	24	(II)
10	(I)	89	(I)	47	(III)	36	(II)
12	(I)	11	(II)	52	(III)	40	(II)
16	(I)	17	(II)	60	(III)	43	(II)
19	(I)	22	(II)	71	(III)	79	(II)
21	(I)	30	(II)	97	(III)	80	(II)
25	(I)	42	(II)	31	(IV)	88	(II)
27	(I)	46	(II)	62	(IV)	5	(III)
33	(I)	54	(II)	$N = 10$		99	(III)
34	(I)	61	(II)			7	(IV)
38	(I)	70	(II)			20	(IV)
45	(I)	72	(II)			28	(IV)
50	(I)	81	(II)			39	(IV)
64	(I)	96	(II)			63	(IV)
67	(I)	44	(III)			69	(IV)
91	(I)	86	(III)			73	(IV)
93	(I)	8	(IV)			78	(IV)
94	(I)	32	(IV)			82	(IV)
1	(II)	100	(IV)			$N = 20$	
6	(II)	$N = 21$					
13	(II)						
18	(II)						
23	(II)						
48	(II)						
49	(II)						
55	(II)						
57	(II)						
58	(II)						
65	(II)						
66	(II)						
68	(II)						
75	(II)						
77	(II)						
83	(II)						
84	(II)						
85	(II)						
87	(II)						
92	(II)						
95	(II)						
26	(III)						
29	(III)						
53	(III)						
98	(III)						
51	(IV)						
74	(IV)						
76	(IV)						
90	(IV)						
$N = 49$							

Note: The variety of language subsequently used by each child in Mode B is shown in parenthesis. Individual children are represented by their identification number in the sample.

Table 15b: *Membership of clusters for Mode B: Informal interview*

Cluster I		Cluster II		Cluster III		Cluster IV	
Children from A I (N = 20)	3	Children from A I (N = 21)	1	Children from A I (N = 4)	26	Children from A I (N = 4)	51
	4		6		29		74
	9		13		53		76
	10		18		98		90
	12		23				
	16		48	Children from A II (N = 2)	86	Children from A II (N = 3)	8
	19		49		44		32
	21		55				100
	25		57	Children from A III (N = 6)	15	Children from A III (N = 2)	31
	27		58		47		62
	33		65		52		
	34		66		60	Children from A IV (N = 9)	7
	38		68		71		20
	45		75		97		28
	50		77				39
	64		83	Children from A IV (N = 2)	5		63
	67		84		99		69
	91		85				73
	93		87				78
	94		92				82
			95				
Children from A II (N = 4)	35			*(Total N = 14)*			
	37	Children from A II (N = 12)	11				
	41		17			*(Total N = 18)*	
	89		22				
			30				
			42				
(Total N = 24)			46				
			54				
			61				
			70				
			72				
			81				
			96				
		Children from A III (N = 2)	56				
			59				
		Children from A IV (N = 9)	2				
			15				
			24				
			36				
			40				
			43				
			79				
			80				
			88				
		(Total N = 44)					

such as games and black magic and witches. When the tapes were transcribed the incidence of the features listed above was quantified, so that each child could be represented by two sets of coordinates – one for his more formal mode of behaviour (Mode A) and one for his less formal (Mode B). The coordinates for each mode for each child are taken to represent the position he or she adopted in that interview in the multi-dimensional sociolinguistic space (see Le Page 1977b) whose external relationships are to the world of Educated Standard English, to that of Barbadian influence in the Eastern Caribbean, to that of the Creole French Patois culture shared with Martinique and Guadeloupe, and to that of the *formerly* French Patois islands of the Windwards and Trinidad. These positions in multidimensional space were then (after a great deal of carefully-refined data analysis by Weekes and Thomson) clustered by applying a Clustan program (Wishart 1978) for each of the two modes. The results of the 'best' clustering are set out in tables 15, 15a, b; they show which children group together on the basis of their linguistic behaviour, (Tables 15a, b) and the average linguistic properties of each cluster (Table 15).

Linguistic properties of the multidimensional sociolinguistic space. We see from the tables that we are indeed confronted with a *multidimensional* continuum. All the children make some use of nearly all the features – thus they share the same repertoire, in the sense in which Gumperz (1972) uses that term. Nevertheless they can also be clustered into groups of similar behaviour according to the *extent* to which they use each component of the repertoire. The scores in table 15 are the *average* for each group or cluster of children.

In this, the most consistent clustering, we find the children falling into four reasonably well-differentiated groups for Mode A and again for Mode B. By examination we can see that Cluster A I has the consistently highest percentage of Standard English features, and is the only cluster having a high incidence of feature SE3. It is one of the three groups making very little use of the Bajan feature C1, or of the Patois-associated feature P4. Some use is made of the features C4P3 and C2P1, common to Bajan and Patois groups, but not a great deal.

Cluster B I is rather similar in the profile of these average scores to A I, when they are compared with the other clusters, except that the score on feature SE3 is rather lower and that on P5 rather higher. As we see from Tables 15a, b, which set out which children belong to each cluster in each mode, the population which makes up B I is different from that making up A I; only 20 of the 49 children are still in the 'most standard English' cluster when the atmosphere becomes more informal and relaxed; and the group's 'most standard' behaviour is now less standard, in the sense of containing more of a Patois-associated feature than in A I. The remaining children from A I are now to be found predominantly in B II, some in B III and B IV. On the other hand four children from A II have, in the informal mode, joined B I – apparently making their usage somewhat more 'standard' when relaxing. We suggest a possible explanation of this kind of behaviour below.

If now we consider Cluster A II we find that the group still has a comparatively high average incidence of the first two Standard English features SE1 and SE2, but only approximately the same average incidence of SE3 as clusters A III and A IV, and of course correspondingly high proportions of feature C4P3 which is the reciprocal of SE3. C4P3 is very much a regional feature associated with the English of the formerly French islands of the Eastern Caribbean, whereas C2P1 is common to all varieties of Caribbean Creole. In respect of the latter feature, A II and A IV are at a half-way position between A I and A III, in other words, in respect of their Creole-ness these two clusters are similar; they are most dissimilar in respect of their Bajan-ness, since the children of A IV are the only significant users of C1. When we turn to Cluster B II we again find a high incidence of Standard English features SE1 and SE2, but the incidence of SE3 has now dropped considerably and the incidence of both C1 (the Bajan feature) and P5 have greatly increased. We see from Table 15a, b that the population of children for B II contains 12 of the children from A II; the other 9 children are now reclustered: 4 to B I, 2 to B III and 3 to B IV, and B II is now joined by 21 children from A I, 2 from A III and 9 from A IV.

If we now consider Cluster A III, we find that only SE1 of the Standard English features is used almost all the time by this group of children, and that they are by far the heaviest users of those *general* creolisms C3P2 and C2P1 – in other words, of invariable, uninflected noun and verb forms. They are also the heaviest users of P4 and P5. They contrast with the cluster A IV, the children of which are by far the heaviest users of C1 – the Bajan feature. Thus, of the two groups whose formal usage is relatively less 'standard', one is characterized by higher use of uninflected forms and specifically Patois-associated forms, and one by higher use of uninflected forms and the Bajan *does/did* constructions.

Comparing A III and B III we find the two linguistic profiles very similar throughout, though with some increase in the use of features P4 and P5 – that is, the Patois-associated features – in B III. The population of 14 children from whose behaviour B III is an abstraction contains 6 who were in A III, 4 who have joined from A I, 2 from A II and 2 from A IV.

Cluster B IV has the lowest over-all percentages of Standard English features and has far fewer of each of these than A IV. As already remarked, Cluster A IV has a very much higher incidence of the Bajan C1 than the other clusters, and in B IV this high percentage is doubled. The use of P5 in B IV is three times that in A IV. Of the population of 18 children from whose behaviour B IV is an abstraction, 9 were in A IV; 4 have joined from A I, 3 from A II and 2 from A III.

The foregoing comments on the apparent average linguistic properties and differences of each cluster of children must be put to the test of the significance or otherwise of variance between the scores or profiles.

What we have tried to illustrate so far is the variable relationship that obtains in a community between such abstractions as 'language varieties' and 'language groups'. Neither of these can be kept constant or internally self-consistent except by a process of idealization which is bound to distort the sociolinguistic model. If we wished to hold 'speech varieties' constant, then we would have to juggle the membership of groups so that their average usage corresponded to an externally-defined stereotype; if we wished to keep the membership of groups constant then we would lose sight of the linguistic patterns. Instead, we have asked 'in what manner do these children draw closer to or distance themselves from one another in their linguistic behaviour, and what sociolinguistic properties can be discerned emerging in this changing society?'

Many attempts have been made in recent years to describe in linguistic terms speech varieties which are socially-determined subdivisions of a language, using labels such as 'register'; here we see the arbitrary nature of all such abstractions – even though many members of speech communities feel that such varieties do exist, recognize them and imitate them. What they recognize and imitate are stereotypes they have created for themselves, in accordance with our general hypothesis. We have noted some features of the two tables which may well allow us to 'stereotype' the clusters for working purposes – the 'high Standard', 'high Patois' and 'high Bajan' clusters, stereotypes tested and illustrated in Le Page 1977b.

But these labels so far are purely for methodological convenience. Our eight 'language varieties' are abstractions made by us on the basis of using the incidence of nine features (socially marked by prestige or stigma) as a surrogate for a sociolinguistic description. They provide one way of relating individual performance to a communal *langue* so as to see the significance of that relationship in terms of our theory of acts of identity. One general comment can be made on the Mode A clusters as compared with those of Mode B – the Mode A language varieties are generally less different from one another than the Mode B. In other words, in formal situations the members of this community have a more highly-focussed *langue* than when they are relaxed. In formal situations they converge on a common model – apart from four children, who seem to reflect their political feelings by doing otherwise, rather as some children may in any country reflect their local allegiances by using a broader dialect than usual when in the company of visitors.

We do not lose touch with the individual informants as we abstract these social language varieties; rather, we can study the membership of the clusters in at least two very productive ways. First, we study it to observe the nature, and speculate on the significance, of the movement of informants from one variety to another in the transition from formal to informal behaviour; the groundwork for this has been laid above. Secondly, we can relate the membership of clusters to the demographic and social data collected by means of an interview with the head of the family or household of each child.

Social distribution of the sample. The 100 children in our sample were distributed over demographic, social and economic categories as shown in Table 16.

Social properties correlating with cluster membership. In our Belizean investigation we sought to proceed by establishing a hierarchy of degrees of association between the membership of linguistic clusters and each of the socio-economic and demographic factors recorded, reaching the tentative hypothesis that what mattered most to Belize children *of school age* was to be like the other children where they lived. With the St. Lucian children, working on a tentative and provisional basis to assess the feasibility of the method, a chi-squared test has produced the significant results set out in Table 17 ($P = 0.057$).

We are left with a series of questions to put to our data, since we wish to achieve two objectives: to characterize both Belizean and St. Lucian society in sociolinguistic terms; and to understand the implications of that characterization as a model which will relate the competence of individual children in a changing society to changes in the 'language' or *langue* of that society.

We have to discover whether our linguistic clusters are meaningful in

Table 16. *Distribution of the sample from St. Lucia*

		Number of children in the sample in each category
1. Age	Approx. 10 years	50
	Approx. 14 years	50
2. Sex	Male	46
	Female	54
3. School level	Primary standards 1–4	48
	Primary standards 5–6	27
	Secondary	24
4. Type of family: parents	Living with only one parent or parent-figure (e.g. grand-parent, uncle or aunt)	43
	Living with two	57
5. Type of family: elder siblings	Having no elder siblings	23
	Having elder siblings	77
6. Type of family: younger siblings	Having no younger siblings	14
	Having younger siblings	86
7. Accommodation available in home: degree of 'crowdedness'	Averaging one person per room	10
	two persons	24
	three	45
	four or more	21
8. Possession of various consumer durables claimed by family	Possessing none of the following:	9
	Radio only	35
	Plus record player	13
	Plus refrigerator also	20
	Plus television set also	23
9. Location of home	Very remote rural	8
	Rural	15
	On main road	29
	In Castries	48
10. Religion claimed for members of household	Wholly Roman Catholic	75
	Wholly other denominations	14
	Mixed	11
11. Apparent degree of political involvement in household	Indifferent or ignorant	35
	Having opinions but not actively involved	61
	Actively involved	4
12. Language(s) claimed as mainly spoken in household	Patois French only	12
	English only	17
	Both	71
13. Colour claimed for family	No claim made	16
	Black ~ Negro ~ Coloured	36
	Brown ~ Dark	27
	Fair ~ light ~ 'clair' ~ middle	9
	'Shabin' ~ 'rouge' ~ red	10
	(East) Indian	2

Table 17. *Chi-squared analysis of demographic and socio-economic data by cluster*

	Clusters			
	I	II	III	IV
Results for Mode A				
1. Sex	+boys	+girls	+girls	+boys
2. School level	+Secondary children	+middle and primary school children		
3. Crowdedness of home	+more crowded homes		+less crowded homes	
4. Claims to own domestic goods	+higher ownership claims	+lower ownership claims	+lower ownership claims	+higher ownership claims
5. Location of home	+urban	+rural	+rural	+urban
6. Degree of political activism claimed in the home	+low political activism			+higher political activism
7. Language use claimed for the home	+mono-lingual English	+bilingual	+mono-lingual Patois	random
Results for Mode B				
1.	Random			
2.	Random			
3.	+more crowded homes		+less crowded homes	
4.	+higher ownership claims	+higher ownership claims	+lower ownership claims	+lower ownership claims
5.	+urban	+rural	+rural	+urban
6.	+low political activism	+higher political activism	+low political activism	+higher political activism
7.	Random			

Note: + means 'a significantly higher proportion than random of children in the following category'

terms of social structure; whether they are meaningful in terms of the 'speech varieties' which can be abstracted from them – as we have done in a tentative way above; and whether the changes of speech variety exhibited by individual children from Mode A to Mode B are socially meaningful. Thus we must examine the statistical–significant results of the chi-squared analysis in Table 17 to see if such questions can be answered. While our work was undoubtedly vitiated in this respect by the weaknesses examined in McEntegart (1980) and McEntegart and Le Page (1981), an examination of the tables reveals some suggestive features.

Some of the significant correlations might be thought only to confirm the obvious. For example, in Mode A there is a significantly higher proportion of secondary-school children in Cluster I – the most 'Standard' cluster – than in the three remaining clusters collapsed together for this purpose; no such result obtains for Mode B. In Mode A, Clusters I and IV contain significantly higher proportions of urban children; this result does still hold good for Mode B. In each Mode, Cluster IV is associated with a high incidence of the Bajan feature C_1, and it is very reasonable that this feature should disseminate outwards from the chief port and administrative centre of the island, through which the Barbadian contact has been primarily maintained in the past. It is not so self-evident why, in Mode A, Clusters I and IV should contain significantly higher proportions of boys, and Clusters II and III of girls. Under our general hypothesis and its riders children would be expected to shift to more standard English in their formal usage if it represented for them a stereotype they wished to emulate. They would do so to the extent that they had access to the necessary repertoire, were motivated to use it, were able to change if it were different from their more informal repertoire and if they received feedback that their society would accept them in the role which more standard English represented. We know from the work, of Trudgill (1973) and others that girls in England are more strongly motivated than boys towards the usage of a higher social class. This would appear not to be so in St. Lucia. Since the numbers of boys and girls in the older age-group, and also in the secondary-school group, are approximately equal, it may be that we must look to the influence of feedback for an explanation: possibly the careers open to boys through a use of more standard English are less available to girls (and indeed we believe this to be the case). We have to look elsewhere for an explanation of the high proportion of boys in A IV.

If we compare the geographical location and the claims made regarding property, political activism, and monolingualism in English vs. bilingualism or monolingualism in Patois in the home, of Clusters A I, A IV, B I and B IV we find the following distribution of significant features shown in Table 18.

Linguistically, Clusters A IV and B IV are marked by the greatest use of Bajan features; A I and B I by the greatest use of Standard English features. In Mode B, this most Bajan Cluster IV contains fewer of those who claim household property as compared with Mode A, but in A it is the only cluster with significantly more claimants to political activism. Moreover, the bulk of the children who move out of Cluster A IV move

Table 18. *Distribution of social features in relation to membership of linguistic clusters*

	A I	A IV	B I	B IV
Location	+urban	+urban	+urban	+urban
Property	+property	+property	+property	−property
Political activism	−activism	+activism	−activism	+activism
Monolingualism in English	+monolingualism in English	Random	Random	Random

into B II, which then shares with B IV an association with political activism. It is tempting therefore to suggest a link between political activism and an aggressive assertion of Creole English (rather than Patois or English or Eastern Caribbean) identity in their *formal* behaviour on the part of one section of Cluster A IV, who then in their more relaxed behaviour become more 'English' – it will be noted that B II, which they join, now contains the *second* highest incidence of Bajan features. The other section of Cluster A IV would then consist predominantly of those who increase their Creole Englishness in B IV. If this hypothesis proves after further testing to be valid, we have discovered something of interest and significance about the structure of St. Lucian society.

The above are simply examples of the hypotheses which the tables suggest. In view of the weaknesses of our method revealed in McEntegart 1980 (see below) they cannot by any means be treated as firm results.

Conclusion. There is a variety of repertoires of various kinds of English in use among the children of St. Lucia, as they take up their respective position in the sociolinguistic space shared with Patois speakers, Bajan speakers, Windward-Islands-and-Trinidad speakers and users of Standard English. The children can be grouped according to their use in formal and informal contexts. The groups cannot be placed on a linear continuum between one particular model language and the Patois. There are suggestions of significant degrees of association between membership of particular groups and factors such as sex, level of education, the locality, crowdedness and claimed relative affluence of homes, and the claimed political awareness or lack of awareness in those homes.

Our statistical analysts for the St. Lucian data, in succession Jean Thomson and Damian McEntegart, felt that the use of formal criteria to identify *possible loci* for linguistic features was unsatisfactory, since it resulted in reciprocal quantities in the cluster-analysis data. For example, Diki-Kidiri had taken as the total number of *possible loci* for past tense indicators all those places where one or another of the specified possible syntactic forms was used, and he left out of the count (because of his feeling that the criteria were too vague) any utterances which might be felt to be semantically 'past' even though none of the specified forms were used. Thus the sum of the percentages for each listed form was 100, distributed over the various forms. Le Page did not feel that this invalidated the statistics; Thomson and McEntegart, however, reworked the data so as to use semantic criteria to establish the total possible loci, thus avoiding reciprocals. Having failed, with this data, to establish for St. Lucia any truly meaningful cluster, McEntegart carried out further analysis using univariate analysis techniques and contingency tables tests (see McEntegart 1980). The conclusion (McEntegart and Le Page 1981: 123) was that there was little evidence of any hierarchy in the effects of the possible explanatory socio-economic variables. However, the variables appearing frequently throughout the models were: location of home, the school standard of the child, the 'colour' claimed for the family, and the language it was claimed was used in the home.

3. Some further problems of variable quantification

Our use of the quantification of variants of linguistic variables was strongly influenced by the pioneering work of Labov, especially in his 1966 New York City study, although Le Page had already been attempting similar techniques in assessing what could be learned from variation within the text of Anansi stories told to him (Le Page 1968b), which he felt gave a diachronic as well as a synchronic social dimension to the selection of linguistic forms because of the oral tradition which lay behind them. The concept of the variable, and its use in practice, as we have already seen, raise some problems which merit further discussion.

In order to be able to say 'Utterance X is an example of variant Y of variable Z' one has to make the following assumptions:

(i)   that linguistic classes – both form classes and semantic classes – are discrete and can be identified as distinct entities
(ii)   that there is a degree of isomorphism within and between bundles of linguistic systems ('idiolects', 'dialects', 'languages', 'registers' etc.)

In very highly focussed linguistic systems there is undoubtedly more validity in these assumptions than in the more diffuse systems we are discussing in this book. The assumptions are, however, never more than *relatively* true, and, indeed, there is an inherent conflict between these assumptions and the concept of idiosyncratic networks of relative values in linguistic systems which underlies our own hypothesis.

The lack of discreteness in linguistic classes – except as imposed by the linguist – can easily be illustrated by looking at the way in which the forms and functions of the Old English cases have been redistributed in modern English – our Appendix to Chapter 5 illustrates this in the case of the so-called 'genitive'. Within our own work it can be illustrated from the difficulties we often had in distinguishing between, for example, punctual, iterative, habitual and generic nuances in predicates. For example, when in St. Lucia a boy said 'my father selling plants in the market' he meant both that he did so habitually and that he was doing so at that moment. If we wished to identify every place where 'past tense' was intended we had in any narrative a stylistic difficulty which can be illustrated by brief reference to a medieval narrative poem, *La Chanson de Roland*, where it is clear that what is normally regarded as a tense distinction, between the past and the non-past of the verb, is in fact being used for stylistic purposes:

> Halt sunt li pui e mult halt les arbres.
> Quatre perruns i ad luisant, de marbre.
> Sur l'erbe verte li quens Rollant se pasmet.
> Uns sarrazins tute veie l'esguardet
> Si se feinst mort, si gist entre les altres.
> Del sanc luat sun cors e sun visage.
> Met sei en piez e de curre s'astet.

'The hills are high, and the trees are very high. There are four shining stones there, of marble. Count Roland faints on the green grass. All the time a saracen is watching him. He pretended that he was dead and lay among the others. He smeared his face and body with blood. He sets himself on his feet and is quick to run.'
                               (*La Chanson de Roland*, ed. and transl.
                 René Hague, London: Faber and Faber, 1937)

Within a story narrative, once the past time of the events has been established, an unmarked predicate may be interpreted as a simple Creole past unmarked for tense because aspect is either unimportant or is non-progressive, or is analogous to the 'historic present,' as used with such effect by Damon Runyon:

Well, I do not hear anything more of the matter for several weeks, but one evening when I am in Mindy's restaurant on Broadway enjoying a little cold borscht, which is a most refreshing matter in hot weather such as is going on at the time, who bobs up but Harry the Horse, and Spanish John and Little Isadore, and I am so surprised to see them that some of my cold borscht goes down the wrong way and I almost choke to death.

> (Damon Runyon, 'Breach of promise', reprinted in
> *Damon Runyon on Broadway*, Picador Books, 1950: 19)

Plurality presents a problem. The plurals of count nouns are normally unmarked in Creole, or else they are marked by a semi-agglutinative suffix *-dem*, the meaning of which overlaps with *an dem* with the sense of 'and that group of associated people':

Sample West Indian texts

(1) Standard English: Where were the children coming from?
     Jamaica: den a we paat di pikini dem bena kom fraam?
     St. Vincent.   a wich paat i pikni an dem bina kom fram?

(2) Standard English: Good children to go heaven
     Jamaica: gud pikni ga-a hebm
     St Vincent.   gud pikni doz gu a hevn

(3) Standard English: John and some others were eating mangoes
     Jamaica: jan an de hada wan bena hit manggo
     St. Vincent: jan an dem bina iit manggu

(4) Standard English: The two cats were squawling
     Jamaica: di tuu pus dem bena kwaal kwaal
     St. Vincent: tu kat bina kworil

Both Jamaican Creole and Vincentian agree in not marking the generic term in (2) above. Otherwise, it seems that Creole-ness is associated with unmarked or *-dem* marked or *-an dem* marked plurals. But in our Belize texts it is difficult to know always from the context whether an unmarked count plural or a generic term is intended:

> Questioner: What kind of trees do you have in your yard?
> Informant: chrii plom ('three plum(s)')

While the use of morphological variables is attractive in that it may avoid to a large extent the minute phonetic transcription needed to identify the variants of phonological variables, it suffers to an even greater extent than phonological variables from this question of identity: how to establish in each case the size of the denominator in the fraction:

$$\frac{\text{instances of x}}{\text{All possible loci where x might have occurred}}$$

Even with phonological and phonotactic variables, however, the problem cannot be entirely overlooked. For example, in our Belize data we had to make the assumption that something which could be identified as the word *work* – which is a unit of written English with various spoken forms corresponding to it – was always a possible locus for postvocalic *r*-colouration, even where the corresponding unit of Creole was the word *wok*; if we regard the Creole as a self-contained system with its own lexical forms, *wok* is not a possible locus for *r*-colouration. All we can do in this case is to suppose that Creole and English each have a lexical item sufficiently similar in form and meaning to be regarded as 'the same word' for purposes of variability – in other words, a speaker wanting to convey 'a particular meaning' might under certain social circumstances use one form or the other, and might hence use an *r*-coloured vowel at times and at other times not. (The limitations of this supposition are easily apparent if for example we ask whether German *hund* and English *hound* are 'the same word'.) Some linguists would prefer to keep the two codes distinct at the level of competence, and to treat performance as code-switching. As we saw in Chapter 1, Labov made the assumption that the Lower East Side New York speakers he studied (1966) all spoke one language, 'English', in which words such as *work* all had potentially an *r*-coloured vowel; his problem then was to define the value of *r*-colouration so as to allow its variation to reflect the social values attached to it. The later challenge to his work with Harlem street gangs (Labov 1972b) was by Creolists who suggested that the non-standard Negro English of these boys contained vestiges of a distinct earlier Creole system.

It is generally agreed that the concept of the linguistic variable, valuable though it has been as a tool of discovery in many sociolinguistic studies, becomes more difficult to work with once one moves out of phonology into morphology, syntax and the lexicon. There is clearly a need for ways to test against performance our intuitive or stereotypical judgments about the linguistic behaviour of others, at all levels from 'accent' to vocabulary; but the quantification of variants of variables involved us in some rather arbitrary decisions as to procedure, and in the end the statistical analysis for St. Lucia, using morphological variables, was the least successful part of our programme. To a greater extent than in Belize this was due to the relative homogeneity of the population, but the quite fundamental theoretical and procedural problems were also a matter of concern to us.

We do not intend to embark here on an extensive discussion of the theoretical issues, which are of only marginal importance to us because of the individualistic and polysystemic nature of the linguistic constructs we are concerned with. The linguist who constructs 'languages' in our Sense 3 (see Chapter 5) tends to construct an idealized grammar and then to see his informants, from whom he obtained his data, as imperfect or varying exponents of that grammar. It is this process which underlies the concept of the linguistic variable 'within a language'. Some of the theoretical issues have been discussed in a series of papers in recent years, notably by Labov (1978), Lavandera (1978), Craig (1980), Romaine (1981) and Winford (1984). They were touched upon many years earlier in a paper to the Royal Statistical Society by Ross (1950).

4. Cluster-analysis and other statistical techniques

As already noted, Labov's New York study, and Trudgill's Norwich study, both rested upon divisions of the sample population into socio-economic classes made prior to the work of sampling their linguistic behaviour. We wished to avoid making such divisions, for two reasons: in the first place, we did not feel as outsiders competent to say what the social hierarchies were, and secondly, we did not wish to predetermine what social information the linguistic data might have for us. Instead, the intention was to find a method of clumping the children together according to similarities in their verbal behaviour, and then to explore the question of what non-linguistic attributes membership of the same linguistic clump implied. It may be asked why, if according to Le Page's hypothesis all the social groups and all their linguistic attributes are properties which each individual has created for himself, we should expect to find any such clumps in the real population? The reason lies in the processes of projection and focussing: the processes through which the individual projects his concepts on to others and receives feedback from them, adjusting his concepts then according to the identity he wishes to focus to and the degree of identification and hence of focussing. This of course does not entirely answer the question: it may be that people who group themselves together, identify themselves with one another, in this linguistic way, have nothing else in common. Certainly our hypothesis allows for the case of the child who might wish to be associated with a group but is rejected by it. Of course, all our intuitive evidence, and all the evidence from other linguistic surveys, goes to show that linguistic behaviour is symptomatic of social groups; our problem is to explore as deeply as possible in a society whose stereotypes are changing the precise nature of the relationships between one set of social symptoms (language) and another.

The recently-developed statistical and computational techniques of cluster-analysis seemed (in 1969 at least) to offer a convenient method of judging which children behaved most alike linguistically. It was felt that the clustering process itself provided a reasonable analogue for what we supposed to be happening in real life. This view has since been challenged (see e.g. Labov 1980; McEntegart 1980) but remains our view. What we cannot dispute is that owing to faults both in the design and execution of the survey, the statistical results have been meagre and inconclusive.

5. The follow-up study

The actual fieldwork records and recordings, however, made it possible for us to understand and illustrate the processes at work in these post-colonial societies, and their linguistic symptoms, particularly in Belize. We have been able in Belize to carry out a follow-up study of 40 of our original sample of children, after an interval of eight years, so that we have a longitudinal record of a sizeable proportion of them. In the case of the informant GM that record covers three recording visits over twelve years. No statistical procedures were attempted here, beyond trying to ensure that the follow-up sample was to some extent representative of the original. Instead, an in-depth study was made of the recorded conversations, many of them up to one hour long; and the opinions of the speakers, the claims they made about education, ethnicity and language, were matched against the data collected about them and their families eight years previously. We draw extensively on this data also in the next two chapters.

6. A qualitative rather than a quantitative study: London Jamaican

McEntegart and Le Page (1981) concluded that in microsociolinguistic surveys of the kind we had attempted, the considerations affecting (i) the 'linguistic identity' of variables, (ii) the choice of variables, (iii) the size of the population, and of the speech-sample for each individual to be studied, and (iv) the analysis of the data, contained so many variable and unknown factors that it was difficult to justify working with the small samples used and the kind of data quantified in St. Lucia. Yet the decisions about St. Lucia were forced upon us by the time, money and personnel available. McEntegart (1980) sets out the case for preferring the alternative statistical technique of factor analysis in surveys such as ours, where we do not expect a 'ghetto' situation and where there are no sharply discrete groups in the population. However, it has been suggested that 300 is a good sample size for factor analysis, so that even our Belizean sample would have been too small.

Both Labov and Trudgill have worked (in New York and in Norwich) with considerably smaller samples than ours; but they worked in each case as insiders, seeking to demonstrate the linguistic correlates of known or given social class, age and sex groups. More recently, in Belfast, Lesley Milroy (1980) has very successfully developed a technique of relating linguistic variables not to such known social variables but to the density and complexity of the networks of relationships in which her informants – whom she came to know intimately – were involved. She has been able to demonstrate focussing processes around a variety of vernacular as well as standard norms in Belfast, through acts of identity on the part of her informants similar to those we have discussed in this book. We referred to her work, and to that of two more recent researchers, at the beginning of this chapter.

It had always been intended that our survey should have a third stage dealing with immigrant children, or the children of immigrants, in Britain and/or France, and for this next stage we decided to concentrate on in-depth studies of a handful of children rather than attempt a quantitative study.

For a number of years now, students in the Language Department of the University of York who were English language specialists have been required to spend their second year working with and studying children who, for one reason or another, have language-related achievement problems in school. Among these are children whose home language is markedly different from that of the school; and among these are many of the children of immigrants from the Caribbean. With the help of the teachers and inspectors of a number of Local Education Authorities and through our students, we had collected – although rather unsystematically – a fair amount of information about these immigrant families. We knew that their situation was changing quite rapidly, in that the problems of the first generation immigrants who arrived in English schools speaking various Caribbean vernaculars were quite different from those of their children, who grew up speaking the local English vernacular. We knew something from the work of teachers, researchers and polemicists, and the publications of, for example, V. K. Edwards, Maureen Stone, D. Sutcliffe (see the Bibliography). We knew also that the general climate, political, social, cultural and economic, in which these immigrants and their locally-born children lived had changed dramatically since large numbers of West Indians were first recruited in the 1950s to meet an acute labour shortage (Patterson 1963). By 1981, when our study began, there was instead an acute shortage of jobs, and in spite of legislation forbidding it, evident discrimination against coloured people in many spheres including employment opportunities.

Frequent references in the literature to what has been called 'London Jamaican' (see e.g. Rosen and Burgess 1980) and the disabling influence on black children at school of the attitudes of white teachers to this or to immigrant vernaculars, coupled with the work done with West Indian children by those teachers and educationalists with whom we discussed these matters at a series of seminars run under the auspices of the Inner London Education Authority's Multi-ethnic Inspectorate in 1980, led us to decide on a descriptive study for Stage 3. We wished to know more about the linguistic and social properties of this 'London Jamaican'.

Stage 3 began in October 1981 with studies by Mark Sebba (see Bibliography) of the speech of schoolchildren in two London boroughs, Waltham Forest and Greenwich. We have printed a short text in Chapter 3 which illustrates the kind of linguistic behaviour which is sometimes referred to as 'London Jamaican'. Once again, as in Belize and in St. Lucia, we must see this behaviour as relating to a constellation of cultural forces. The acts of identity reflected in Mark Sebba's recordings are of solidarity with, or imitation of, peer-group West Indians or more distant models such as the Rastafarians, the Afro-Caribbean London poet Linton Kwesi Johnson, or the Jamaican singer, the late Bob Marley. In Belize we are dealing with the emergent form of a common Belizean vernacular as a first language, and in St. Lucia with the gradual shift of a population from a French-patois-like vernacular to a creolized English as their native language, via an intermediate stage of 'Standard English as a second language in the classroom'. In London, in contrast, we are dealing apparently with an in-group argot invented and constantly renewed as a second language by each generation of teenagers as an act of Afro-Caribbean Londoner identity. (We return to this question in Chapter 6.) Three hypotheses are possible in this connection:

(i)   That each child has at least a passive competence, possibly a bilingual active competence, in the West Indian dialect of its parents which it draws upon when, in its 'teens, it wishes to join the Afro-Caribbean peer group; it has, in addition, full competence in the London English of its peer group.

(ii)   That each child has a passive competence in the teenage peer group 'Jamaican' but does not exercise this option until it becomes a teenager.

(iii)   That each child as it enters its 'teens takes part in a fresh creation of a linguistic system as part of an assertion of in-group identity, drawing on many available but fragmentary resources to do so.

These hypotheses are not mutually exclusive; indeed, it is our contention that all three reflect factors involved in the creation, not only of an argot like London Jamaican, but in the language of every social group in every society.

Sebba has recorded and analysed the linguistic behaviour of two groups of young people (not all of them black) attending schools with fairly high percentages of children of West Indian descent: in East London (Waltham Forest) and in South-East London (Catford). We have given in Chapter 3 a short sample of a conversation between two black teenage girls. In Chapter 5 we quote his findings, that in spite of great inherent variability in the code (illustrated there from the pronominal system as he has analysed it) there *is* nevertheless a discrete code which can be labelled 'London Jamaican'; it forms part of the repertoire of black teenagers of West Indian descent in London (and of some white teenagers also), is closely associated with the identity of the black peer group, and members of that group can switch into it as a conversational strategy – the text in Chapter 3 illustrates the switching process.

Of his method in collecting such data, Sebba says:

The remainder of the examples in this paper are drawn from recordings made by my informant Brenda (I have changed her name and the names of other members of her family), an 18-year-old woman of Jamaican parentage who lives in London E10. She herself was born in the East End of London, when her parents had already been settled there for five or six years. The recordings were made in her home, on a cassette machine which I lent her. She was asked to record her family and friends (with their consent) in informal conversations and without trying to set up an 'interview'. This she did very successfully and the tapes (despite some technical problems) promise to be a very rich source of socio-linguistic data.   (Sebba 1983: 6)

The method he has used for the analysis of the techniques and meaning of the code-switching evidenced by the data uses the insights of conversational analysis into the organization of conversation; he quotes Gumperz and Hernandez-Chavez (1972: 98): 'Code-switching is also a communicative skill, which speakers use as a verbal strategy in much the same way that skilful writers switch styles in a short story.' He has modified the techniques of conversational analysis in order to take account of information external to the linguistic corpus, information such as the age, sex or race of the speakers.

He draws attention to a variety he refers to as 'Black London English', in addition to London Jamaican and 'London English'; 'Black London English' is an identifiably black variety of London English, as London Jamaican is a London variety of Jamaican Creole. 'Thus' (p. 5) 'all of the following are possible realisations of the Standard English sentence 'they're black':

dɛm blɐq   dɛm ɪz blɐq
ðɛm blɐq   ðɛm ɪz blɐq
dɛm blæk   dɛm ɪz blæk
ðɛm blæk   ðɛm ɪz blæk

([q] here represents a post-velar voiceless stop, usually with aspiration or frication; it is a variant of /k/ following a rather low back vowel.)

However valid it might have been for the Caribbean, Sebba rejects the concept of a continuum for the description of the repertoire of his London informants. He prefers to consider them as having basically two discrete varieties in their repertoire (London English and London Jamaican), and a variety of conversational or discourse-related strategies for mixing them – in different proportions and for different purposes – to produce in talk the effect of a language which is neither wholly one nor wholly the other.

We shall return to Sebba's findings in Chapter 5. For the moment, it is sufficient to note that it is the use of the repertoire, and of the appropriate conversational strategies for mixing, which are the 'acts of identity' for this particular group of young people.

5 Towards a general theory of the evolution of languages

We consider in this chapter in what sense the individuals we have studied in our survey can be considered members of linguistic communities – and, if they can, how their linguistic behaviour can be described as a property of their community. This, after all, is what descriptive linguists are usually doing; and it is what the Linguistic Survey of the British Caribbean, begun in 1951, set out to do for each of the then colonial territories in turn: to produce a phonology, a grammar and a lexicon for each. So far this aim has only come anywhere near achievement for Jamaica, with Guyana perhaps next in the descriptive work done upon it. The Guyanese descriptions have raised in an acute form the problems of variability within the usage of the community with which this book opened (see e.g. Bickerton 1975, W. F. Edwards, 1977, Devonish 1978, Gibson 1982).

I. Individuals and communities as linguistically polysystemic complexes

Narrative in Belize and St. Lucia

Let us consider a sample of four children from Cayo District, Belize, each of whom told Pauline Christie the story of 'The three little pigs' (we refer to the children by their initials).

Phonological properties. Table 19 shows the phonological properties of their story-telling in terms of the three variables studied in the survey. The four children reflect different accents. The two most similar are SH and SM; both exhibit properties associated with Creole speech in the degree of nasalization. SM has reached Standard V in a Roman Catholic rural school at 12; SH is only in Standard IV in an urban Anglican school at 13; SH is rather more Creole than SM, but at the same time exhibits symptoms of Hispanization which SM lacks. The other two children have nasalization only to a very small degree; they both have a high proportion of *r*-coloured vowels; but DG, like SM, has none of the devoicing associated with Hispanization while the little boy FN, going to school in the 'Spanish' township of Benque Viejo, not surprisingly shows this feature to a

Table 19. *Incidence of three phonological properties in the story-telling of four Cayo District children*

Child	Sex	Age	Denomination and situation of school	School standard	Degree of nasalization %	Degree of r-colouration %	Degree of devoicing of /-z/ %
SH	F	13	Anglican Urban	IV	67	30	37
DG	F	13	Anglican Urban	V	2	75	0
SM	F	12	RC Rural	V	53	21	0[a]
FN	M	10	RC Benque Viejo	IV	2	67	73

Note: [a] There were not enough occurrences to calculate a reliable figure here; the figure in brackets is supplied from her late conversation, having generally comparable properties otherwise.

considerable extent. These four children live within a few miles of each other and are all 'native Belizeans', but we need at least three dimensions to describe the variation in their accents. That is, it would not – if they made up a representative sample – be possible to predict the other two values from any one. One cannot therefore arrange these four children on a linear continuum.

Grammar of openings. Next let us look at the grammar of their openings:

SH: wʌns apɔna taɪm ðɛʙ wɒz θri lɪdl pɪgz dɛm mɪ lɪv wɪð ðɛ maða...

DG: wʌns ʊpɒna taɪm deɜ wʊz čri lil pɪgz de jʊstʊ lɪv wɪt deɜr madɜr...

SM: dɪ ma mɪ ha čri a di li pɪg dɛ̃...

FN: wʌns ɣpɒn taɪm deɜr wɜr čri lɪtl pɪgs ðat de wɜr bɪg an...de haf deɜr mɒda...

SM here has the most uncompromisingly Creole opening, using the past marker [mɪ] from the outset where SH starts with [wɒz] and moves on to [mɪ] only in her second verb phrase; SM using the Creole plural marker in [pɪg dɛ̃] where all the others use the {-z} plural suffix as in Standard English. It is she also who uses the broad Creole form [li] for Standard *little*. SH and DG both use a form of *was* as their first past marker, where FN uses a form of Standard *were*. SH, whose phonology is in a number of respects closer to Standard than DG's ([ðɛʙ] vs. [deɜ], [θri] vs. [čri], [wɪð] vs. [wɪt]) nevertheless uses the less Standard past marker [mɪ] compared with DG's [jʊstʊ]. FN not only devoices the final consonants of [pɪgs] and [haf] but shows clear non-Creole interference in the way he introduces the adjectival clause [ðat de wɜr bɪg].

Once again, therefore, it is not possible to arrange these openings on a linear scale from less Standard to more Standard, or from more Creole to less Creole. Each child has produced its own unique set of datum-points in relation to any external models – 'Standard' or 'Spanish' or 'Creole'. Moreover, the incidence of phonological features does not necessarily parallel exactly that of grammatical features.

Internal variation in a single story. If we now look at the full text of SH's version of the story (printed in Le Page 1973) we find the following internal variation in her grammar (the orthography here is as on pp. 84–5, except that it has been necessary to retain the symbols ɜ, ɜɜ for the short and long non-rhotic or *r*-less vowel as in RP *hurt, heard* and the symbol ð for the voiced initial consonant of RP *that*):

'Past' contexts: use of the Creole marker *mi*

> *States:*
> dem mi liv wið ðe maða
> 'they lived with their mother'
> di man mi gat som schraa
> 'the man had some straw'
> wan ulf mi liv dea
> 'a wolf lived there'
> ði ulf mi kripl
> 'the wolf was crippled'
> ði pig mi ga wan ting a waata di bail
> 'the pig had a thing of water boiling'
>
> *Change of state:*
> weng ði pig mi gaan aut bai i gyaadn
> 'when the pig had gone out through his garden'
>
> *Desires:*
> di ulf mi wan iit am
> 'the wolf wanted to eat him'
> i mi waang klaim in di hous
> 'he wanted to climb into the house'
> di ulf mi wan klaim op di hous
> 'the wolf wanted to climb up the house'
>
> *Progressive aspect:*
> engtaim i luk ði ulf mi di kom
> 'whenever he looked the wolf was coming'
> weng i mi di kom hom
> 'when he was coming home'

'Past' contexts: use of the unmarked Creole form

> *Actions:*
> ðe staatu get big
> 'they started to get big'
> di fɜɜs litl pig fain wan man an i se
> 'the first little pig found a man and he said'

i as fi sel am som schraa
'he asked (him) to sell him some straw'
di man sel am som straa
'the man sold him some straw'
ði ulf se...
'the wolf said...'
aftawɜdz ði ulf blo dong ði hous an i iit ði fɜɜs litl pig
'afterwards the wolf blew down the house and he ate the first little pig'

Serial constructions:
i rol gan hom
He rolled home (in the barrel)'
i ron gan hom
'he ran home'
hi hori put ðɜ baril ingna ði hous
'he hurried and put the barrel in the house'
i tel ði ulf se
'he told the wolf'

Progressive aspect:
ði pig mi ga wan ting a waata di bail
'the pig had a thing of water boiling'

In addition SH uses a few Standard constructions. However, there is no continuum of forms in between. It is clear that in a large part of the story SH conforms to the grammatical rule for Belizean Creole – and for some other Anglophone Creoles in the Caribbean – that 'past actions' with punctual aspect can be unmarked, but that 'past states' or changes of state or constructions that necessarily imply some progressive or continuative aspect must be marked with *mi*. Note, however, that this is not true for those constructions where the progressive construction is used adjectivally:

> ði pig mi ga wan ting a waata di bail
> 'the pig had a thing of water boiling'

and from TA's story of Mariquita Plata:

> (dem) gaan gaan dans di kik yanda
> '(they) had gone to the dance being danced yonder'

It may well be that some of the Standard constructions SH uses are formulaic; one of them at least is direct speech. The serial constructions on the other hand are generally (although this is disputed in Bickerton 1981) associated with the influence of West African grammar.

Variation in forms for 'habitual' meanings in St. Lucia. A further illustration of our point is provided by the data from St. Lucia discussed in Le Page (1977b). There (2.21) we discovered variation in the use of forms for *habitual* meanings which reflected the different usages both in various neighbouring islands (Barbados, St. Vincent, Grenada and Trinidad for example) and in written Standard English, and in other non-Standard British dialects, as well as common 'inter-language' forms and hypercorrections.

We do not wish to suppose that there is a semantic universal [HABITUAL], but simply here use the term as a convenient abstraction for a number of relationships between predicates and their subjects which are undefined as to tense and aspect except that they imply that what has been done in the past continues and is likely to continue.

Among our texts we find versions of the model sentences from the grammar questionnaire being given as follows in Jamaica, St. Vincent and Grenada.

Standard:	He always writes like this
J:	him rait so aal di taim
St. V:	a so i doz aalwez rait
G:	i aalwez raitin so
Standard:	I live at the crossroads
J:	mi lib rait a di kraas ruod
St. V:	mi liv we tu rood kraas
G:	a livin in di jongkshan a di tuu rodz
Standard:	What kind of company does he keep?
J:	a we kain a kumpini him kip?
St. V:	wot kaind ov komponi shi doz kiip?
G:	wot kainda kompini ⎧ hi doz kip? ⎨ hi kipin?
Standard:	He seldom stays at home
J:	him haadli tan a yaad
St. V:	i doz haadli de hom
G:	hi doz seldom ste hom
Standard:	Good children go to heaven
J:	gud pikni ga-a hebm
St. V:	gud pikni doz gu a hevn
G:	gud childrin go-in tu hevn

Habitual meanings overlap with other continuative or progressive constructions, and this part of the semantic field is focussed variously from culture to culture and by a variety of formal items in each code (see Appendix to this Chapter). The West Indian *do/does* forms derive to some extent from West of England and Irish uses, to be found in the *EDD*, e.g. East Devon *Sheep da browse*, Cornwall *As fast as I do go to one, they do go to another*, Gloucestershire *I do like, I do feel* etc., Irish *Your cow does be threspassin on my fields*. In our Bajan texts we find (we have standardized the spellings here):

> I does sell sweeties there at the school
> I does make about three or four dollars a day
> He does tell me to bring it to court...

The habitual *-ing* forms (e.g. *hi kipin* etc., above) are common in Grenada, co-exist with *does* forms in Trinidad, and do not seem to occur in Barbados. The Bajan forms are common in St. Vincent and do occur in Grenada and St. Lucia, but both habitual *-ing* and habitual *does* are rare in our data from Jamaica, Belize and the Leeward Islands.

The other forms used by the St. Lucian children are:

(i)   normal Standard, e.g. 'I live at 53 Mount Coco Road', and (on three occasions only in the data examined here and generally rare) 'I am living...'

(ii)   the generalized inflection in *-s*, common in many non-standard British dialects, resulting in non-standard 'I, you, we, they lives...'

(iii)   a number of other forms most of which can be listed as hyper-corrections (although in some cases they may equally well be regarded as translating a French or Patois idiom) or over-generalizations of rules, as in 'he live...'

Our particular working hypothesis here, derived from our pilot survey and from the materials in *Sample West Indian texts*, is that Standard English forms are associated with book-learning; *-ing* forms are associated with a quite widespread regional English vernacular with its roots in former Patois-speaking territories and *does* forms with another widespread regional English vernacular with its roots in Barbados and influencing St. Lucia via the urban vernacular of Castries. We hyphothesize also that hyper-correction is associated with a desire to be identified as a Standard English speaker (the generalized incidence is too low to be very sure about this), or perhaps as an urban Castries speaker. Forms which were originally marked as being the usage of various immigrant groups, and as having the prestige or stigma of those groups, now retain that prestige or stigma within a complex stylistic or dialectal hierarchy or polysystem.

We must emphasize once more what we have said above: we do *not* assume that there is some universal category of aspect, 'the habitual'. Indeed, some of the children seemed to be inclined to make a semantic distinction of various kinds between one form and another, for example between habitual punctual and habitual progressive, whilst others did not; e.g. in this extract the child identified by the number 082 in the survey speaks of an evil spirit (the spelling has been normalized):

They say he taking your hair and go with it...they [spirits] does go with you...they say they does take you and kill you and take your blood for the devil...they giving theyself to the devil and they does give them money...

The people be in the roads and the people come, they coming, they making something and when they reach they seeing a man paying in front of them and they asking him what he want and he telling them what they want...

Later, talking about the games people play:
In the shop they play for sweets they drinking rum

The model we would wish to present here is one, as we have said, of semantic distinctions being variously focussed in relation to the forms available for use (see Appendix to this Chapter). Some verbs are inherently more 'punctual' than 'continuative' in meaning for some speakers; for example, *hit* tends to be punctual, *love* tends to be continuative, *live* varies depending on whether we mean *be alive* or *stay in residence* (for which the Scots, incidentally, regularly use *stay*). Thus the relationship between aspect and tense is a variable one; it may be that in a highly-focussed Creole like that of Belize City it is more possible (as Gibson 1982 does for Guyanese Creole, and Gibson and Levy 1983 do for Jamaican Creole) to list verbal predicates as using *either* state verbs *or* action verbs, but at least in an emergent situation like that of St. Lucia the situation appears more fuzzy in this respect – individuals seem more diffuse in their usage. It is however clear once more that all the children we worked with in St. Lucia were influenced by several models of English usage, that more than one variety of St. Lucian English was emerging, and that these varieties could not be placed on any linear continuum from Standard English to some supposed basilect. The cultural links reached out to St. Lucia's past and to the influence also of all the other islands, Francophone and Anglophone, as well as to that of the education system and the printed word.

Although the Caribbean Creoles generally share certain features (as described particularly in Alleyne 1980) they nevertheless differ from each other in quite surprising features – for example, in the form of the second person plural pronoun (*unu, yu-aal, amongs-yu* etc.) and in the form of the progressive marker (*a-, di, -ing* etc.); but it is not possible to arrange these regional variants on a linear continuum. The point here, once again, is that even in the most homogeneous of our texts, and far more so in most other texts, there is no linear continuum from Standard English to a 'broadest' creole vernacular; and if we turn to Sebba's London Jamaican we find again evidence not only of the cultural effects of parents from various Caribbean islands, but also of London Cockney, educated or Standard British English, and educated West Indian English.

Diachronic variation and its relation to claims about language use

Let us now return to Belize to look at some diachronic variation. We will examine the differences between our two informants, GM and TA, both living at one time in Santa Elena; and between GM at 12, 16 and 24 years of age.

Both these informants were 'bilingual', if that is the appropriate term – and we see shortly why it is not very appropriate – in varieties of 'Spanish' and varieties of Creole and of more standard English.

The case of GM. The text of GM's Creole (['kri·ɐ] as she called it) Anansi story is given in part in Chapter 3; she then immediately re-told the same story in 'Spanish'. It was noticeable however that her Creole was somewhat more fluent than her Spanish; when she stumbled in the Creole version it was because of her excitement at having a recording made of her skill as a raconteuse; when she stumbled in the Spanish version it was because she had forgotten the Spanish word or slipped unconsciously back into Creole. In 1970, when she was 16, she explained some of the background to her childhood; she was by this time living as the wife of a Government Agricultural officer who had been to college in Guatemala. Her narrative explains in detail how her mother spoke to her, how her father spoke to her, how the children spoke to each other at school and how she and her husband now conversed; it is a fascinating personal linguistic history:

LeP: Yes, we've been all over the district...When you were a little girl, what language did you speak first of all with your mother?
GM: Oh, (it) was Creole, from ever since I was learning to talk.
LeP: But your father was a Mexican, wasn't he?
GM: No, my mother. My father is a...Creole...Belizean...
LeP: When you say Belizean what does that mean?

GM: His mother was a Belizean from here an' his father is an Irishman but he grew up in Belize so...they call him a Bay-born...he was born in Belize anyhow.

LeP: Yes – so he spoke Creole and your mother spoke Spanish?

GM: Well she spoke both.

LeP: But with you she spoke Creole?

GM: No well she don't...she doesn't exactly speak Creole to us you know but we...by going to school an' hear other children...well we pick it up...No she tried to talk to us the proper way but...you know children...we want to go our way...we pick up Creole...

LeP: But she learnt English at school, did she?

GM: Mhm.

LeP: So she wanted you to speak proper English?

GM: (Laughs) Well, at all of us...Now whenever we'd say something out the way like...something funny like [bi'ka·z] and we don't say [bi'kɔ·z] she'd put [bi'kɔ·z]...and we'd say [bɪ'ka·] because we heard that in school you know, [bɪ'ka·] that's the way it is,...we never finish a word...we always...cut it short or put more to it.

LeP: That school you went to in Santa Elena...the Catholic school...did most of the children there speak Creole?

GM: Mhm. And Spanish...but this...broken-up Spanish you know. We call it Creole Spanish too because that's not grammatical Spanish.

LeP: But most of the families round there speak Spanish at home, don't they?

GM: Mhm.

LeP: So what did they talk in the playground, the children?

GM: Some Spanish and some ['kria].

LeP: Which most?

GM: That's [fʊ] tell...I guess it's both! Balance half of each!

LeP: Did they ever mix the two up?

GM: Mhm.

LeP: So there was a sort of Creole Creole Spanish and a Creole Creole English?

GM: (Laughs) Mhm. Have a language spoken like...for instance you would want to say, em, 'bat the ball', they wouldn't say, well 'bat the ball' or...how you'd say 'bat' in Spanish now I've forgotten...or 'catch the ball' or something like that... they wouldn't say 'agarrame la bola' or something like that they would say [ka'čiə ˌla 'bola] you know an'...that's 'catch' (laughs). They wouldn't...em...finish it.

LeP: Did your mother ever do that kind of thing when she talked to you?

GM: Hng! [i.e. No!]

LeP: She spoke good Spanish, did she?

GM: She spoke good Spanish, yes, because she learned good Spanish from her father...her father is a pure-bred Mexican...

LeP: Was she proud of that?

GM: (Laughs) Well I guess so! I suppose!

LeP: And when you spoke Creole Spanish, did she correct that?

GM: Always...idea to put us on...Daddy the same way, because Daddy never spoke to us in...broad Creole...although he is...right from Belize...he never spoke to us in broad Creole...he always...em...you know try to correc' us an'...(get us to) speak correctly but we never...we never give up to them...(laughs) as we get to bear children...there it is!

LeP: What will you do with your children?

GM: I guess I'll try to do the same but they'll come out the same! (laughs)

LeP: You think so? Come out talking what?

GM: They'll come out talking Creole! Only if I go away an'...they don't come back to BH (British Honduras)...that's...the only remedy [fʊ] do [fʊ] that, you know...right from getting them speaking this Creole...but... you notice...most of the [ˈtuˑrɪsɪz] an' the...the outside visitors, their children usually go back to their home town with this Creole.

LeP: My children did!

GM: It's...it's a easy thing for children to catch on to...an'...my mother...husban' now...sh...he em he's here over ten years an' he can't...speak a word of Creole.

LeP: Why is that?

GM: He never did try! An' either Spanish...he's an American...that's all he speaks...never did try...the Creole, never did try the Spanish.

LeP: This is your husband?

GM: No – he speaks both! Spanish Creole and English.

LeP: What does he use with you?

GM: Oh he tries to let me speak grammatical Spanish but...(laughs) that's a problem. You know whenever I say something funny like...[ˈaːwa] he'd say [ˈagwa] an' he'll laugh at me, you know, but I guess...it's because he laugh at me I don't try any more...you see...an' I tell him I say don't laugh at me because I won't try...So well I...

LeP: I suppose he learnt this grammatical Spanish in Guatemala?

GM: Mhm – in school.

LeP: He went to school there?

GM: Sure – where he was studying for agriculture.

LeP: Yes – but as a little boy did he go to school there too?

GM: Well – as a little boy he went to school in Sacred Heart in Cayo, and, he went to the College and from the College he went over there.

LeP: Mhm. The L..... family (her husband's family) – what did they speak at home when he was a little boy?

GM: Spanish – but the same broken-up Spanish.

LeP: Are they pure Spanish?

GM: Well – by the mother side they're pure Spanish but the father is a – you know, just like me – a half-Creole (laughs).

She then went on to record another Anansi story; it took her a little longer this time to get into her stride:

Alligator and the eggs

brada taiga an aligeta wɜɜ gud frenz. taiga yuztu aalwez wantu kuot sista aligeta. sista aligeta had a nes da di rivasaid, (at this point her language becomes markedly more Creole) ang hi hav baut wan dozn eg iinga ðis nes...

(spelling normalized; for full original text see Le Page 1980)

When we called on GM the last time, in 1978, she had left Cayo District and was living in Belize City, married by now to a Creole man, and doing a responsible supervising job in a factory. Part of the conversation went as follows:

LeP: Do you still speak Spanish?

GM: Well em I speak Spanish enough to hold a little conversation. I've lost a bit of it.

LeP: Does your husband speak Spanish?

GM: A very little.

LeP: Do you ever use Spanish in the house here?

Gm: Mhm. Sometimes. I would more use it for a joke to hear the answer. You know – to hear, how he would answer, or I would tell him, answer me in Spanish or...for the fun of it.

LeP: Do many of the people in this part of Belize speak Spanish?

GM: No. The only Spanish-speaking district is San Ignacio, Corozal, up in Orange Walk, North.

LeP: But people in San Ignacio nowadays are becoming Creole speakers.

GM: Aha...It's changing quite rapid...Because even the children that are going to school, the parents would speak to them in Spanish and they would answer in English or refuse to speak Spanish, for what reason I don't know...

LeP: ...What will your little girl speak when she grows up?

GM: She's only speaking Creole right now...

GM this time was unwilling to record a story. She felt she had put her childhood and youth behind her.

The case of TA. TA (whose story about Mariquita Plata is given in part in Chapter 3), by contrast, had grown up in the frontier region of Orange Walk, only accessible in her youth (and for a long time afterwards) by river. She had had less education than GM. In her childhood, Cayo District really was frontier territory, being exploited primarily by the mahogany-loggers and the chicle-tappers. It is difficult to know whether she originally heard the story of Mariquita Plata in a mixture of Spanish and Creole, or wholly in Spanish; to begin with, Spanish is reserved for the dialogue, although it is noticeable that dialogue with the carpenter is in Creole (TA herself comments on this in passing) and that much earlier in the story the division between Spanish and Creole is blurred; the mix is sometimes quite intimate (the 'Spanish' here is italicized):

> i...hib am we...*lo boto*...*kwando lo boto*
> *lo yebo el chilang*...aii nau *ya empeso*
> *a yora*
> i se...mai daahta...*de ke stas yorando?*

TA gave us the impression of being much more fluently bilingual in Spanish and Creole than GM, and of being fully at home in a community where, in earlier years, as much Spanish as Creole was heard, perhaps (in Orange Walk, as in Benque Viejo) far more. On the other hand, her more Standard English was more fragmentary, more fixed with Creole features, than that of GM.

The case of EO. The next pieces of evidence come from further conversations with some of our informants whom we interviewed again in the follow-up survey in 1978. For example, Miss EO, who had left the primary school in San Ignacio from Standard VI at about 14 to go to do domestic work at a new motel built by a local businessman of Lebanese descent. His house in the centre of San Ignacio was one of those completely destroyed by a disastrous fire; when she told us about the fire she slid into broad Creole:

EO: Well, when the house burn we mi gaan by [she then corrects herself] em...we went to...to his other house in Cool Shade. And I work there with him. By I lef and I went to Belize to work.

LeP: Can you tell us about the fire, what was it like? Where did it start?

EO: Em...from a little house, from...the lady name Miss Rosie.

AT-K: I think I knew her.

LeP: How did it start?

EO: fang iina ði haus wi ði noiz evribadi sii ði fleemdem fang iina ði haus...fang datawe i kech di hotel...fang ang awe spred...da fang mis eskanda haus wi mi di bring daung a lat av klooz a lat av θingz...

It is not, however, the broad Creole vernacular of Belize City, where for *a lat av klooz* would be heard *wan lat a klooz*, and *wan lat a ting* for *a lat av θingz*. Notice in this respect the shift made by GM in her story above about 'Alligator and the eggs', from *had a nes* to *hav baut wan dozn eg iinga ðis nes*. On the subject of languages, EO told us she could speak a little Spanish; her mother spoke Spanish most of the time. Her father was Spanish, her mother 'Mixed' – half Spanish, half Creole. Her own little daughter Salomé could understand if the 'great-great-grandmother' (*sic*), who could only speak Spanish and no Creole, spoke to her, but Salomé herself could speak only Creole. Most of the neighbours round about, she said, were 'Spanish', but the children all spoke Creole. We shall be returning to the discussions with EO when we discuss ethnicity later, in Chapter 6.

The case of DGL. Another informant was DGL, part of whose conversation went as follows:

LeP: How old were you when you started teaching?

DGL: I was fifteen years.

LeP: What languages can you speak?

DGL: English and Creole, and Spanish a little.

LeP: Do you ever use Spanish?

DGL: To outside...outside. But in school I don't use Spanish, only English.

LeP: Do any of the children come from Spanish homes?

DGL: Oh, a lot.

LeP: Can you tell me any of the difficulties they have when you are teaching them?

DGL: Well, em, we put them along with the children that know English, so that they can have a...can know how to talk the...em...English, you know. After a while they can talk it.

LeP: Do they learn to talk English or Creole?

DGL: Yes, English. There's mostly Spanish as long as they ...em...heard...they hear someone talking English they would pick it up. Then the Creole would come right in.

LeP: The Creole comes in...why is that?

DGL: Well, because most people talk Creole.

LeP: The people living round here, what would you say they are, mostly?

DGL: Oh, em, some well...some of...most of them are Spanish.

LeP: Any...any other kinds?

DGL: Oh, English...em...Kekchi, Mayas...

LeP: Any Creole?

DGL: Creoles, yes.

LeP: Any mixed?

DGL: Mixed, yes.

LeP: Any Carib?

DGL: Carib – well, my husband is a Carib.

LeP: Is he? But your own family, when you were a child, was not Carib, was it?

DGL: Yes, I am mix too. My father is a Carib and and my mother is a Spanish...

LeP: How would you describe yourself?

DGL: Mixed.

LeP: You'd say mixed? Have you ever heard any one describe themselves as a Belizean?

DGL: I am a Belizean [laughing]...

LeP: How do Belizeans talk?

DGL: Creole. Mostly Creole.

LeP: What does Creole sound like? Can you tell me any story in Creole?

DGL: brada hanansi an em bra tuod de had baagin...brada tuod mi tel...ai med a misteek...bra-a nansi had tri childrin...hi didn...hi mi gaan naa wɜrk an i neva hav noting fu iit...sa i miit brada rabit...i aas bra rabit if i no hav eni plaanting...so i tek an i gaan houm...bra-a nansi tek an i roos it...an i kaal i children...so em de sidaung raung di teibl...bra hanansi onli mi smaat...so i staatu shee di plantin bitwiin di chrii children...an di childrin dem bigan di se papa bot hav yu no gat notin fu iit? etc...

There are a number of features in this narrative which mark it off from the focussed Creole of Belize City; for example, *bigan di se* for *bigin tu se*, 'began saying'. It is significant that when asked to tell a story in Creole she straight away launches into an Anansi story, and the story has a faintly 'literary' flavour about it. Her father she describes as a Carib, her mother as a 'Spanish'. She herself had been a pupil-teacher and then a teacher since she was 15. In other words, she represents yet another slightly different region of linguistic competence from GM, from TA, and from EO, though sharing with them three similar ingredients: 'Spanish', 'Creole' and 'English'. In her case there is the added ingredient of Carib.

The case of LG. Our final informant was another teacher, this time at the Sacred Heart College in San Ignacio, and we talked to her with her brother at their home. Her case is interesting because of her very strong attachment to Spanish, her resentment that her brother uses Creole, even to her when she speaks to him in Spanish, and that her own little four-year-old boy learned Creole first and only started using Spanish well when he was over three. She herself claimed that, though she had presumably learned Creole as a child, after an absence of 17 years in the United States she finds it very difficult to speak Creole and people laugh at her mistakes. Her brother had not been away. She was proud of the fact that, in contrast to the United States, racial tolerance and intermarriage were increasing in Belize; but at the same time she was upset that Creole was replacing Spanish.

Here she is talking about the difficulties the Creole-speaking children have with English, as compared with the children from Spanish- and Maya-speaking villages:

LG: They have a tremendous amount of trouble with em subject and verb agreement. Em, they also have much difficulty using adverbs. In the correct pers...correct em, person...They will write *they gone, they gone to the show*. Or em, *I will went*. You know, which is completely wrong and most of the times they're not even aware that they have made that mistake. Well I, I taught, I taught English last year and I...it was terrible when it came to compositions, you know, because it was...If I started correcting them, one paper, usually would take me half an hour just for one. The children from the Mayan villages don't usually seem to have so much trouble with the English because they don't learn Creole. They don't learn as much as to talk Creole as the children here in Cayo do, nor the children in Benque. Usually we don't have quite the trouble with the children around here because they learn Spanish and they learn Creole and people from Benque learn Spanish and the ones from the smaller villages that are Mayan learn Maya, and so in school they're taught English, and they're taught it in the correct way, and so they don't encounter the difficulties of having to switch from Creole to a correct English which to them usually...people that speak Creole that's as far as they're concerned they speak proper English you know; an' then when they have to do it in another language, which is English, they have got difficulty doing it, so...The kids from the town have more difficult time learning the correct English.

LeP: In the town...you mean where?

LG: That's from here...San Ignacio.

LeP: You've forgotten your Creole?

LG: Yes, I, I don't think I ever learned it really. Because I only studied French a little bit, and I remember that well. And I can't remember my Creole – in fact everybody makes fun of my Creole...When we were small, when we were growing up *all* of us spoke Spanish, *all* of us. Whereas now my little...my little four-year-old boy, em, he learned Creole first and it hasn't been until the last eight months or so that he has learned Spanish to the point where he can speak it very well. Because most of the children learn Creole. I have a little eight-year-old sister who barely talks Spanish. Barring bare necessity when she has to talk to my mother and she speaks Spanish, which is a shame.

We shall return to her very interesting testimony when we consider, in Chapter 6, the question of ethnicity.

Parents' claims compared with children's claims. LG and her family are by no means an isolated case, but the complex of cultural loyalties and individual perception of the linguistic behaviour within families is clearly illustrated from the following data to which the case of LG can be related (Tabouret-Keller and Le Page 1983).

In the 1978 follow-up survey two-thirds of the former pupils still lived in their families' homes. It was therefore interesting to compare their 1978 declarations on the languages spoken within their families (a) with the declarations made in 1970 by their parents who had been asked what the usual language in the family was, and (b) with the declarations they had made themselves when interviewed as schoolchildren by Pauline Christie. Thirty-eight of our informants were studied in this way. The questions asked by Dr Christie were on language use with father, mother, grandparents, older and younger brothers and sisters, when talking about schoolwork or when telling jokes. Table 20 shows these three sets of data. It illustrates that in 1970 parents and children described their common language situation in terms that differed in quite important ways. Where parents mentioned Spanish as the only language spoken in 15 cases and Creole only in four, the children's information reversed these proportions, mentioning Creole in 14 cases and Spanish only in eight.

We wanted to know how general such a discrepancy in the description

Table 20. *Family language situations as described by parents and children in 1970 and by children in 1978*

Languages	Parents 1970	Children 1970	Children 1978
Spanish	15	8	7
Spanish, English	2	1	—
Spanish Creole	1	—	8
Creole	4	14	19
Creole, Spanish	—	1	3
English	2	2	—
English, Creole	1	—	—
English, Spanish, Creole	2	2	—
English, Spanish	—	1	—
Maya	1	1	—
Maya, Spanish	1	—	—
Maya, Spanish, English	—	—	1
{ Spanish with parents ⎰ English with brothers, sisters	—	6	—
Creole with father, Spanish with mother	—	1	—
Not known	9	1	—

Note: Mention of two or more languages is given in the order as indicated by the informant, the first mention being generally the language referred to as most spoken.

Table 21. *Language use as stated by parents for the family (overall question) and as stated by their children (questioned as to their usage with parents, grand-parents, older and younger siblings) in the 1970 survey*

	Spanish only %	Creole only %	Spanish mentioned %	Creole mentioned %
Parents	37	20	62	38
Children	12	35	31	76

Note: N = 96, all the children in our sample attending San Ignacio's primary schools.

of languages as used in families would be, and therefore made a check of a fairly large sub-set of the original sample, that of all the children in our sample attending San Ignacio's primary schools (N = 96). Table 21 shows a clear-cut pattern: in 20 per cent of the families parents specify Creole as the only language in their family; in 37 per cent of the families they specify Spanish; but 35 per cent of the children specify only Creole whereas 12 per cent specify only Spanish. And whereas parents mentioned Spanish as one of the languages being used in 62 per cent of the cases, and Creole in 38 per cent of the cases, the children, in contrast, mentioned

Spanish, often as used with grandparents, in 31 per cent and Creole in 76 per cent of the cases. This information indicates of course that people's perceptions of language situations differ. It indicates also that in 1970 Creole usage was already fairly widespread among schoolchildren in San Ignacio but that they did not feel the same inhibitions as their parents about mentioning it.

Returning to Table 20 we see also that in six cases children described a mixed situation where Spanish was spoken with parents but 'English' with brothers and sisters. 'English' here is to be understood as 'Creole' and was probably used in preference to the latter term as a result of a defence mechanism against Creole on the part of the parents, but it may also to some extent result from the interview situation where members of our team appeared as more or less official persons to whom 'English' was more to the point than 'Creole'. However, one of the mothers when asked what she meant by English answered: 'the same English them learn at school we call it Creole'.

So we come once again to the question with which we started this chapter: In what sense are all these people members of linguistic communities? Their cultural gravitational forces operate in many directions; each of them occupies an individual position, and yet they give evidence of sharing various loyalties and hatreds and alliances and identities within many different spheres.

Comparison with Malaysia and Singapore

At this point it is worth while turning aside briefly from the Caribbean to look at what is happening today in Malaysia and in Singapore, since the problems and processes we are discussing are in fact universal, and can be illustrated from all parts of the world (including Britain and France), and from all periods of history.

Malaysia and Singapore achieved their independence of Britain, first as a Federation and then separately, in 1957 and 1963 (see Le Page 1964). Leaving East Malaysia (Sarawak and Sabah) aside, each has a similar ethnic and cultural mix, but in quite different proportions: Malay, Chinese, Indian, Negrito, Eurasian but with Malays predominating in Malaysia, Chinese greatly predominating in Singapore. Each country is trying to unify its people through a common cultural and educational policy. Whereas Malaysia once had English-medium, Chinese-medium, Malay-medium and Tamil-medium education, today it has only Malay-medium (*Bahasa Malaysia*, 'the Malaysian language', having been adopted as both the 'National language' and the vehicle of national unity). Singapore retains Malay as its 'National language' from the days before the Federation broke up, but for economic reasons (unlike Malaysia, which has resources of natural gas, oil, tin, rubber, timber and other agricultural products Singapore has nothing except a deep-water harbour and the work and brains of its $2\frac{1}{2}$ million people) Singapore parents have more and more opted for English-medium education for their children and the Government has provided considerable resources to meet their wishes, while at the same time urging all Singaporeans to become 'bilingual', and urging the Chinese who speak Hokkien, Hakka and other non-Mandarin 'dialects' to speak Mandarin instead.

In both Malaysia and Singapore, therefore, the families of Chinese ethnic origin have been faced with a crisis of identity. The overseas Chinese have always, like other immigrant groups in other countries, been strongly motivated towards economic success. They have always – with some exceptions – looked back culturally to China, with strong feelings of Chinese ethnicity which we discuss in Chapter 6. But today pressures are strong for them to adopt in one case a Malaysian, and in the other a Singaporean, identity. In Malaysia this means using *Bahasa Malaysia* and in Singapore, being 'bilingual' in English and their 'native language' (so called) which – for the Chinese – is now officially deemed to be Mandarin although in fact it is most likely to be felt by the people themselves to be Hokkien or some other southern Chinese dialect. Such evidence as we have points to the fact that the younger generation in each country is, perhaps *faute de mieux*, perhaps because they are rather conformist and disciplined people accustomed to accepting Government pressures, perhaps out of a genuine sense of identity, accepting that they must be Malaysians or Singaporeans first and 'Chinese' second, while continuing to want economic advancement. They use, or attempt to use, *Bahasa Malaysia* in Malaysia, and English and Mandarin in Singapore. In both countries, however, this has led, inevitably, to a great deal of code-switching, code-mixing, interference, and the evolution of various vernacular norms of speech behaviour very different from the official norms of Standard *Bahasa Malaysia* or Standard English or Chinese *putonghua*. There have been strong official reactions in each country – attempts to insist on 'correct' *Bahasa Malaysia* or 'correct' English – the Minister of Education in Singapore going so far as to state that they could not countenance the 'Caribbeanization' of English there. These vernacular norms are not yet highly-focussed; they are quite diffuse, in fact, since the population learn their Malay or their English from a wide variety of sources, and themselves start from a wide variety of different language backgrounds. Nevertheless, all linguistic history tells us that more focussed local vernacular norms *will* emerge through close daily urban interaction and similar processes (National Service in Army camps, for example), and that these will become the target varieties. There will, however, be no linear sequence of varieties from these vernacular norms to Standard *Bahasa Malaysia* or Standard English, any more than in the Caribbean region from one broadest Creole to a single Standard (see, for further discussion, Le Page 1984).

The situation then in both Belize and in St. Lucia can be paralleled in many other parts of the world, and illustrates the processes by which, as Hugo Schuchardt pointed out a century ago (Schuchardt 1882), new languages are constantly coming into existence in response to new needs.

The case of London Jamaican

A further example is provided by the so-called 'London Jamaican' of the children of West Indian immigrants in London, which the last of our texts in Chapter 3 illustrates. (Similar argots are to be found in other urban areas with West Indian immigrant populations.) Sebba and Le Page (1983) report on the characteristic features they discovered in a pilot study among adolescent boys and girls in three schools in East London (Waltham Forest) and two in South-East London (Catford). At this pilot stage they were only able to deal with the pronominal system, the complementizer *se*, methods of handling tense and aspect of predicates, the copula, and one specific phonological alternation between ʌ and ɐ. (Local, Wells and Sebba 1984 deals, further, with very interesting aspects of the systems of intonation and the demarcation and focussing of speech varieties within the linguistic behaviour of these adolescents; Sebba 1983, which we have cited in Chapter 4, deals with conversational analysis as a technique for establishing the characteristic code-switching in the use of their repertoire by his informants. Further work is in progress.)

Most of the London-born informants appeared, with the exception of some of those born in Catford, to have as their dominant vernacular a variety of London English (LE) virtually – although not wholly – indistinguishable from that of other London children in the area. The London Jamaican (LJ) was reserved for a relatively limited range of uses. Sometimes it is clear that they are code-switching between LE and something more like LJ. Moreover, what is identified as LJ itself owes aspects of its phonology and grammar to LE; it clearly owes others to West Indian influences – primarily to Jamaican Creole, but also possibly to Bajan, Vincentian and other varieties, and to more educated Jamaican usage. Nevertheless, Sebba and Le Page's conclusion is that 'any attempt at analysis must, we feel, come to terms with "London Jamaican" as a system of its own, with high internal variability, drawing on both London English, and Jamaican and other Creoles for its substance.' They further speculate that 'there are 'trade-off' relationships between syntax, morphology, phonology and phonetics, so that (at least sometimes) when the syntax tends more towards Standard English there is a compensatory "Jamaicanization" of, say, the intonation and rhythm'. They report that:

'fifth-formers were generally better informants than sixth-formers, although two sixth-form girls provided us with excellent recordings. There are two possible reasons for this: firstly, that sixth-formers tend to be pressed for time . . . but more important, there is a sociolinguistic reason as well: sixth-formers have taken a decision to stay on at school, to try to 'do well', and this aim is felt to be consistent with being heard to speak only Standard English or London English and not London Jamaican. Some of our sixth-form informants denied that they ever spoke London Jamaican, though when pressed they admitted that they would use it just for 'joking or the like'.

Clearly, the evolution and use of this argot is the outcome of many 'acts of identity' by young people growing up in a multidimensional linguistic and cultural environment to which their parents, their teachers, their peer group and 'the establishment' all contribute. The precise linguistic outcome, as the analysis seems to show, is not that of any single external model but the result of focussing around a repertoire of forms in relation to meaning-potentials (see Appendix to this Chapter) so that a polysystemic system of multifunctional units develops its own internal coherences and contrastive potential, both in phonology and grammar. This can be illustrated by relating their pronominal system to that which we described for Jamaica, St. Vincent and Grenada in Chapter 3. The idealized broad Jamaican vernacular system described by Bailey (1966) (Table 22) has just six forms, undifferentiated for case or gender (although a 'possessive' may be marked by the preposition *fi* with any one of these forms). Other, less broad, varieties of Jamaican, and the vernacular usage of other islands (as the texts in Chapter 3 show) have systems somewhat closer to those of English and American dialects: the West African form *unu* for *you* (plural) is replaced by *yu, yu-aal, aal-a-yu, amongs-yu* and so on; there can be alternation between, e.g., *ai* (unstressed *a*) and *mi* in stressed subject position (in Belize to use *mi* in subject position is regarded today as old-fashioned or rural); and gender differentiation of the third person singular can be marked by *shi, hi, hit* etc. Both London English and Standard English mark the possessive (*my, your, her, his, its, our, their*) and some of the other oblique cases (*me, her, him, us, them*) as well as third person singular gender (*she, he, it*). The London Jamaican system analysed

Table 22. *Jamaican Creole pronominal system (Bailey 1966)*

Person	Singular	Plural
1	mi	wi
2	yu	unu
3	im	dem

Table 23. *London Jamaican pronominal system*

Person	Subject	Oblique	Possessive
singular			
1	mi ~ ai	mi	mi ~ mai
2	yu	yu	yu ~ yɔə(ɹ)
3 masc.	(h)ii ~ (h)im ~ in	(h)im ~ in	(h)im ~ (h)in ~ (h)iz
fem.	shi	shii ~ (h)ə(ɹ)	shi ~ (h)ə(ɹ)
neut.	it ~ i	it ~ i	ʔits ~ im
plural			
1	wi	wi ~ ʌs ~ ɒs	wi ~ auə(ɹ)
2	yu ~ unu	yu ~ unu	yɔə ~ unu
3	dɛi ~ dɛm ~ ðɛi ~ ðɛm	dɛm ~ ðɛm	

by Sebba is as shown in Table 23; he describes it as 'a rather "messy"
system with alternations between variants coming from the LE and LJ
systems', and comments 'we have not found any way of predicting which
of the available variants will be used by a speaker on a particular occasion,
but it seems that speakers do make a clear distinction between pronouns
belonging to a "Jamaican" set and pronouns belonging to an "English"
set'.

It should be noted that this paradigm is a linguist's abstraction from the
behaviour of a number of young people when, according to his criteria,
each of them was speaking London Jamaican. It is a statement about a
language in our Sense 3 (see below, p. 190). It is not a statement about
the usage of any individual speaker. Part of the planned further investigation will be to see to what extent it might be reasonable to extrapolate
these properties as those of London Jamaican speakers as a community,
that is, of a language in Sense 4 (see pp. 190–1) called London Jamaican.

Sebba and Le Page (1984) emphasize the distinction to be made between
the indigenous culture of the teenage children and that of their immigrant
West Indian parents, towards whose 'deep Creole', if it is used (and their
parents may well try to avoid it or modify it in the presence of the children),
the children's attitude may be one of perplexity and even derision,

especially if their parents are from different islands or from the Eastern Caribbean. As most of the children have native competence in London English they feel most comfortable using that in any public situation. It seems that only a minority of the London-born Afro-Caribbean children have a native-like command of Jamaican Creole. 'London Jamaican' is more a set of norms to be aimed at than an internally coherent and consistent system. Speakers behave as if there were a language called 'Jamaican', but often all they do (perhaps all they *know how* to do) is to make gestures in the direction of certain tokens associated with Jamaican Creole which have a stereotypical value. In other words, the 'idealized' London Jamaican is a language close to the 'deepest' form of Jamaican Creole, and is identified as such by all those features above the level of awareness which distinguish Jamaican Creole from Standard English (with minor exceptions, noted below). In practice, most speakers cannot achieve the ideal. The result is a variety of speech which is (a) highly variable from speaker to speaker, (b) highly variable internally, (c) tends to 'revert' to London English – i.e. speakers often seem to find difficulty maintaining London Jamaican over long stretches.

2. Linear continuum or multidimensional model?

One cannot avoid using a multidimensional model to accommodate these 'acts of identity' and as a framework for considering our question. The statistical analysis program we used on the linguistic data collected from each of the 280 children in our Belize sample, and from each of the 100 children in our St. Lucian sample, as described in Chapter 4, was one of cluster-analysis; and although we had only partial success with this in relation to the Belize data and very limited success with it in relation to St. Lucia, nevertheless the concepts behind cluster-analysis do seem to provide a useful analogue for what is going on in a community as people speak to each other. We return to the details of this analogue below. Even in relation to London Jamaican, no linear continuum is adequate, but rather, complex social rules for switching between and mixing items from two (or more) codes in a shared repertoire. It is a weakness of our method of investigation that we are obliged to select just a handful of linguistic features as a surrogate for a linguistic description.

Further weaknesses are (i) that it is in some ways easier to work with phonological features than any other, and (ii) the analytical program forces us to quantify them in such a way that we have to assign each feature equal weight until we have discovered the relative importance of each feature in the hierarchy of degrees of association with various socio-economic and cultural factors. In regard to the latter, Trudgill, at the end of his paper applying our general hypothesis and riders to the phonology of British pop singers, who for professional purposes make certain adjustments in the direction of their stereotypes of American pronunciation, lists as one of its inadequacies (as of sociolinguistic theory in general) its inability to explain why *particular* consonantal, vocalic or other variants are retained, rejected or selected (Trudgill 1980: 159–60). However, the differential weighting of prestige or stigma attached to particular linguistic features in people's stereotypes about groups is clearly shown by Milroy's work in Belfast, as we see below (p. 185). It might also be alleged against us that we have never collected samples of an informant's 'real' dialect – our samples have always been affected by the nature of the audience, the setting, and the topic. This is quite true – in telling traditional stories, for example, the children who knew them most intimately went into a 'story-telling' mode. Sebba, however, seems to have collected at least some samples of very uninhibited peer-group behaviour. Nevertheless, our answer to this last objection forms a major bastion in our general theory; it is that *all* utterances are affected by the audience, the topic and the setting, and that in general terms – to modify our original hypothesis – 'the individual creates for himself the patterns of his linguistic behaviour so as to resemble those of the group or groups with which from time to time he wishes to be identified, or so as to be unlike those from whom he wishes to be distinguished'.

Projection, focussing, diffusion. There are constraints upon the individual's ability to create these patterns, which we shall deal with in a moment. Within this general theory we see speech acts as acts of projection: the speaker is projecting his inner universe, implicitly with the invitation to others to share it, at least insofar as they recognize his language as an accurate symbolization of the world, and to share his attitude towards it. By verbalizing as he does, he is seeking to reinforce his models of the world, and hopes for acts of solidarity from those with whom he wishes to identify. The feedback he receives from those with whom he talks may reinforce him, or may cause him to modify his projections, both in their form and in their content. To the extent that he is reinforced, his behaviour in that particular context may become more regular, more focussed; to the extent that he modifies his behaviour to accommodate to others it may for a time become more variable, more diffuse, but in time the behaviour of the group – that is, he and those with whom he is trying to identify – will become more focussed. Thus we may speak of focussed and of diffuse, or non-focussed, linguistic systems, both in individuals and in groups, with each individual's knowledge of the systems of his groups the lynch-pin upon which the shared concept of communal languages or varieties turns.

The constraints upon our acts of identity. Our ability to get into focus with those with whom we wish to identify, however, is constrained, as we have already said, and the constraints can in general terms be categorized under four heads; each can be illustrated from the data given above. We can only behave according to the behavioural patterns of groups we find it desirable to identify with to the extent that:

(i)   we can identify the groups

(ii)   we have both adequate access to the groups and ability to analyse their behavioural patterns

(iii)   the motivation to join the groups is sufficiently powerful, and is either reinforced or reversed by feedback from the groups

(iv)   we have the ability to modify our behaviour

(i) *The identification of groups.* It should here be noted that our general theoretical approach to the evolution of languages is intended, by Le Page at least, to be universally applicable. For most infants creating their first 'language' the most easily identifiable group is that of their family as contrasted with the less familiar world; but even within a family of two parents and one child there are four possible groups for the child to discern, each of which may be – in a multilingual household almost certainly is – linguistically differentiated: Mummy and me; Daddy and me; Mummy and Daddy; all three of us. The vaguest group – though one frequently invoked – for most people is 'They', a group to which it is easy to ascribe bad attributes but perhaps difficult to clothe with precise linguistic characteristics.

In the case of our Belizean informants, the identity 'Belizean' was a comparatively recent one and to some extent a vague one, as we shall see in Chapter 6, meaning primarily people who were born in or lived in Belize. The country had in any case changed its name. Belize, when we began our work there, was the name of the capital city at the river mouth; the country was called British Honduras, or ('BH', the term GM still used from time to time). Older identities were more clear-cut: 'Spanish' or 'Guatemalan' or 'Mexican'; 'Bay-born' or 'Creole'; 'Carib'; 'Maya' or 'Kekchi'; 'Waika'; 'English', 'Irish', 'American'. Each of these groups could in the past be seen to have their own language, each with cultural connections reaching out into Central America and beyond that to Spain; down the coasts of the isthmus to Panama and into the Caribbean; into North America and Britain. But today, as we shall see when we consider ethnicity, these identities have crumbled and are being replaced by concepts of 'mixing' and of being a Belizean; Belizeans speak 'Creole'.

(ii) *Access to groups.* Belize is a sparsely-populated country, and before the road was built there was not all that much contact between Benque Viejo, San Ignacio and Belize (City). There was close daily interaction within towns and villages but not between them. Very few people in Cayo District had access to users of Standard British English; even in the schools, a number of the teachers were nuns from a German teaching order, or Caribs, or a few Creoles. Contact with the systems of Standard English was through school books and through a handful of administrative expatriate Government officers and their families. In the past, therefore, most people had close access to one fairly highly-focussed group, and slight contacts with others. Today all that has changed; there is much greater movement up and down the country, both because transport is better and because work is more scarce and people are more reluctant to live by subsistence farming; moreover the mahogany and the chicle are finished. Thus the villagers of Succotz, most of whose inhabitants claimed a 'Mayan' identity and spoke Maya when we started our work, had by the time of our last visit become Spanish-speaking and were claiming 'Spanish' identity.

In St. Lucia, on the other hand, there was greater internal homogeneity, the most consistent differences being between urban and rural children. Communications within the island were very poor until a road was built from the former US air base (now the international airport) at Vieux Fort, at the southern end, and the capital, Castries, towards the northern end. A network of paths and tracks linked inland villages and subsistence-farming settlements in the interior, and it was to this inward-looking, focussed Patois-speaking community that children had daily access. The port of Castries provided access to the outside world, most commonly via Barbados. The St. Lucian schools however did tend to provide rather better access for children to native speakers of English, in that the Roman Catholic mission which supplied teachers was an Irish, as opposed to a German, mission.

As to ability, it is generally assumed that all children, unless disabled in some way, have the same innate capacity to learn the linguistic systems of their community. It does not seem that this has been demonstrated beyond the earliest years; whether or not there are in later years complexities of grammar or lexicon beyond the capacity of some to cope with is unknown. But apparent differences in capacity to cope with more than one language-system in multilingual situations are more likely to stem from differences of access and, as we discuss in the next paragraph, from differences of motivation, rather than from differences of capacity.

(iii) *Positive and negative motivation to identify with groups.* This appears to be by far the most important of the constraints governing linguistic behaviour. The importance of motivation, of the desire for group solidarity or personal individuality, has been shown over and over again in the work of, for example, Labov, Trudgill, Lesley Milroy, and in our own results. It is the area in which the individual has the greatest appearance of 'choice'. In highly-focussed monolingual communities it may appear as if there could be little choice, and because a great deal of work in linguistics and psycholinguistics in the past has been done in what were supposed to be such communities it is common to speak of children 'internalizing the rôle-system' or 'the language' of the community. But even in such communities there are always linguistic changes in progress, and it is possible for the individual to adopt or not to adopt these changes, to practise identification with some, and distancing from other, perceived groups. Very often – perhaps always – the changes are socially marked, being innovations associated with particular social, economic, regional, age, occupational, sex, educational, political, religious or cultural groups. In multilingual communities such as those of Belize or St. Lucia, or among the West Indian or other immigrant communities in Britain, motivation governing choice over the adoption of one rule-system or another is far more clearly apparent. One adopts the supposed rules of those groups one perceives to be socially desirable, *to the extent that* one wishes to be identified with them. Motivation is of course usually mixed. It is very common, for example, for the language of economic opportunity to be different from that of one's home; very often economic opportunity lies through passing examinations in the education system, and this may mean becoming bilingual or bidialectal or even accepting that for educational purposes one's home language is 'wrong' and should be rejected. The conflicts set up where the norms and standards of the examiners require the rejection of the norms of home usage are evident in a great many societies, including most Creole-speaking countries (Le Page 1968a). On the other hand, many children can become quite happily bilingual or trilingual, keeping one variety for their home, another for school and so on, without conflict.

We are not, however, for the moment concerned with conflicts of motivation except insofar as they illustrate the importance of motivation as a factor. It may well be that our apparent freedom to 'choose' is so powerfully constrained by universal social and psychological factors – as envisaged, for example, by Sapir (1921), by Whorf (1956) or by Bernstein (1971) that it is no real freedom; nevertheless, until we know far more about psychological 'freedoms' it is reasonable to speak of motivation in choice between possible alternatives as a heading for the third of our four sets of constraints.

The motivation governing choice is reflected in listening and understanding as well as in speaking. The phenomenon of hearers refusing to acknowledge that they can understand the speech of those of whom they disapprove and with whom they do not wish to be identified, is very familiar to linguists; we could cite many anecdotes, from many communities. Grenadian schoolteachers, during Le Page's fieldwork there in the 1950s, steadfastly refused to acknowledge that they could understand Patois, although they were then caught out laughing at some Patois jokes.

Not all of our Belizean informants wished to be Creole-speaking Belizeans. One 'Spanish' boy in particular, from Benque Viejo, told us he was determined *not* to speak Creole, as all the other boys did, when he went to St John's College, the boys' secondary school in Belize City. He tried to keep his English as 'correct' as possible, and intended to further his studies in Guatemala through the medium of Spanish. One of the clearest cases of overtly-recognized hostility to Creole is provided by the conversation we reproduce with LG in the next chapter.

Very often motivation appears to affect single linguistic features, and to operate in a quite complex way within a community. Examples of this are provided by Milroy in *Language and social networks* (1980). Particular features (such as 'dropping their *h*s') form parts of the stereotypes we create about the way a particular group speaks. Milroy cites the fact (p. 156) that although women in general in a particular community had lower levels of use than the men of *vernacular* variants of the variables (a) and (th) – that is, they had on average a less frequent use of a low back variant of their /a/ phoneme, and they tended more than the men to use an intervocalic /ð/ in words such as *mother* – nevertheless *individual women* could use these variables 'to symbolize their level of integration into the local community'. One of the most important findings of Milroy's study is to underline the fact of vernacular, as well as more standard, norms – of loyalty to the focussed usage of very local groups, a loyalty which can be demonstrated by the use of particular variants of the variables needed to describe the usage of the larger community in grosser terms. This finding is borne out by Sebba's studies of London Jamaican.

(iv) *Ability to change one's behaviour, to accommodate*. This constraint is normally interpreted in terms of age. It may well be however that a greater generalization would be in terms of the relationship between what is new in incoming data and what can already be accounted for in terms of existing models in the mind of the percipient, best described perhaps in terms of Piaget's 'assimilation' and 'accommodation'. The data of interference and of over-generalization or under-generalization, as described for example in Weinreich (1953), show that we perceive fresh linguistic data in terms of the models we have already constructed – the units are either 'the same as' or 'different from' what we can already handle. Frequently we simply cannot hear differences or contrasts in another language which are not contrastive in our own – most English speakers, for example, have difficulty with French nasal vowels or Chinese or Bantu tones. Since a contrast between /t/ and /θ/, and between /d/ and /ð/, is rather rare in the phonemic systems of the world's languages, we find /θ/ and /ð/ replaced – by /t/ and /d/ in Caribbean Creoles, by /s/ and /z/ in French speakers, by /s/ in the Polynesian ancestors of the Pitcairnese, and so on. If the fresh data can be assimilated to an existing model we do so; if the differences are too great or the cultural associations too important to us, we construct a new model. Children generally have far less difficulty in accommodating, in building new models for fresh data, since their existing models are comparatively limited anyway; the older one gets, however, the stronger the motivation has to be to overcome the inertia which says 'I can get by with some slight adjustment of what I already have – there's no need to construct a whole new system.'

So much for the general constraints which act to inhibit our perception of, and selection from among the data of the linguistic systems of those around us as we grow up. In theory the possibilities for our own personal symbolic systems are limitless; in practice the creation of systems, sets of rules, is constrained by our gregarious needs and the projection and focussing which follow from those.

3. The question of linguistic description

We now have to consider the question of description, both synchronic and diachronic. It is clear that, diachronically, nothing so simple as Uriel Weinreich's classic cases of interference is possible because of the multiplicity of sources from which the data come. We can recognize among the agencies which promote focussing: (a) close daily interaction in the community; (b) an external threat or any other danger which leads to a sense of common cause; (c) a powerful model – a leader, a poet, a prestige group, a set of religious scriptures; (d) the mechanisms of an education system.

We must recognize the activity which goes on in our multidimensional space as processes of diffusion through initial contact, and then, in the right circumstances, of focussing, or convergence, towards various vernacular norms. Then subsequently – possibly under the influence of literacy or (today) of broadcasting or television, there is focussing towards more regional norms, and the subsequent *institutionalization* of some *prestige* norms as standard languages which may form the basis of education systems and become the basis of prescriptivism within a society. *We then find prestige or stigma being transferred from the group whose norm has been so marked, to a construct which comes to be thought of as autonomous – such as ' Standard English' or ' the Cockney dialect'.* People come to believe that a particular way of speaking is *intrinsically* 'good' or 'bad', 'correct' or 'incorrect', and unchangeable. We shall return to this process when we discuss Language X in Sense 4, below.

Thus, as we can see from our Belize and St. Lucia data and from the sample West Indian texts in Chapter 3, a variety of local systems have emerged from what were in general terms the same kind of socio-historical situation: colonization and slavery. The various West Indian Creoles have features in common; they also have locally-distinctive features. Each one of our 'Three little pigs' informants has some personal features and some shared features in his/her story-telling language. In their interaction with Pauline Christie they reveal something of the social and psychological values they set upon telling a story for her to record, their attitudes to her, to the story, to the varieties of language they are able to command.

Descriptively we need some polysystemic apparatus which provides for social marking, and we have not yet evolved one.

A model for pidginization and for creolization : the individual, and the systems

Various attempts have been made to devise an apparatus to meet the needs we have outlined – a seminal book, *New ways of analyzing variation in English* (Bailey and Shuy 1973) contained the proceedings of a symposium devoted to that end, and the debate continues. Usually the attempts are concerned with how to construct *grammars* (in the Chomskyan sense) in order to contain an historical process which is seen as a linear sequence in time:

pidginization — creolization — decreolization

We do not ourselves see the process quite in this way, nor does the evidence from current contact situations giving rise to new languages (e.g. in Papua-New Guinea where Tok Pisin is evolving – see *inter alia* Hall 1953; Sankoff and Brown 1976; Mühlhäusler 1980) support such a model. It is true that the languages we currently refer to as creoles – 'locally born' or 'crioullo' varieties of various languages transplanted during the European colonial expansion described in Chapter 2 – derive many of their properties from a contact pidgin, a *lingua franca*; but it is clear that such contact varieties continue to exist alongside both the nascent creoles and the native languages of the pidgin speakers; and that decreolization affects some speakers far more than others. The simplistic process depicted by the linear sequence above owes a great deal to traditional views framed within a family-tree or genetic model of linguistic descent. In order to state our own view, it is necessary first to consider what we mean by 'a language'.

Four meanings of the term 'Language X'. The terms of the linear sequence refer to languages, not to people, and it is here that the weakness, for our purposes, of most current theory lies. We should constantly remind ourselves that languages do not do things; people do things, languages are abstractions from what people do. Moreover the words 'Language X' are used by both linguists and non-linguists to refer to at least four distinguishable phenomena, without the users always knowing which one of these they mean.

Sense 1. Language X in Sense 1 is used to refer to a supposed property of an individual, his 'native language' (or dialect). It is frequently supposed that we all have such a 'mother tongue' or 'native language' which represents some really fundamental properties of us as individuals who have grown up in a particular society. This concept is often made use of for political purposes, as in Wales or Belgium or Quebec or a hundred other countries. For some people in the world it is true that one particular variety of linguistic behaviour has a peculiar force and intimacy from being powerfully associated with early childhood; for others it is not true. But whether true or untrue, such a variety is likely to be only one of several learned in childhood, since no society is totally homogeneous. Moreover, –

other than through performance, which is always to an audience, even if only to one's self – we have no means of access to such a variety, of finding out about it, except possibly through some kind of psychoanalytical procedures. Introspection does not lead us to it, since either the questions which introspection is supposed to answer are meaningless to the naive informant, or they lead to a very 'tutored' concept of language if the informant is linguistically sophisticated enough to answer them. (As an example, Beryl Loftman Bailey, a 'native speaker' of something we have called 'Jamaican Creole', when she described this language (1966), described what she herself later confessed was an idealized version of what she remembered of her childhood usage, focussed by linguistic theory subsequently learned.)

Nor is it ever possible to isolate such a 'native language' by recourse to the strategies Labov and most other sociolinguists have developed for recording relaxed peer-group usage. As Labov himself has noted (1972a), and as we ourselves observe about our London Jamaicans, and as Lesley Milroy has demonstrated in Belfast, relaxed peer-group usage is still oriented towards some social target, the establishment of identity with a group; and that target varies from occasion to occasion.

Moreover, the concept of 'native language' or 'mother tongue' is, like all concepts, culturally conditioned. In multilingual settings the term 'native language' or 'mother tongue' may have little meaning because children are exposed to many linguistic systems from birth. In immigrant communities in Britain, where efforts have been made to provide instruction for children in their 'mother tongue', it usually turns out that their home dialect is in any case different from that in which tuition might be provided, and the children's version of the home dialect is different again from that of their parents (cf. Smolicz 1979). In Malaysia, many Malays are accused of not knowing or using their 'mother tongue' correctly (Le Page 1984). In Singapore, because of the enormous importance attached by Chinese to the written language, 'mother tongue' is used – quite arbitrarily – to refer to that spoken language (Mandarin) which is culturally most closely connected with written Chinese, regardless of the fact that most Singapore Chinese speak Hokkien or Teochew or Hakka or Cantonese or Hainanese, i.e. languages from the south of China. Even these are likely to be spoken in a mixed, Singaporean way.

The description of the processes of pidginization and creolization generally distinguishes pidgin languages from creoles on the basis that the former are nobody's mother tongue, while the latter are the outcome of children growing up in pidgin-using societies and creating their mother tongue out of the pidgin. But this is always a gross over-simplification. No children have ever grown up in a pidgin-only-using society, since by definition each pidgin speaker has another, his own, 'native language'.

The 'rules' of a child's 'native language' in this first sense are in any case likely to be tentative hypotheses, easily modified by fresh semantic needs, fresh contacts, fresh analogies. 'Syntax' in the grammarian's sense is what emerges from this process, not what it starts from. The process, in pidginization and creolization, is vividly illustrated by Sankoff and Brown (1976) from New Guinea.

However, Language X in Sense 1 appears to be a concept very important to the personal identity of a great many people, and an important hypothetical base for many linguists and educationists. We must therefore accept it as part of our data on social institutions; we deal with the processes of institutionalization in the next chapter.

Sense 2. Language X in Sense 2 is used to refer to the actual behaviour of people, and to whatever system may be supposed to motivate it – but not a description of that system, only to the behaviour. We say such things as 'As she spoke, her language became familiar' or 'She used the sort of language she would use to a child' or 'I can't understand the language of this book'. This is the only kind of language to which we truly have access – the data of linguistic behaviour, of performance. Even the 'intuitions of the native speaker' depend really upon performance; when we ask somebody, 'Can you say '——' in your language?' the answer depends upon the informant trying to contextualize '——' to make it an imaginary speech event.

Sense 3. Language X in Sense 3 is the kind of description made by linguists using data from Sense 2 performance. They bring to this task their prior conditioning as to what constitutes a description of a language and their theories about language, their own perceptual apparatus and their fieldwork or data-collecting and data-scanning methods. Their data are always incomplete, their theories and methods various and their perception idiosyncratic. Thus there can never be two descriptions of 'a language' that are in complete agreement, that would always generate exactly the same 'set of sentences'. Nevertheless, once linguists and lexicographers have produced their grammars and dictionaries these frequently tend to become 'the language' for prescriptive or reference purposes, and are used as objects of classroom study.

Sense 4. Language X in Sense 4 is the sense most familiar to the layman; it is what he means when he speaks of 'French' or 'English' or 'Yoruba' or 'Chinese': that is, the systems assumed to be inherent in the linguistic behaviour of a community and in their literature (whether oral or written). Again, as a totality it is inaccessible and indefinable; each of us has only partial experience of it. Many attempts have been made to define a language in social terms, such as 'The language of Community X'; but when we have to devise a test for membership of Community X it frequently includes – as we shall see in the next chapter – speaking Language X, and the definition therefore becomes circular. (The problems of defining a language community or a speech community, and various discussions of these problems, are summarized in Hudson 1980 and in Romaine 1982b.)

Language X in Sense 4 has a sub-category, that of the standard language. 'Standard' may be understood in two senses: that of a *norm*, as when we say 'it is standard practice now to pack coffee in vacuum bags'; and that of a prescriptive yardstick against which things or people are measured. This involves, in the case of language, the concept of correctness, very often tied to puristic theories about language, to the institution of academies or other regulatory bodies, and also, as we have mentioned under Sense 3, to the descriptions of grammarians and lexicographers. Descriptive linguists themselves often appear to be supporting prescriptive norms in designating or starring some constructions as 'ungrammatical' when they mean 'not normal'. We describe below the ways in which 'standard' in the sense of 'norm' often becomes converted into a prescriptive standard used as a yardstick; through the education and examination systems as a test for admission to various occupational elites, and through social convention as a test for admission to social elites.

This is not true of all societies. The processes by which 'standard' languages have emerged or have been legislated for are many, varied, and complex. They have been described for a wide range of countries in three recent publications, among many others concerned with language standardization: Haas (1982), Fodor and Hagège (1983), Scaglione (1984). They are of particular concern to newly-independent nations and to those nations for whom the vernacularization of literacy has become urgent as a condition of political coherence and of modernization.

In some societies such as those described by Ferguson (1959) as diglossic, the standard language has become far removed from the verna- cular. It is an object of study, rather than an effective vehicle of mass education. It depends for its focussing upon the projections provided by literary or other written use, or upon various legislative bodies such as the academies mentioned above, to sustain the 'correct' standard. Thus in Malaysia, the Dewan Bahasa dan Pustaka, the Language and Literature

Agency, is charged with defining 'correct' or Standard *Bahasa Malaysia*, even though no educated Malay would speak according to its rules. (It may be observed in passing that it may be precisely those members of a community who are most confident in their command of its cultural norms or standards who will feel most free to innovate among themselves; the contradiction here with the concept of 'focussing' is however more apparent than real, since such innovation is itself rule-governed even if by rather arcane rules.)

The concept or stereotype of being a 'correct' user of the language, or alternatively, of being somebody *capable* of using 'correct language', is a powerful one in many societies, and the standards of correctness may be, as in Arabic-speaking countries, those of a body of scripture which has divine sanction and which it is the duty of each generation of scholars to pass on intact. In diglossic societies there may be a double standard: that of the written norm of the 'High' variety, but in addition, the concept of 'the real old dialect'. Thus, in Belize City we have been told that it is only the old people, and among them the Belize City Creoles, who use the 'real Creole'; younger people may well be discouraged by their Creole-speaking parents from using it because it can be a bar to advancement. In Cayo District we were told 'of course, all the young people speak Creole – but you know, we don't speak the real Belize Creole'. In most countries wholly pragmatic considerations are invoked in support of standardization; the Chinese Government might justify basing *putonghua*, or Standard Chinese, on the Beijing dialect on the grounds that that is already the language of most Chinese literature and of the traditional Civil Service; attempts have been made elsewhere (e.g. by missionary sects in Nigeria – see Ndukwe 1984) to create 'standard languages' by finding a common core from a number of related dialects.

The manner in which various standard varieties of both spoken and written English have evolved is still very imperfectly documented. (There is of course a flourishing industry worldwide in the publication of prescriptive descriptions of 'correct English' – no two descriptions being totally in agreement except through plagiarism.) It is now generally accepted that American English, Canadian English, Australian English and New Zealand English have regional educated norms distinct from those of educated British English (the processes of linguistic emancipation for the United States have been documented at some length by, among others, Mencken (1919/63) and Gleason (1965)). In India, where English is an official second language, efforts are being made to describe an educated Indian English which could replace external standards. In the Anglophone

Caribbean, where external examination bodies have been replaced in many instances by indigenous bodies (e.g. the Caribbean Examinations Council) similar efforts are being made to describe an acceptable educated Standard Caribbean English. Meanwhile both spoken and written usage goes on developing, sometimes relatively unaffected by these prescriptive descriptions, sometimes taking rules from the grammarians into the language of education and hence into the stereotype of the educated standard, as with the prohibition on double negation in English that we referred to in Chapter 1. In both spoken and written varieties, Language X in Sense 4 is commonly being affected from generation to generation by contact with other cultures.

Where a standard language is highly focussed and highly codified, for example through literature, the effects of such contact are also commonly resisted by purists and linguistic nationalists. The stereotypical standard language is often tacitly or explicitly referred to by descriptive linguists to authenticate their rules, thus completing the circularity of the descriptive-prescriptive process which we refer to below as 'the logic of closed systems'.

Shared, or overlapping, linguistic systems : polysystemic description

If we now return to the description of the properties that the linguistic behaviour of groups of individuals may have in common – if we take the four children telling their 'Three little pigs' stories as an example – we see that they appear to have overlapping linguistic systems. Two major systematic descriptive devices have been put forward in recent years; one uses the concept of 'variable rules', the other, that of an 'implicational polylectal grammar' (see below). Variable rules are part of an attempt by William Labov, Gillian Sankoff, David Sankoff, Henrietta Cedergren (see Bibliography) and others to preserve the Chomskyan concept of individual 'competence' (that is, knowledge of the rules of the grammar of a language) while taking account of the observable variability in the behaviour of speakers of 'the same language'. They attempt this by applying statistical constraints, based on the observation of performance, to those rules which might otherwise be classed as 'optional'. Here it is necessary to make another digression, this time to consider various meanings of the term 'a rule', since we often confuse different meanings.

Some meanings of the term 'a rule', and their predictive implications. Type 1 : observed regularities. The first meaning is based on observed regularities in behaviour. There may be a high degree of observable regularity or a comparatively low degree, but rules based only on observed regularities can only be applied to the future at risk, that is to say, with a probabilistic value. The series:

He has always had a bath on Sundays (past observation)

He always has a bath on Sundays (extrapolation into habitual aspect)

He will have a bath next Sunday (prediction)

is only valid if we can be sure that *all* the factors which led to his past behaviour will hold good in the future. In the behavioural sciences generally (and indeed in much science outside the laboratory) there are too many variables, many unknown, for such rules to have anything more than a probabilistic value; nevertheless, that fact tends to be overlooked. Most linguistic descriptions have in fact been based on the observation of regularities in behaviour, but the rules derived in this way tend to become idealized and converted into a more firmly predictive kind of rule. (The informants on whose behaviour the resultant grammar was based, when they fail always to confirm its predictions by future behaviour, are frequently then to that extent labelled as deviant.)

Type 2 : The logic of closed systems. The second kind of rule is that which would obtain within a closed system. It is 100 per cent predictive because of the circularity within the process of rationalization. If we take a set of sentences, and analyse them so as to discover the 'rules' or grammar which will relate them most economically and efficiently to each other, we can then use that grammar to generate fresh sentences which will by definition be grammatical, and therefore members of the same set. However, to use such a grammar in an attempt to predict human behaviour, or to appeal to real-life speakers or hearers in order to test the validity of its construction, is silently to transfer a closed system into a situation where only open systems can operate. The grammar of the closed system, and its predictions of 'grammaticality', become confused with the empirical judgments of people whose concept of 'grammaticality' – if they have one at all, which is in fact comparatively rare among the world's population at large – is subsumed within a much wider concept of 'acceptability', a concept which takes account of creative, innovative, analogical, inventive and tolerant capacities of the human mind ignored by the closed systems of many grammarians.

Type 3 : 'Universals'. First let us consider inductively and deductively based universals. The third kind of 'rule' is the universal law. These are predictive to the extent that we have formulated them correctly. Formulations may have their origins in induction from observation, as in the first kind of rule, in which case they may be progressively refined so as to take more and more accurate account of the variables involved. Alternatively they may originate in deduction from the nature of things, such as the law of probability that a true penny will on average when tossed come down heads half the time – simply because the penny has two sides and, *as far as we know*, there is no reason why it should fall one side up rather than the other. Some grammarians have attempted to formulate 'universals' of grammar – which they have then reasoned must be part of an innate human competence – by empirical observation of many languages; some have tried to approach these by a more and more minute refinement of the observations to be made about a particular set of sentences, mostly 'English'; some, like James Harris, have attempted to rationalize a deductive process from 'the nature of things', as the following quotation shows. Harris attempts to justify a classification of sentences into Assertions and Volitional Statements by arguing that this classification reflects the two 'powers of the Soul', those of perception on the one hand and those of the will, passions or appetites on the other:

– What then shall we say? Are Sentences to be quoted in this manner without ceasing, all differing from each other in their stamp and character? Are they no way reducible to certain definite Classes? If not, they can be no objects of *rational* comprehension. – Let us however try.

'Tis a phrase often apply'd to a man, when speaking, that he *speaks his* mind; as much as to say, that his Speech or Discourse is *a publishing of some Energie or Motion of his Soul*. So it indeed is in every one that speaks, excepting alone the Dissembler or Hypocrite; and he too, as far as possible, affects the appearance.

Now the Powers of the Soul (over and above the meer nutritive) may be included all of them in those of Perception, and those of Volition. By the Powers of Perception, I mean the *Senses* and the *Intellect*; by the Powers of Volition, I mean in an extended sense, not only the *Will*, but the several *Passions* and *Appetites*; in short, *all that moves to Action, whether rational or irrational.*

If then the leading Powers of the Soul be these two, 'tis plain that every Speech or Sentence, as far as it exhibits the Soul, must of course respect one or other of these.

If we *assert*, then is it a Sentence which respects the Powers of Perception. For what indeed is to *assert*, if we consider the examples above alleged, but *to publish some Perception, either of the Senses or the Intellect?*

Agen, if we *interrogate*, if we *command*, if we *pray*, or if we *wish* (which in terms of Art is to speak Sentences *interrogative, imperative, precative,* or *optative*) what do we but publish so many different Volitions? – For who is it that *questions?* He that has a *Desire* to be inform'd – Who is it that *commands?* He that has a *Will*, which he would have obey'd. – What are those Beings, who either *wish* or *pray?* Those, who feel certain wants either for themselves, or others.

If then the *Soul's leading Powers* be *the two* above mention'd, and it be true that *all Speech is a publication of these Powers*, it will follow that every Sentence will be either a Sentence of Assertion, or a Sentence of Volition.

(James Harris. 1751. *Hermes*, Bk 1, ch. 2: 14–17)

Secondly, we turn to *logical universals*. Universals have sometimes been based on an appeal to logic. If the appeal is to systems akin to mathematical logic, which involves only a discussion of the internal properties of systems without regard to any possible external applications, so that the units and combinations of units always have fixed, unchanging values whatever processes they are subjected to, then the logic may be valid but the rules are similar to our Type 2 rules, above. If the appeal is to 'natural' logic, through which it is supposed 'truth values' may be approached through natural language, then the argument is based on a fundamental fallacy as to the nature of language. It may well be, as we suggest below, that what is inherent in mankind is a universal longing for reason, so that a grammar capable of framing logical truths about the universe is a target towards which we all strive, towards which all languages ought theoretically to evolve (in which case logically all languages would become steadily more alike), and to which the descriptions of grammarians ought to approximate as closely as possible. We can represent this as a left-to-right process on our 'focussing diagrams' (see p. 202). But to leave a theory of language there is to overlook the right-to-left process: the fact that every use of language is a fresh application, a metaphorical extension, of existing systems, made at risk on the basis of rules of Type 1. It is an instant pidgin, expressing not truths about the external universe but views of the universe modelled by a particular speaker or hearer – and they, in the last analysis, are the only repositories of language, the only creators of systems, the only, and idiosyncratic, links between language and the 'real world'. 'Truth value semantics' has indeed very little to say about the properties of natural language, and logical models of human language overlook the fact that we do not know until words are used the precise values they will bear in the new context or the precise part of the sentence they will form. Grammars that appeal to any kind of test of the usability of sentences (whether through overt performance or the covert performance of introspection) must in fact always take account of the inherent (and utterly necessary) openness of linguistic systems: that is, they work by being mediating systems, symbolizing the internal models each of us creates of the universe we inhabit, providing a means (not the only means – all art forms resemble language in this) by which we can analyse and project our fantasies on to the social screen.

Logic and universal grammar, then, are targets towards which, rather than the starting point from which, human linguistic activity proceeds. The origins of that activity are like those of a game which gradually develops among players, each of whom can experiment with changes of the rules, all of whom are umpires judging whether new rules are acceptable. This process may be observed quite clearly in the evolution of pidgin languages and argots, and is illustrated by work on London Jamaican where each generation of children tends to change the rules so as to keep 'their' language their peculiar property. It is illustrated also by the processes reported by Elton Brash from New Guinea (personal communication), or by Sankoff and Brown (1976) from the same country, as a pidgin evolves into a creole and we can be shown 'the origins of syntax in discourse'.

Thirdly, we consider '*natural*' *universals*. A rather different kind of 'universal' is sometimes invoked, in which language is thought to reflect directly the properties of the real world. Obvious examples of this 'naturalness' are found frequently in the literature on pidgin and creole languages; for example, in echoism or onomatopoeia in phonology, syntax or the lexicon, or among the many and complex ways in which iteration or reduplication may be used – for example, to reflect the distribution of the action of a verb in time:

JC: im kom, im kom, im kom, im kom – im ton bak!
        'He kept on coming, kept on coming – then he turned back!'
Belize: i di wosh, di wosh, di wosh di gots
        'She went on washing and washing the tripe'

or of an adjective in space:

JC: poto   mud, muddy
        poto-poto mud all over the place

        prikl-prikl (see *DJE*: SPRICKLE-SPRICKLE)
        having a great many small prickles

Here one must be careful, since nearly all such examples are to some extent culturally conditioned. It may seem to us undeniable that cocks say 'Cock-a-doodle-doo', but French cocks say 'cocorico' and German cocks, 'kikeriki'. In other words, once again our perception of the external world is filtered through the linguistic models already available to us, and our language has reference to these percepts, not directly to objective reality. We frequently find models for our Creole echoisms in the substrate languages e.g. of West Africa.

Type 4 : Prescriptive rules. The fourth kind of rule is prescriptive, similar to *It is forbidden to feed the animals – Penalty ten pounds*, or *Good children must clean their teeth before they go to bed*. The predictive value of such rules is constrained by the extent to which those addressed fear the sanctions attached – in the first place, the fine, in the second place, being labelled as 'bad', or 'not good'. Many grammars are prescriptive in that they tell you how you must behave if you are to be accepted as 'a speaker of Language X' – the term 'Language X' being used either in Sense 3 or Sense 4 above. Otherwise, however much you may be understood, you will not be accepted as a 'correct' or 'standard' or 'good' speaker of Language X. The foundation of such prescriptivism is, as we have said, the prestige attached originally to the behaviour of a particular group, and then transferred to that abstraction made from their behaviour on the basis of rules of Type 1.

Variable rules and polylectal continua. We mentioned in the first paragraph of this chapter treatments of observable variability within the Guyanese community. In particular, we have developed an argument against the treatment best exemplified by Bickerton (1975), which links variability with language change in what we consider to be a simplistic model, and presents us with a picture of a community whose communal 'language', 'the Guyanese language', can be represented as a series of 'lects' or grammars each internally consistent but each in order representing a step towards the grammar of a more standard variety of English, a polylectal continuum reflecting language change in progress. The lects were arranged on an implicational scale; that is, in such an order that if one were affected by rule-change C it implied that one had also already been affected by changes B and A.

Such a model necessarily implies a linear sequence of varieties within 'a language', with the implication that all innovation starts from the same source and travels in the same direction; and that innovation in phonology is paralleled by a similar sequence of innovation in different parts of the grammar and lexicon. None of these suppositions can be sustained; as we have seen, our four children do not exemplify such a unidirectional continuum; nor did the St. Lucian children in their use of various 'habitual' constructions, nor do Lesley Milroy's Belfast informants, nor Bortoni-Ricardo's Brazilians.

Although it is clear from our Belize and St. Lucian examples that language changes are taking place, it is also clear that not all change is in the same direction, towards the same target; moreover, a good deal of the variability observable either in the usage of individuals, or in any abstraction made from communal behaviour, seems to be of a kind which has been inherent for many centuries in many English-speaking parts of the world (see e.g. Romaine, forthcoming). To the extent that it does not derive from factors inherent in linguistic systems – such as the assimilation of sounds to one another in certain environments – such variability may be ascribed to us fluctuating in imitating the usage of the group or groups with which we wish to identify; it is not necessarily a symptom of change in 'the language'. At any moment in time each of us can select from a variety of possible models, each socially marked; change only takes place when the social values of the possible models change, and the behaviour of the community is re-focussed as a result.

The attempts that have been made by Labov and his colleagues to quantify observable variability in the form of variable rules modifying the individual's competence, take Chomsky's (1965) ideal speaker-listener with perfect knowledge of the language of a completely homogeneous language community and adapt him in the direction of having knowledge of the variable behaviour of different groups within the community. To that extent, Labov's model seeks to accommodate the kind of performance that our own data resemble. Nevertheless, it seems to us that there is in the concept 'variable rules' an inherent confusion of two or more meanings of the term 'a rule'. The observed statistical regularities in the past behavioural events in a community are being converted into part of the knowledge the individual has of his community; and that knowledge in turn is converted into something which specifies the behaviour of the individual towards his community. This seems very close to our own formulation of events; but what is left out of account is the fact that the 'rules' which govern the performance of the individual towards his community are not purely grammatical rules, but rather socially-marked rules constrained by our general hypothesis and its four riders.

Labov's variable rules are probability statements based on rules of our first kind. Such probability statements are obviously never intended to predict precisely what a particular individual will actually do on a particular occasion. They do, however, imply that each individual member of a community has as part of his competence – that is, as part of his knowledge of how his community works – knowledge of such statistics. Bickerton (1975 *et seq.*) has objected to such rules as if they were intended to determine the precise outcome of a particular situation, but that is not so. One might however more seriously object that we do not know, except in small, highly interactive and therefore highly focussed communities, how much knowledge the individual has of his community, nor indeed what constitutes his community. Within our own theory, he will have stereotypes about the groups which he himself perceives in his community – that is, he has endowed those groups with some linguistic characteristics constrained by our first two riders – but the observations of two individuals, and therefore their 'rules', are likely to differ. To go back once more to our four children, each is likely to have a stereotype for the group that he/she feels each of the others represents – 'typical Spanish kid', 'typical rural Creole kid', 'typical middle-class Creole kid' and so on, but these stereotypes do not amount to the same thing as 'competence in the grammar of the Cayo District language'.

4. The universality of contact phenomena, of diffusion, and of subsequent focussing

If we now return to the processes of pidginization, we must consider the various models which have been put forward to account for these processes in the light of what we have said about the meanings of 'Language X' and 'rule'. Before we temporarily divorce pidginization from creolization, however, we must note that such a divorce is for methodological convenience only, since there is no necessary historical chain or divide between pidginization, creolization and decreolization. The processes may overlap, or a stable pidgin may develop without creolization, or a creole language may come to exist in a stable diglossic relationship with another language without being decreolized, and so on. Moreover, the processes we are going to talk about are inherent in cultural contact of many kinds. What is more, the processes may be put into reverse, so that we have also to speak of 're-creolization', or the adoption of a vernacular norm as the prestige variety, as when 'Frankish' became 'French'.

We may think of two parallel processes, best described as having an oscillatory relationship, each inducing changes in, and feeding back into, the other. The first process is concerned with the evolution, the processes of diffusion through contact and subsequent focussing through nativization, of 'languages' in Sense 4. The second is concerned with a scale of abstraction and idealization on which linguistic descriptions of a language in Sense 3 may be placed in relation to one another. We suggest that the goal towards which much linguistic theory works – the highly abstract description of a grammar and a lexicon as a closed system, with rules of Type 2 which are then transmuted into universals – provides also a model for the stereotypes of the layman who wishes to reify and totemize the (basically Type 1) rules of what he conceives to be his community, to provide for some kind of constancy and loyalty and communal support in a changing world. Of course, our processes never do in fact converge, since the accommodation inherent in each speech act sends us back, as we said, towards the starting-point of 'instant pidgin' once again. Our targets are permanently hull-down on the horizon. Moreover, despite the linearity of stereotypical thinking, in fact at any one moment not only is there inherent variability and polysystemicity in any community, but different groups in that community may well differ in their targets.

In the first process, the left-hand side, the instant pidgin, has all the potential creativity of pidginization. It is diffuse, opportunistic, involves all kinds of contextual cues to convey meaning. It may rely heavily on the mutual semantic delimitation which words exert on one another in juxtaposition (i.e. on the lexicalization of syntax) without these having to be defined in grammatical terminology; on the prosody of utterance, and on any kind of gesture such as pointing; the most basic sentence being the single word uttered with a particular experimental prosody in relation to body-language and context. As we move towards the right-hand side the language becomes more highly focussed, highly-regularized. The functions of words and the relational functions between words have been grammaticized; the grammar is to some extent context-free, the subject as well as the predicate is fully explicit and there is a sanction attached to breaking the rules in that 'the rules' are now marked by members of the community as symptoms of identity. Models memorized and stored for use in future linguistic contact at the pidgin stage now become the basis of predictive rules, either in a stable pidgin, or in a creolizing situation. With creolization we are in a 'normal' language situation, in which close daily interaction constrains the creativity of contact, and in which the norms of different groups within a society become marked with the attributes of those groups. A prestige group's norm may then become a standard, and institutionalized as such; the usage of other groups may now be seen as variations on that standard or a departure from it or an imperfect variety of it. 'Language X', from being the property of a group, takes on an autonomous existence, sometimes endowed with divine authority (for example in the case of classical Arabic). This is not to say, nevertheless, that it will necessarily continue to be the standard; at any time social values may change, a new prestige model emerge; literacy may be vernacularized, or some new written language be imposed; the selection of forms by individuals to create their languages will be constrained by fresh variables under our four riders;

the apparently inexorable processes of linguistic history can be halted, or put into reverse, or given new direction, and are in fact seen – though not by the layman – to be the artefacts of hindsight.

In the second process, at the left-hand end the linguist regards the variable data of one or more informants as what he must account for, and he has constant recourse to the context in order to understand fully the significance of every aspect of the linguistic data. Linguistic theory – even the very processes of perception and transcription – compel him from the outset to idealize to some extent, to attempt to distinguish between the context-bound and the context-free elements. Our problem is always that if we bring a powerful theory prematurely to our data we may miss much that is significant; yet linguistic theory tends to be highly influenced by the search for very abstract universals and at the same time to be conceptualized in terms of the standard forms of highly-focussed languages. In its most extreme right-hand form it tends to be thought of as a description of the competence of Chomsky's idealized speaker-listener in a totally homogeneous community, with complete knowledge of the language of that community. The starting point of such a grammar must however inevitably be rules of Type 1.

Thus, both varieties of linguistic behaviour, and stereotypes and beliefs concerning language, can be placed at points along this dual continuum; from the highly-diffuse to the highly-focussed, from the actualities to the highly abstract. We can represent the two continua in Figure 2. We believe these processes to be common to all linguistic communities.

← ———— diffuse		focussed ———— →
'Instant pidgin' trading on analogy and metaphor; context-bound	Natural languages in Sense 4, including Creoles	Unchanging and eternal 'language' capable of expressing 'truth'
Descriptions of behaviour, highly data-oriented, context-related	More idealized and abstract descriptions, more context-free	Wholly abstract 'grammar'

Figure 2. Focussing in linguistic behaviour related to focussing in linguistic description

'Projection', 'diffusion' and 'focussing' as a model for pidginization and creolization. It is clear that our four children do not in their story-telling represent a highly-focussed language community. The forms used in the book from which they had heard or read the story; the forms of the broad Creole vernacular of Belize City which had been carried into Cayo District

by settlers from the east; the forms of a more educated Creole class; the forms learned by a Spanish boy learning English as a second language and then having his usage creolized in the school playground, are all reflected in their story-telling. Any description of their community language will therefore have to be polysystemic. Each of the four children, even if they did not know one another, at least knew plenty of other children in the district similar to the other three. They would all understand one another. The shared norms of Cayo District are, under social pressures, evolving towards a more focussed shared system; and that system will be neither the broad vernacular of Belize City nor any external norm such as Standard British English. For descriptive purposes we will have to continue to idealize the systems, to simplify them, to give them far greater homogeneity than they will ever possess. The kind of description we produce, *Language X in Sense* 3, will depend on the particular theory with which we approach the data; but no theory should blind us to the fact that all linguistic performance is mediated by socially and psychologically constrained choices by which possible forms are selected to be matched with possible meanings in actual contexts; and that we can never predict with certainty, even in the most homogeneous society, what systems will emerge from this process.

We believe that these same considerations hold true for any kind of pidginization and post-pidginization situation. What happens in contact situations may be 'explained' *post hoc* (but not predicted) with reference to one or more of the following factors:

(i) The degree of necessity for communication and therefore of careful attention to all possible clues, both linguistic and contextual

(ii) The consequent reduction possible in paradigmatic and stylistic redundancy, holding as many factors as possible constant

(iii) The perception and reinterpretation by each party involved of the speech-data of the others in terms of systems they have already constructed for themselves (with possible consequent 'interference' *in either direction*)

(iv) The recourse they may have to the phonology, grammar, lexicon and semantics of those already-constructed systems when at a loss

(v) The quick apprehension of any coincidences or partial coincidences between their existing systems and incoming data

(vi) Recourse to pointing, gesture and body-language, some parts of which may be virtually universal

(vii)   Recourse to such universals as 'natural' syntax (for example, iteration over a period of time to indicate the progressive nature of a predicate)

(viii)   Recourse to genuinely innate linguistic universals (of which, as yet, we know hardly anything)

(ix)   Focussing of the multiple output from contact around models whose dominance is due to the interplay of systematic linguistic, social and demographic considerations

Multiple and complex input and output. In nearly all known pidginization situations there has been a multiple and complex input – even in the simplest contact situations of which we know, such as that of Pitcairn Island (Ross and Moverley 1964) where the Bounty mutineers who carried off Tubuai Islanders to Pitcairn to start their new colony spoke various different dialects, Scots, English, Cornish, Channel Islands, St. Kitts. The initial output by the Polynesians must have been highly diffuse. The form which 'Pitcairnese' eventually assumed – highly focussed by all the factors we have mentioned: external threat, a common cause, dominant models, close daily interaction – has been strongly influenced by the dialect of the longest-surviving mutineer, the Londoner Adams, by his reading aloud of the Bible and the Prayer Book. To a less extent it has been influenced by the St. Kitts usage of Midshipman Young, and the general maritime usage of the mutineers accustomed to modes of pidgin communication with South Sea Islanders. Of all the many possible outputs, the usage of those two, who were both favourites with the Polynesian women (the Polynesian men and most of the other mutineers having killed one another off within a few years of the founding of the colony), was selected, within the constraints provided by our general theory as to the way in which we create our linguistic systems.

Similar considerations hold good for the evolution of a common language among our Cayo District informants; their usage being refocussed under the influence of the new social circumstances we have described. It may be that one day in the not-too-distant future the '*langue*', or 'Language in Sense 4', of the District will become sufficiently homogeneous, sufficiently focussed for a description of the Sense 3 kind to be attempted for the community as a whole. One most important theoretical consideration does however emerge clearly from all our data, and from a general consideration of the processes by which new languages evolve. Our attention is directed back to the nature of the linguistic sign, as depicted by Saussure. It is not form, it is not content; it is the relationship between these which is the unit which combines and re-combines in linguistic systems. In contact situations one can observe the search on both sides for a *fit* between nascent contextually-relevant concept and nascent contextually-acceptable form (see Appendix to this Chapter). It is these *relationships*, rather than universals of concept or form, which are the key to linguistic systems, and it is similarly the relationships between people, as symbolized by and inherent in the linguistic systems of each individual, which are the key to personal and social identity.

At present each individual gives evidence of partial knowledge of a number of systems which can to some extent be defined in terms of external norms which they have identified as the properties of the groups they have perceived. A community, its rules, and its language only exist insofar as its members perceive them to exist; this is the nature of linguistic competence, and no satisfactory model is yet available for its description. In Chapter 6 we discuss similar problems in relation to concepts of ethnicity.

APPENDIX:

FORMAL AND SEMANTIC RE-FOCUSSING: AN EXAMPLE

As an illustration of what we mean by re-focussing, we can consider the distribution of forms and meanings conventionally referred to as 'genitive case' in Old English and in Modern Standard British English (since 'possession' is among those meanings).

Old English had various noun paradigms, most of which distinguished the 'genitive plural' from other forms and some (the strong declensions) also distinguished the 'genitive singular'. Only the -*s* suffix of the strong masculine singular has survived, being used now for both singular and plural. In addition to the various senses of possession and attribution (which overlap and shade into each other: the king's head, the king's army, the king's wife, the king's command, the king's argument, the king's nationality, and so on) the 'genitive' case was used adverbially with a wide range of meanings as in *dæges ond nihte* 'by day and night', *hiera þances ond hiera unþances* 'whether they wished to or not'. As can be seen, except where fossilized idiomatically, as in *He works nights* or *Needs must when the devil drives*, where the -*s* endings of *nights* (which replaced the feminine genitive -*e* by analogy with masculine *dæges*) and of *needs* tend to be thought of as plurals, most of these adverbial uses have been redistributed among other forms, and sometimes semantically modified, in Modern English. Thus, *We go to work on weekdays* not only introduces *on* as a preposition (which in OE would have governed the dative case), and shows *days* to be regarded as plural which is used here to reflect iterative and habitual predication of going to work, but, being used thus, requires a new prepositional construction *by day* or *in the daytime* for the original meaning.

At the same time we have had a redistribution from OE to Modern English of the functions and meanings of *of*. These overlapped with both the genitive and the dative (e.g. *away from*) inflexional functions in OE and there is an overlap also in Modern English – but the areas of overlap have changed. The re-focussing that has taken place is extremely complex; we cannot do better than indicate its complexity by quoting the *OED* (OF prep. *General signification*):

Whether *of* might have come independently in English to be a substitute for the genitive is doubtful. In the expression of racial or national origin, we find *of* and the genitive apparently interchangeable already in the 9th c. *wæs þes wer...of þæm æþelestan cynne Scotta...Se nyhsta wæs Scyttisces cynnes* – [this man was...of the noblest race of the Scots...The next was (of) Scottish (+genitive) race (+genitive)] and this might have extended in time to other uses; but the great intrusion of *of* upon the old domain of the genitive, which speedily extended to the supersession of the OE genitive after adjectives, verbs, and even substantives, was mainly due to the influence of F[rench] *de*...the uses derived from F. *de* have so blended with those derived from OE *of*, giving rise again to later uses related to both, that it would be difficult, if not impossible, to separate the two streams, with their many ramifications.

(There follow seventeen columns of illustrated citations of various uses of *of*.)

Readers are invited to scan their own usage to discover how they decide whether to say, for example, 'Dublin's fair city' or 'The fair city of Dublin'; 'my right thumb's nail' or 'the nail of my right thumb'; 'head downward' or 'head downwards'; 'the King of England' or 'England's king'; 'the banks of the river' or 'the river's banks'; 'a moment's work' or 'the work of a moment'; 'a month's notice' or 'the notice of a month'; and so on. It is improbable that any two speakers will agree in all such cases. Not only will their selection of forms vary, but their rationalization of their selection will reveal variability also in semantic and analogical justification.

6 The place of ethnicity in acts of identity

In this chapter we shall propose that 'ethnicity' and other related communal groupings present conceptual and behavioural problems very similar to those of 'language' discussed in Chapter 5, that they may profitably be approached in the same way, and are, as the evidence from our survey shows, interrelated with those of language.

1. Concepts and stereotypes of ethnicity

Definitions of ethnicity as ideal

Throughout the chapter, as elsewhere in this book, we must try consistently to distinguish in the evidence between how people think they ought to behave, how they say they behave, and how they are observed to behave. Fredrik Barth (1969/70: 14), when discussing the theoretical framework of ethnicity, demands that anthropologists should concentrate on cultural features of the first kind:

It is important to recognise that although ethnic categories take cultural differences into account, we can assume no simple one-to-one relationship between ethnic units and cultural similarities and differences. The features taken into account are not the sum of 'objective' differences, but only those which the actors themselves regard as significant. Not only do ecologic variations mark and exaggerate differences; some cultural features are used by the actors as signals and emblems of differences, others are ignored, and in some relationships radical differences are played down and denied.

The 'objective' differences to which Barth refers here would correspond to the percepts of the linguist writing a description of 'a language' (Language X, that is, in our Sense 3 in Chapter 5). Barth gives an account of anthropological attempts to define the term 'ethnic group' only to show that such attempts are misleading. They imply that such a group (the following quotations are from Barth 1969/70: 10–11):

1. is largely biologically self-perpetuating; 2. shares fundamental cultural values, realized in overt unity in cultural forms; 3. makes up a field of communication and interaction; 4. has a membership which identifies itself, and is identified by others, as constituting a category distinguishable from other categories of the same order.

This ideal type definition is not so far removed in content from the traditional proposition that a race = a culture = a language and that a society = a unit which rejects or discriminates against others. Yet, in its modified form it is close enough to many empirical ethnographic situations, at least as they appear and have been reported, so that this meaning continues to serve the purposes of most anthropologists.

Barth's main objection to this ideal type definition is:

that such a formulation prevents us from understanding the phenomenon of ethnic groups and their place in human society and culture. This is because it begs all the critical questions: while purporting to give an ideal type model of a recurring empirical form, it implies a preconceived view of what are the significant factors in the genesis, structure, and function of such groups.

Most critically, it allows us to assume that boundary maintenance is unproblematical and follows from the isolation which the itemized characteristics imply: racial difference, cultural difference, social separation and language barriers, spontaneous and organized enmity. This also limits the range of factors that we use to explain cultural diversity: we are led to imagine each group developing its cultural and social form in relative isolation, mainly in response to local ecologic factors, through a history of adaptation by invention and selective borrowing. This history has produced a world of separate peoples, each with their culture and each organized in a society which can legitimately be isolated for description as an island to itself.

Barth's discussion, here and elsewhere, echoes in many respects our discussion of language; and we also maintain that the assumptions of linguists about living in a world of separate languages begs all the critical questions. Nevertheless we have to recognize among our data the fact that people *do* believe themselves to live in a world of discrete or distinct ethnic or racial groups – these among other social groups they also believe in. That belief is grounded in the use of terms of identity, words that are used in discourse which illuminates the concept each user attaches to each term (as we can exemplify from the use of 'Spanish...Yellow Belly Spaniards' in the discourse of our informant Mr DeS: see p. 228). Such terms function as symbols ready at hand for identities to hang on, providing the links between individuals and groups, the instruments therefore of identification. They allow the members of a group to achieve unity by 'focussing' their use of the terms; at the same time, they mediate the concepts of differences between (perhaps also of barriers between) individuals, and between groups. No term is ever used in an *identical* way by two different people; meaning is always to some extent idiosyncratic.

Table 24. *Criteria used in self-allocation to an ethnic group (from Le Page and Tabouret-Keller 1982)*

Number of times used	(a) by non-British students	(b) British students
Physical features	9	26
Provenance	8	16
Language	6	12
Family descent or race	6	8
Nationality	2	7
Culture/tradition/religion	3	8
Other	2	4
Total 'mentions'	36	81

Note: The British students were very inclined to use more than one criterion; many of the non-British felt that one sufficed. Taking this into account, only 'physical features' seems to distinguish the British from the non-British answers; one-third of the British criteria mentioned were physical, only one-quarter of the non-British criteria mentioned were physical. In the description of others, there appears to be a tendency among the British students to use crude colour categories Black, Coloured, White, and two crude regional categories Chinese and Indian. But many caveats must be issued before these results are interpreted.

The variety of ethnic criteria

A convenient survey of recent studies concerning the beliefs held both by scholars and by laymen on ethnicity, on the maintenance of ethnic boundaries and on the role of language in these matters, is provided by Haarman (1983); many such studies have been published under the aegis of Joshua Fishman, and also by Howard Giles and his associates (see Bibliography).

The basis of these beliefs which people hold is various; the variety can be illustrated from the results of a set of simple questions put to a class of students from different parts of the world at the start of their course at York University. They were asked to look around them at the other members of the class, and then to write down the terms they would use to describe the various ethnic groups in the class in a letter home (there were 51 British and 21 non-British students). They were next, after they had done this, asked to write down which of those groups they themselves belonged to. When they had done that, they were asked to set down the criteria on which they based that claim. Table 24 summarizes the answers to.the third question.

Each of the criteria in Table 24 can be illustrated in use by our Belizean informants. *Physical features* were given prominence by informant OM, who had referred to a division into 'Spanish' and 'Creole':

LeP: What are the main differences between Spanish and Creole?

OM: Well, the main, the main erm thing is the way they look. Their...their faces are...you can see it in their faces.

LeP: But what's the difference?

OM: Their hair.

LeP: What about their hair?

OM: Their hair are straight.

LeP: That's the Spanish – Spanish hair is straight?

OM: Yes. Some of them that...those that they are real Spanish, have their hair straight, an'...their, their erm, their way of talking, their way of, some of them, their way of acting. They are sh...very shy, an'...when you talk to them they don't want to answer you. Or, some, by looking at them, you can see that they are Spanish. Because you know, we are...we are used to, we...we can tell who...who is Spanish, an'...

LeP: What else apart from their hair being straight? What's Creole hair like?

OM: Well, it is...it's very short and it's very erm, their hair are very different, the Creole hair from the Spanish hair...tight...

LeP: Creole hair?

OM: Creole hair, yes.

LeP: And what about skin?

OM: They are very clear, the...some of Spanish, some Spanish are very clear and the Creoles, they are dark. You have some Creoles that are clear too.

LeP: Do you have any Spanish that are dark?

OM: You got some, some Spanish that are dark. An'...they have the...erm their hair just like Creole. But you can see it's Spanish. You know it's Spanish.

LeP: But some people have said to us, 'We are Spanish', although they have quite dark skin and quite crinkly hair.

OM: Yes.

LeP: Why is that?

OM: Well we would say they are...maybe a Spanish girl married to a Creole, and their children would be like that.

LeP: And what do Indians look like?

OM: Well, I don't erm, I don't erm, know the Indians from...'Cause you know I don't see the difference when they say Indian hair from Spanish.

LeP: Is there any difference in skin?

OM: Well, to me, no.

Throughout Central America there is widespread fear among those who claim 'Spanish descent' and 'White' colour status (and this of course includes many Mestizos) of the 'Blacks' – that is, the Afro-Creoles who have established pockets of settlements right along the Caribbean coast from Belize to Panama, and in the off-shore islands. The hostility and fear is based on many factors, but in Belize the resulting tensions between the two groups seem to have diminished since we began our survey there in 1970. Nevertheless it is interesting that in a village where most of the inhabitants identified themselves as Maya Indian in 1970, on our most recent visit in 1978 they identified themselves as Spanish. There is in fact a possible physical bridge from 'Maya' to 'White' which is not available to 'Creoles'. The Maya, although dark-skinned, have straight, black hair. Mestizos – that is, those of mixed Maya-Spanish descent – also have straight hair. The richest families in the Cayo District of Belize are 'los Turcos' – the descendants of Syrian or Lebanese merchants – who have light skins but a tendency to rather frizzy hair. Whereas at one time their grandparents went back to Syria or the Lebanon for their wives, recent generations have married locally – from among the 'Spanish' (which includes Mestizos) – and all generations have taken mistresses from among the Mestizos or Spanish. In this way there is a continuum of skin pigmentation and hair texture from Maya to 'Spanish', so that it was possible for a Maya boy to say to us, 'The Creoles don't like us Whites'. Again, among our informants, of two daughters of the same Creole mother, one was of slightly lighter skin colour than the other. She powdered her face with rice powder to make it seem even lighter, straightened her hair, and was eager to marry a 'Spanish'. The other, darker, daughter would have nothing to do with such practices or ambitions, wore her hair Creole-style, cherished her independence and worked in the fields on her mother's farm. 'Spanish' society in the region is strongly patriarchal and 'Creole' society strongly matriarchal; a lot therefore is at stake in the acts of ethnic identity made by the younger members of the growing 'Mixed' population.

Physical appearance loomed large also in GM's responses:

LeP: Most people looking at you would say you were Spanish, wouldn't they?

GM: Mhm – they usually take me...mistake me for a Mexican or something like that you know...they have dark Indian...they never did em...an' the same with him an'...although his hair is curly...but...the way he speaks when he go outside you know, they take him for a foreigner or a San Salvadorian or...they never did em mist...em...tell him that well you are from Belize or you are British Honduran...they never did.

LeP: But he doesn't have hard hair, does he?

GM: No!...he has family that has...hard hair...

LeP: And you too?

GM: Well...as far as I can remember, no...because even my grandmother although she was a Creole her hair was crimpy you know...sof' an' curly...never did have the...the...dead em type hair you know...I would say most of my blood is Spanish more than...more than Creole...I have more Spanish in me than Creole...

Provenance was emphasized by informant MB:

MB: Oh, well, well my grandfather, my father's father he's from Syria. So...
AT-K: You look rather English to me.
MB: Well my grandmother's mother is from Spain, somewhere. Then my mother's parents are from Mexico. An' we have some German blood somewhere along...So I really couldn't tell you.

Nationality was usually referred to as 'Belizean'. As we have already seen, it was sometimes used as an escape-route from what was felt to be a problem of one's ethnicity or race if one was 'mixed'; MB again:

LeP: But if somebody asked you what you were, what would you say?
MB: I'm Belizean, that's all. That's all I can say.
LeP: You wouldn't say you were Creole or Spanish or...
MB: How can I say that? I cannot say I'm a Creole because I'm not, I can't say I'm English because I'm not.

In Mexico, from which she had just returned:

MB: Oh, well from the fact that you say Belizean they know you're not one you know, just...you're either Spanish or you're English, right, they know you're a mixture of something or the other. You don't even know what so you...I mean you just can't say...you...you just can't curse anybody because they're you know they're Spanish or something because you don't know, you can be...s...you might have some Spanish blood in you.
LeP: Yes...Yes...
MB: You can never tell.
LeP: Yes, but do you think people *do* say they're Belizeans nowadays?
MB: Oh, yes...*I do.*
LeP: You have a sense of identity, do you?
MB: Yes. Well we can't...you see it would be difficult to classify ourselves with the British, right? I mean, well, we're British according to laws right, but we're not really British.
LeP: What is really British?
MB: Well, the people from England (laughs). You. The same as you say 'What is really a Belizean?'
LeP: People from Belize.
MB: Yes.

One informant at least did use the term 'Belizean' as an ethnic term parallel to 'Creole' or 'Guatemantican':

LeP: When you say he, what race would you say your father belonged to then?
LV: Erm, I don't know. His dad is em, half Mexican and his mother em, is mixed you know with Spanish and I don't know if it's Creole or what. But she's mixed.
LeP: And what about your mother?
LV: My mother erm, she, her dad is Creole and her mother is mixed too.

LeP: What do you mean by mixed?

LV: Like em, maybe her father is erm, Creole and her mother is Spanish, you know that's what we call Mixed, or erm, like if erm, my father is er, Belizean and my dad might be a Guatemantican you know, like that you would say they are mixed, different.

LeP: If I had asked your father what race he was what do you think he would have said?

LV: Creole.

LeP: He would have said Creole?

LV: Aha.

LeP: And if I asked you what race you are what would you say?

LV: Creole.

Genetic descent too was invoked. The father of one informant (RC) felt that he was so mixed in his descent that he could *only* define himself as 'mix-up':

LeP: Is he a Spanish man?

RC: English.

Father: No, no – mix-up, just mix. I got black...some black blood, English blood, an' Indian blood. Three blood, yes. My grandfather was an Englishman. Come from England. Well, you know, when you get, when you get to different part of the world, you want to marry, your father want to marry, the children they cross over right so. We're still Christian. Everybody in this world is the same thing, white, black or blue, whatever you are. All, I've got to tell you, even Englishman.

But as we shall see later, 'mix-up' appears already in the 1970 survey as a cover-term for various identities, particularly 'Spanish-Creole'. It is certainly the term that has been used most frequently as the first answer to our question 'there being many different kinds of people in British Honduras, what would you call yourself?', usually followed by specifications like 'Creole, Black...' (see all the 'Mixed' names on figure 3, page 218).

The negative criteria for deciding on a personal identity as 'Belizean' were emphasized also by GM; she began by referring to family or genetic descent 'in the blood' – that is, the property many people think of as 'race':

LeP: How would you describe yourself now if somebody said well what are you?

GM: Hm!! Well that's what I would like to sit down and ask myself. All I could say I'm a Belizean – I don't know how I would – you know.

LeP: Would you say you're Spanish?

GM: No and I wouldn't, 'cos as long as you have that...Negro in your blood they say you're a...you're a coloured, so I wouldn't say I'm a Spaniard! (laughs)

LeP: But you have good hair.
GM: Yes, well – I guess I only have a quarter of my...blood...you know.

The same point about genetic criteria in defining 'Creoles' was made by others, including SH:

LeP: And em supposing I said to you now wha...what race do you feel you are then?
SH: I would say a Creole. A Creole is er anyone er that is called a Creole. If the race is white, Spanish, Indian, whatever, as long as you're...you had a mixture of Negro then you're a Creole. Otherwise you would be Spanish, Indian or something else...all races born in Belize, they are called Belizeans no matter what colour, what race.

EE however clung to her claim to be 'Arab' in spite of the acknowledged admixture of 'Spanish':

LeP: But, would you...and what would your father have said your family was?
EE: My family?
LeP: If I had asked your father what is your family what would he have said?
EE: Well em...Because em, he's a half Arab. My mother is a Spanish but my father is...was a full Arab you know, and her mother was a Mex...em Guatemantican. So he was a half Arab. Then my...my grandfather by my mother's side used to be an Arab too, you know? an' our mother used to be a Spanish.
LeP: So what answer do you think he would have given me, if I said well what do you reckon your family is?
EE: Well...A half Arab, I don't know.
LeP: Rather than Spanish?
EE: Rather than Spanish. 'Cos the two of them half Arabs in them, right?
LeP: But if somebody said to you now, well, what do you reckon your family is, what would you say?
EE: I would say Arab.
LeP: Arab?
EE: Mm. Anybody ask me I would say an Arab.

Later, she said that she would only use the term 'Belizean' when in another country, to explain where she was from.

'Belizean' as a geographical and as a linguistic criterion. The schoolteacher LG, despite her prior commitment to being 'Spanish' and speaking Spanish, became fiercely 'Belizean' in the context of refuting Guatemala's claim that all Belizeans were Guatemalans:

LeP: What is stopping you getting independence?
LG: That's a very good question. I don't really know. I know that Britain will certainly be grateful to get rid of us because we are nothing but a financial burden to them. And I feel that most Belizeans don't realize that. I don't know. I know that Guatemala's quite a threat.

LeP: D'you think it's a real threat?

LG: Well I know they talk a lot. But as long as... I feel that as long as England and the United Nations keep up this noise about Belize that they wouldn't dare do it. So far Belize has had so much world support that I don't think Guatemala has the guts to do that.

LeP: So you think you really could get independence and Guatemala wouldn't carry out its threat?

LG: I hoping not. I don't think they would. I really don't.

LeP: But I believe there was quite a scare when they...a few months ago.

LG: In June? em, through July.

LeP: People left?

LG: Oh, yes, people from Benque and people from Cayo even left. A lot. But I think it was mostly because of the propaganda on the radio, you know. Very bad.

LeP: From Guatemala?

LG: From Guatemala because Belize Radio hardly had anything to say about it...anything.

LeP: Do people listen to Guatemala radio a lot here?

LG: Quite a bit. Well you know, they're very, those people have a little bit of brains. I have to give them a little bit to credit. They've set up that radio in Melchor. 'Course and it gives nothing but music all day and in between the musics they give you 'All of we are Guatemalans'. You know and the little children...Well we listen to it, but every time they say something like that we contradict what it says, so even when they're having their noise we make our noise also but that's just happens to be this family and you know they may not convince the younger people like me but small children...I know my little son here...They will say 'Todos son los Guatemala'. And I've said 'No you're *not*'.

Language was occasionally, but not often, used as an ethnically-identifying criterion, although many informants claimed that Creole was the Belizean language; one example of it being used as an identifying characteristic came from a boy who claimed both his parents were Spanish, but that they spoke Creole as well as Spanish at home (informant DR):

DR: In my home I speak Creole, you know, usually m...

LeP: Why is that?

DR: Well, that's the language that we were taught you know, from home you know. An' a bit of Spanish, you know?

LeP: Is your...what would your father say he, he was originally?

DR: My father is a...er watchman, fire-lookout you know, he work up in the fire lookout, right? On the hill above.

LeP: What...what race is he?

DR: He's Spanish. Yeah. My mother is Spanish too.

LeP: And yet you speak Creole at home?

DR: Yeh, we speak Creole enough.

LeP: Why is that?

DR: Many of them are very surprised at it you know. But...well, my father usually speak Creole, you know, that's the way he was, he came up, you know, with that language. So he just carry on that way.

LeP: Where did he learn that?

DR: Well, he learn it in the Cayo District, you know? Right in Santa Elena, you know, where he grow up. Along with people you know. He was a Spanish chap, but he grew up in Santa Elena.

LeP: Yes. And the other children spoke...

DR: Yeh.

LeP: ...Creole did they?

DR: They all spoke, speak Creole here, especially in the school, the playground and all...all over, you know? Creole is the major language in here. So that's what we use, you know, all about.

LeP: When you say your parents are Spanish, what would you say you are?

DR: Well, I would say I'm a Spanish too. I speak a bit of Spanish – not too good, you know? But I try.

LeP: And have you ever heard people call themselves Belizeans?

DR: Yeh.

LeP: What does it mean?

DR: Well, I would say I'm a Belizean too. Co...Because erm, born in Belize you know I got to know about Belize a bit in history. An' originally, everybody called themselves Belizean, so I call myself a Belizean.

LeP: How do you recognize another Belizean?

DR: Well, usually in Belize you find the language, the main language you know is this slang, that I tell you about. The Creole. And you'd recognize them by that you know. They usually have this you know, very few of them speak the English or some of them usually speak Spanish.

One girl who denied the use of the 'Belizean' label nevertheless went straight on to agree that one could recognize Belizeans abroad by the way they talked (informant MM):

LeP: So you'd say you are Spanish?

MM: Yeh.

LeP: Have you ever heard people say they're Belizean?

MM: Have you...what you say?

LeP: You haven't heard anyone say that they are Belizean?

MM: They're Belizean? No.

LeP: You haven't. Would you say you are a Belizean?

MM: No, I wouldn't say that.

LeP: You wouldn't? What does it mean?
(Silence)

LeP: If you heard, if you were in another country and you heard someone talking and he was a Belizean would you, would you recognize from his voice that he was a Belizean?

MM: Yes.

LeP: How?

MM: By hearing how him talk.

LeP: What would it be about him talking?
MM: Well, the way him talk his language.
LeP: You, you'd recognize him.
MM: Yeah.

Patterns of ethnic identities : the example of Cayo District
The evidence from which we have cited the above statements, consisting of long conversations with about 40 informants in 1978, was analysed in detail by Andrée Tabouret-Keller as to the claims of ethnic identities, and compared with data of our 1970 survey (see Tabouret-Keller and Le Page 1983). As we have already seen, in between these dates the former colony of British Honduras came close to full independence under its new name of Belize, the final steps being delayed only by the threat of Guatemala to annex the territory as its own as soon as the British left. We are, then, concerned with ethnic identities and their evolution at a time when the emergence of a new identity, that of being a 'Belizean', is called for by the political situation, and with the evolution of the concomitant language situation – one important feature of that common 'Belizean' identity being a tacit recognition of 'Creole' as the Belizean language, whatever this term 'Creole' might mean and/or imply.

When Le Page first visited the colony in 1952 'Spanish', 'Maya', 'Creole', 'Carib', 'Mestizo' were only the five main labels out of many applied to a wide range of cultural and ethnic identities. In 1970 the range was still very large: 38 different names in response to a question on ethnic identity in the sociological family questionnaire (the question was normally put obliquely in the form 'What sort of people live round here?' and then 'What sort of people would you say you were?')

Figure 3 shows the distribution of identity assessment in 253 families of the original sample of schoolchildren (27 having been discarded for various reasons) (see Tabouret-Keller 1975a). Two-thirds of the families called themselves by names that referred to one of three main ethnic groups in Cayo District: 30 per cent Creole, 25 per cent Spanish and 12 per cent Maya. Whereas the Spanish and the Maya had a very limited number of alternative names – as if one either is or is not Spanish or Maya, the Creoles had a fairly large and open set of different names – more or less synonymous, as their meaning was given as 'mix-up' in most cases. Primarily 'mix-ups' then, the Creoles nevertheless kept themselves distinct from families whose complex names explicitly referred to two (or even three) of the main sets, as in 'Spanish Indian' or 'Mixed Spanish Creole' (the Mixed 'a' group in Figure 3, a sub-set of 17 per cent of the families in the sample). The remaining families (16 per cent illustrated by the Mixed 'b' group in

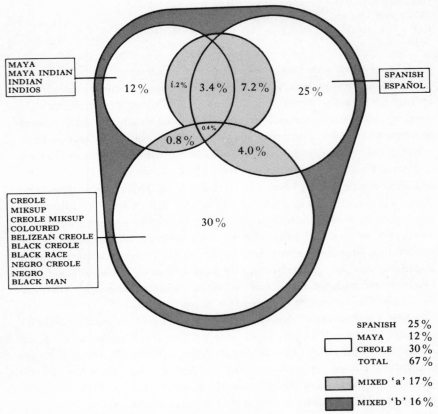

Figure 3. Ethnic identity of the families from the 1970 survey
The Mixed 'a' sub-group includes the following 20 names: *Spanish Mestizo, Spanish Indian, Mixed Spanish, Mixed Maya Spanish, Mixed Indian Spanish, Yellow Belly Spaniard, Spanish and Maya are all the same, Revueltos, Trigenos, Latino, Spanish Latino, Mixed Lebanese Spanish, Mixed Maya Indian, Indian Mestizo, Halfs, Mixed Creole Indian, Pure Black Spanish from San Benito, Mixed Spanish Creole, Mixed Indian Spanish Creole*

Figure 3) belonged also to that 'crossed' set but included all cases where no decision as to the identity of the family could be made. This arose, for example, when the father said he was 'Creole' and the mother said she was 'Spanish' and both agreed that their children would have to decide for themselves; the mother added that she would prefer the children to be 'Spanish' but she felt they were 'Creole'. At the time of our first study we suggested that at least for this group a common Belizean identity would be welcome.

The overlapping parts of the sets on Figure 3 (the Mixed 'a' sub-sets) illustrate how intermarriage fits into the general pattern of ethnic identities: it is easily acknowledged between Spanish and Maya (11.8 per cent of the families) but far less between Spanish and Creole (4.4 per cent of the families) and almost not at all between Maya and Creole (1.2 per cent). This betrays not only a high consciousness of ethnic identity but a sense of hierarchy among the three main ethnic groups, that ranks 'Spanish' identity at the top. A further study (Tabouret-Keller 1976) supports these results: information given by the families on the pupils' *grandparents'* identity and place of birth showed that loyalty towards Spanish identity was stronger than towards any other, and also that Spanish descent was overestimated: we recorded more Spanish grandmothers (or great-grandmothers) than any Census of the beginning of the century allowed for!

In our 1971 survey only one man claimed his family and himself to be 'Belizean'; he was of Lebanese descent and as such generally referred to as a 'Turk'; he had married a 'Spanish' wife from Benque Viejo and he explained that he felt a sense of duty towards British Honduras in the independent Belizean future, in which he placed his faith and money. He was indeed a rich man and had decided not to export his fortune to the USA. With independence Belizean identity was advertised and supported in many ways and in the follow-up survey (1978) seven out of the 36 former pupils interviewed introduced spontaneously the term 'Belizean'. In the interview with the schoolteacher LG she told us that 'for National Day, they put out sweat shirts and posters and everything that says "Belize is for ever", "Belizeans for Belize"...'; here she was corrected by her younger brother: "Belize is for Belizeans!" In most cases the term was introduced in contrast to the names of other countries as in 'Belizean students in Guatemala' but it was mentioned also in a more personal context, that of ethnic identity. In those cases the term was clearly identified as a common name superseding ethnic particularity; for example 'No matter what colour, what race, you are a Belizean if you are born here'; 'They are all coming to one thing, calling themselves Belizean'; 'Everyone call themselves Belizean' and 'We are all Belizean.'

Despite the progress of a Belizean identity the traditional ethnic identities were still quite vigorous and the weight of the loyalties they carried was still present. Table 25 shows the ethnic identities claimed in 1970 by the parents of 36 of the children whom we interviewed again in our follow-up survey in 1978. It will be seen that whereas Spanish identity was largely maintained, there was considerably more willingness among the children (now grown up) in 1978 to call themselves 'Creole' or

Table 25. *Overall view as to identities proclaimed and languages used by parents and by their children in 1970 and in 1978* ($N = 36$)

Identities I.	Languages L.	Parents 1970		Children 1970	Children 1978	
		I.	L.	L.	I.	L.
Spanish	Spanish	14	15	8	11	7
Creole- (Mixed[a])	Creole- (English[b])	3(2[a])	6(2[b])	16(2[b])	14(8[a])	19
Maya	Maya	1	1	1	0	0
Indian	—	0	—	—	2	—
Belizean	—	0	—	—	2	—
Complex names	Complex situations	7	7	10	0	10
No inf.	No inf.	11	7	1	7	0

Note:
[a] refers to those who used the term 'Creole' + 'mixed' of their identity
[b] refers to those who used 'English' as the name of their language in a context which made it clear they meant Creole

'Mixed' than among their parents in 1970. The term 'Maya' was not used by the younger generation to name themselves; they would use 'Indian' although they might call their parents (or grandparents) 'Maya'. And indeed in Succotz, which we had known largely as a Maya village in 1970, we now came across many young people who claimed Spanishness. More generally there was less attempt to be very specific about their ethnic 'descent' by using complex names (like 'Indian Spanish Mixed' or 'Mixed Spanish Creole') – in fact none of them did this in 1978 and the names most chosen were either plain 'Creole' or a kind of neutral 'Mixed'. In 1978 specific genetic claims seemed to matter less than in 1970. In addition to the category 'Mixed' the category 'Belizean' now appeared.

We have established how in 1978 'Belizean' denoted citizenship of the state of Belize, but we must now stress the very strong connotation it had with the use of Creole. In most of the cases where Belizean identity was referred to, Creole was mentioned as 'the Belizean language'. But not only was Creole felt to be 'the Belizean language', it was also mentioned as the everyday common language in two-thirds of the follow-up families: of the 36, 19 mentioned Creole as their only spoken language, whereas in 1970 within the same set of families not more than 6 mentioned Creole as their only language. In 1978 the extension of the use of Creole was often mentioned and stressed, as for example (each example is a quotation from a different interviewee):

> 'the Creole brought bit by bit wiping out the Spanish'
> 'here we speak mostly Creole as they call it'
> 'we usually speak Creole, most useful the Creole, you know?'
> 'with their mother is mostly Spanish but with the little school-mates and some of the time...Creole more'
> 'what we talk is broken Spanish and broken Cr...English, so I would call myself Creole...though if she (the mother) talk Spanish to us we answer her in Creole'
> 'we just run right off into the Creole again'
> LeP: 'What language do Belizeans speak?' – '...well, Creole. That's the way we call it round here'
> 'most of them talk Spanish' (in families in Bullet Tree Falls)
> 'in school they learn the Creole' LeP: 'How do Belizeans talk?' – '...Creole, mostly Creole'
> 'but still Creole is everywhere'
> 'but of course all races speak Creole'

On the whole there is an acute awareness among the younger generation of the extension of the use of Creole although, as it was illustrated in some of the case-studies earlier on, often there were still traces of resistance to the fact.

It seems from Table 25 that for the parents' generation ethnic choice had to coincide more or less with language choice. Members of the younger generation however seemed to be able to establish their ethnic identity separately from their language identity. This had the advantage of allowing respect for the parents and for their Spanish loyalty while giving voice to the social linguistic evolution towards Creole that would by now be difficult to deny. The 'Mixed' identity seemed also to allow them to keep some Spanishness, as we could establish from a case study of one of the families (Tabouret-Keller 1980a) and as is illustrated from answers such as: 'like her father is Creole and her mother is Spanish, that's what we call Mixed'. Young people who identified themselves as 'Mixed' might be those who did not want to make a choice or who preferred to avoid one. We must in any case remember that 'Mixed' was more or less synonymous with 'Creole' for many of our informants.

The concept of 'race'

Barth spoke of 'the traditional proposition that a race = a culture = a language'. Such a proposition lay behind Hitler's 'Ein Volk, Ein Reich, Eine Sprache'. Although today the concept of a 'German people united by their language' – a product of nineteenth-century romantic nationism – is still strong among Germans, the general proposition could not be maintained for a moment.

First perhaps we should, as social anthropologists have done by coining the term 'ethnic', draw attention to the difficulties raised by the concept of 'race'. It is interesting that one of the very earliest citations of this word in the *OED* (from Dunbar, the Scottish poet, at the beginning of the sixteenth century) is in the sense of 'a group or class of persons...having some common feature or features'. (Dunbar speaks of 'backbiters of sundry races' – that is, of various kinds.) By the end of the century it was being used much more in the sense of 'a group of persons...connected by common descent or origin', and by the end of the eighteenth century with the sense of 'one of the great divisions of mankind, having certain physical peculiarities in common'. In this last sense it is of course related to theories about the genesis of mankind itself, and in the nineteenth century in particular these theories were associated with the linguistic evidence of comparative and historical philology which, based on the written records of the comparatively recent past (that is, not more than 3,000–5,000 years) primarily of the Indo-Aryan languages, reconstructed family trees which led scholars back to the supposed 'Ur-sprache' or original language. The time-scale of the known history of man was then that of written or incised records; theories based on a reconstructed history of 'the Indo-Aryans' were then extrapolated to take account of the rest of the population of the world, and they were theories of family descent which spoke where necessary of people of 'mixed race' (or 'Mestizo' or 'half-caste') as opposed to those of 'pure race'. They were accompanied by concepts of 'pure' language also.

Underlying the use of the word *race* – as also of the older word *kind* – are two concepts, one of typological classification, the other of genetic or family descent. If we were to classify mankind according to its various physical or behavioural 'kinds' we might sort the fat from the thin, the long-nosed from the snub-nosed, the males from the females, the meat-eaters from the vegetarians, the dark-skinned from the light, and so on. 'Sorting' according to genetic inheritance is done for us, were we only able to read the code. In assessing the genetic evidence, however, there are problems.

The first is that the surface, easily observable typological evidence, which in the past has been held to betray genetic evidence, only holds good for a few generations back, except in very cut-off communities. Secondly, we know absolutely nothing about the vast majority of anybody's ancestors. Thirdly, the less visible, less easily observable typological evidence when applied by modern genetics does not by and large support the earlier concepts of racial descent.

Let us take the last point first. It has been examined in some detail by J. S. Jones (if discontinuous variation of a character in a population, such as colour blindness or the ABO blood groups, is such that the incidence of each genetically-determined form is higher than could result from chance mutation, the population is said to be *polymorphic* as to that character):

It is generally accepted that the human population can be divided into groups which differ from each other in obvious characteristics such as skin colour. The classical (and most popular) views of race are typological; they imply that each race is a homogeneous group of individuals, and that the members of such a group are biologically similar to each other, and different from the members of other racial groups. Each race is assumed to represent a genetically differentiated human type.

There are serious problems in defining races in this way, as it is now obvious that each human population, rather than consisting of a uniform group of individuals, contains within itself a large amount of genetic variation for many of those characters originally used to define racial 'types'. Faced with this variation, supporters of typological views have been forced into increasingly unlikely models involving the mixture by migration of originally pure populations. Physical anthropology has found it difficult to come to terms with genetic polymorphism. This very diversity can, however, be used to provide information for an estimate of the differences among human populations.

Rather than defining race on the basis of a few conspicuous variants such as skin colour (which may be based on genetic differences of as few as four loci), it is now possible to use information on the distribution of genetic polymorphism at scores of loci for blood groups, histocompatability entigens, enzymes and the structure of DNA revealed by restriction enzymes...

Even a superficial examination of the geographical patterns of allele frequency in man shows that the typological view of each race as a genetically well differentiated group is not correct. The geographical trends of gene frequency for a sample of human polymorphisms hardly ever parallel those for skin colour or body form. New statistical techniques which combine all the available information on biochemical polymorphism make it possible to quantify the extent of genetic differentiation within and among human populations and give a new insight into the nature of race.

Latter has developed an index which uses data on 18 polymorphic gene loci from 180 different human populations from each of the six major racial groups (classified as European, African, Indian, East Asian, New World and Oceanian) to give a measure of the proportion of genes which two randomly chosen individuals have in common. Comparison of the value of this index obtained when the two individuals come from the same 'race' with that obtained when the two are members of different 'races' gives a clear indication of the degree to which the human population is divided into genetically different groups. His analysis shows that by far the largest component of the total genetic diversity of mankind – about 84 per cent of all genetic variation – results from the genetic differences which exist between individuals belonging to the same tribe or nationality. About six per cent arises from differences between tribes or nationalities (such as those which are found, for example, between the populations of France and Spain, or between different tribes in the east and west of Africa). Only about ten per cent of the total biological diversity of mankind arises from genetic divergence between 'racial' groups. In other words the genetic differences between the classically described races of man are on the average only slightly greater than those which occur between nations within a racial group, and the genetic differences between individual human beings within a local population are far larger than either of these. Mankind as a whole, far from being divided into a number of discrete entities which could be defined as racial 'types', is in fact rather a homogeneous species in terms of geographical variation...

Although the races of classical anthropology and popular myth do not represent genetically differentiated entities, it is of course possible to use the geographical variations in gene frequency which do exist as the basis of a taxonomy of mankind. Several trees showing the evolutionary relationships of various population groups have been constructed. Until recently there was considerable disagreement between those based on skeletal characters and those based on molecular polymorphisms. It now appears that this arises largely from the strong correlations which exist between skull form and climate. These lead to a convergent evolution of populations living in similar climates great enough to obscure the patterns due to common ancestry. Once these climatic effects have been removed by statistical means, both skeletal and biochemical measures of identity produce trees which show that Africans and Europeans are more closely related to each other than either is to Amerindians or Australasians...

A confusion between these two measures of genetic identity – the proportion of genes which members of different races have in common, versus the probability of being able to identify to which race an individual belongs – has led to a recent controversy about the real extent of the genetic differences in the races of mankind. Mitton claims that, as by multiplying the probability of identity of individuals of different racial origin for one polymorphic locus after another it is possible to assign them with some precision to the racial group from which they come, then human races must each represent a rather major level of genetic divergence. However, the index of identity used by Mitton is a multiplicative one; it does not give information as to the extent to which races show overall genetic differences among themselves. Several authors have pointed out that Mitton's measure of the genetic identity of populations cannot be used to assess the average genetic differentiation of human races. The idea of 'racial' type – and some would argue, of 'race' itself – is no longer a very useful one in human biology.   (Jones 1981: 189–90)

Nevertheless, 'race' remains a very powerful concept in our stereotypical thinking. If we then take the two earlier points, the shakiness of our racial claims is made clearer if we think for a moment what they are based on. For example, in spite of the rigidity of the South African classification of every person in the country on supposedly genetic grounds, the classification must to a large extent rest on appearances and popular report. It is rarely possible for any child to be utterly certain who its father was (and the statistics showing the relationship between claimed putative or supposed fatherhood and the possibility of that claim being true as demonstrated by an examination of the blood-groups of 'father' and 'child' make it clear that the illegitimacy rate in some communities is far higher than is generally realized). Also there is the fact that very few people in the world know who all their supposed eight great-grandparents were. If one remembers that one has had 16 great-great grandparents, 32 great-great-great grandparents and – if one reckons four generations to a century (a conservative estimate) – that one only has to go back 500 years to have had 2^{20} (or more than one million) ancestors, it is clear that, even if we reduce this number drastically by allowing for in-breeding, what one knows about one's ancestry is infinitesimally small in comparison with the chances that one's suppositions are mistaken. This holds true for every single member of the human race, even for those who most confidently display their family trees.

We hear people speak of 'direct descent' – but this normally means 'patrilineal descent'; no descent is in fact more 'direct' than any other – most of the population of Britain is 'directly descended' from King Alfred, and equally directly from his serfs. The mother makes an equal genetic contribution to that of the father, and in any case the genetic chances are very thoroughly shaken up at conception. We each carry 23 pairs of chromosomes in each of our cells. The fertilization of a female egg involves the combination of half of the chromosomes of a male egg with half of those of the female, in such a manner that the theoretically possible combinations are 2^{23}. But that is not the whole story, since at conception a redistribution of genes takes place among the chromosomes in such a way that the theoretically-possible combinations of *genes* is in fact very, very much greater – quite large enough to ensure that, identical twins apart, each human being is unique in its genetic potential, or genotype. To this we must add the fact that many genotypical characters (such as hair texture, eye colour, skin colour, potential for height etc.) are transmitted independently of each other, so that it is perfectly possible to combine blue eyes with a dark skin and tight curly hair. Finally, the transmitted potential, the genotype, may or may not be realized in the actual person;

the phenotype depends on the favourability or otherwise of the environment to that potential. (It has, for example, just been reported by the National University of Singapore Student Health Service that the average height of a random selection of 40 male undergraduates has increased from 1.63 m (5′ 5″) in 1970 to 1.72 m (5′ 8″) in 1982, due possibly to improved diet.)

In the face of all these considerations it is likely that racial or ethnic stereotypes in popular thinking are much more sharply focussed than the genetic facts of dispassionate scientific observation warrant. Nor is this true only of popular thinking, as two news items in the London *Times* in February 1984 vividly demonstrate. The first reported that the South African Government changed the racial classification of 690 people in 1983; two-thirds of these, who had been Coloureds, became Whites, 71 who had been Blacks became Coloureds and 11 Whites were redistributed among other racial groups. The second reported that the French Communist leader M. Georges Marchais had expressed his offence at a new Soviet book, *Populations of the world*, in a letter to *L'Humanité*. The Russian book claimed that the population of France consisted of 'French, Alsatians, Flemings, Bretons, Basques, Catalans, Corsicans, Jews, Armenians, Gypsies and "others". 'For us' said M. Marchais 'every man and woman of French nationality is French. France is not a multinational state: it is one nation, the product of a long history...'

Focussing and diffusion of ethnic concepts

Thus we have, as far as the 'racial' basis for ethnicity is concerned, stereotypes which rest largely on certain aspects of external appearance and largely also on misconceptions about 'genetic' evidence. The first kind of evidence is, moreover, very much culturally conditioned. What one notices about other people, one's percepts about them, both physically and behaviourally, are conditioned by the concepts important in one's own culture, just as what one perceives about their language is conditioned by the models one has already built around one's own language. Thus, a man in Singapore claimed that he would never have any difficulty in telling the difference between a Tamil and a Chinese. If he had said 'between dark-skinned non-Malays and light-skinned non-Europoid' his statement would have been more valid. He was interpreting such observed data in terms of the official Singaporean 'ethnic' categories: Chinese, Malay, Indian, Others. Had he been presented with the same visual data in another context his racial classifications would probably have been different. We are always more acutely aware of more minute classification on our home ground than at a distance, and the cues on which we base these classifications – whether of known provenance or descent or physical or behavioural characteristics – are perceived in terms of the extent to which they match or contrast with classificatory concepts in our own society. The stereotypes themselves are important in binding together groups of individuals who interact according to their stereotypes, or in providing and maintaining boundaries around social groups. In Europe we may hear people say 'All Chinese look alike to me'; in China, 'All Europeans look alike to me'; but within each of these regions more minute distinctions are made: the northern Chinese have strong stereotypes about southern Chinese; northern Europeans about Latins and so on. Each culture has what Roger Brown (1965) has called 'categories of low codability and of high codability'.

'Racial' and 'ethnic' awareness and focussing in Belize

Within our data from Belize we find variable degrees of awareness of physical features, family provenance, and behavioural characteristics of different individuals and groups of individuals. A set of questions in the family questionnaire was devoted to ethnic identities and the answers show that there is a socially well-established knowledge of the characteristic physical features of 'Negro', 'Spanish', 'Maya', etc., characteristics to the point of stereotypes. Nevertheless in many instances people themselves did not observe these stereotypes when it came to state their own identity. The case of the shoemaker's wife in Benque Viejo, the 'Spanish' border town, illustrates the point. He belonged to the poorer part of the population and lived in the very last house of the town, a rather decrepit wooden thatched house; within the last ten years his business had been shrinking because people no longer bothered to have their shoes mended, the shoes being made now of synthetic materials. The shoemaker was not very dark and called himself a Creole man; he called his wife a 'true Spanish from Bullet Tree Falls', a former Maya chiclero village. Great was our surprise when she arrived during the interview (she had been at the river doing some washing). She was not only very dark, much darker than her husband, but she had also all the stereotyped features of 'Negro' (lips, nose, hair, etc.). However, she spoke only Spanish.

Another case is worth mentioning, of a family established along the road between the 'Mayan' village, Succotz and the 'Spanish' town, Benque Viejo. The family consisted of a widowed mother living with her unmarried children, and her two eldest sons, already established in adjacent houses in the same yard. They were all very consistent in their ethnic choice, calling themselves 'Spanish', using Spanish as their home language, both with the small children and with the mother who indeed ignored 'Creole' totally. After a time of prolonged acquaintance and friendship, and looking at some family portraits, the question was raised again (out of mere curiosity, no longer in an interview situation) 'was he (the grandfather) a Spanish man?' to which the eldest son replied laughingly 'we are all yellow belly Spaniards' (probably meaning Mestizo) but the old mother said 'este español'.

Many factors are at work to influence the degree of physical and ethnic focussing or diffusion in a community. This confluence of factors can be illustrated by the case of a pupil Irma F., whose history was explored in some detail in Tabouret-Keller (1980a). Irma F. grew up in her father's parents' home. The language situation of the child was constrained by two processes: the need to use Spanish and Spanish only with the grandmother who dominated the household, and the decision of Irma's father to use Creole with his three daughters. This decision was due to the fact that Irma's mother had been a Creole woman and that the father was married again to a Creole woman, this new family also containing three daughters living some distance away. The ethnic and linguistic situation of Irma as a child (she was 14 at the time of the first survey in 1970) is illustrated by Figure 4.

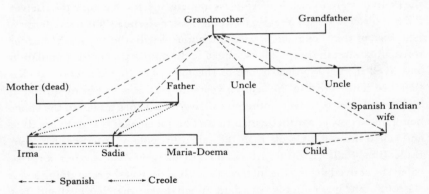

Figure 4. Language use as observed in Irma Fairley's family during the interview in 1970

At the time of the follow-up survey in 1978 Irma, whom we interviewed, was already married and had two children. She was living with her husband's family where the ethnic and linguistic situation was as illustrated by Figure 5.

It is interesting to note that the R. family, into which Irma F. married, duplicated somehow the combinations of the F. family where she grew up.

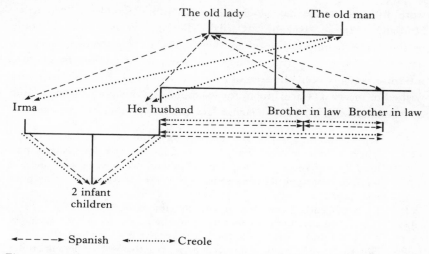

Figure 5. Statements made by Irma Fairley as to language use in her husband's (Ramirez) family, 1978

Among the focussing factors we see that in both cases 'the old lady', that is, Irma's grandmother in the F. family (Figure 4), and her own children's grandmother in the R. family, focussed both on Spanish identity and the use of Spanish. The mere existence of such an 'old lady', the term used in both families, is in itself a focussing factor. Both families were described as Spanish but in 1978 Irma specified, on second thoughts, that her own family was 'Spanish' but actually 'Mixed': 'we call it Mixed but it's Mestizo I guess, you see but we call it mix, we are mixed with different types of races'; she also specified, during the same interview, that her husband's family was mixed indeed: 'Well, we would say Spanish but I guess it's more a mix with Spanish than with Creole, because they have some...Creole families.'

In both families we see also the same pattern of diffusion: the younger generation uses Creole alongside Spanish and Irma specifies that she will bring up her children to speak both Spanish and Creole. And also, as we have already shown, the younger generation quite easily combine their parents' claim to Spanishness with their own consciousness of mixing. It is interesting to recall that, when asked in 1970 about the husband she would like when older, Irma replied that the best husbands were the Spanish – she herself expected however to marry a Creole man.

We have seen that informants in Belize themselves have commented on the greater degree of intermarriage today than in the past between what were hitherto somewhat aloof ethnic groups: 'Creoles', 'Spanish', 'Indian', 'Maya', 'Kekchi', 'Carib', 'Turks', 'Waika' – to use some of the names commonly used in Belize. We have ourselves observed instances of very powerful prejudice on the part of parents preventing intermarriage between children of different groups: a 'Spanish' girl who wished to marry a 'Carib' man, for example. On this point, parts of our conversation with the schoolteacher LG and her brother are relevant:

LeP: What about the sort of racial composition of the area, has that changed?
LG: There is more intermarrying...more Spanish marry the Negro than used to be when...(I) left here. But em, we have always been a homogeneous type of people so it...doesn't seem to unbalance anything very much.
LeP: By homogeneous you mean mixing up all together?
LG: Yea...that is...that's one beautiful part about...my country, you know. I...I like that...Because in the United States it's not like that.
LeP: But the people in Benque used to regard themselves as something separate. Very Spanish, didn't they?
LG: Is that so? They used to think themselves better?
LeP: Well, separate.
Br: They wouldn't like to associate themselves with the Negroes.
LeP: That's right.
LG: Well that's probably true because they don't have very many Negroes there. They still don't.
LeP: But now they have to come out in search of work?
Br: That's true. Most of them...
LeP: You said earlier on that one of the things you liked about your country, which is...
LG: Belize.
LeP: Was the homogeneity of the population. D'you think that er, will continue to grow or do you see any signs of it not continuing?
LG: Oh, no I think it will continue to grow. I think...
LeP: You think it's getting more homogeneous or less homogeneous?
LG: Oh, yes, more homogeneous. I see it in the High School when the students you know they date one another and like one another, all that business and...they don't respect colour and race, they really don't.
LeP: We know a family in Succotz where the mother is very much against her daughter, who is in love with and wants to marry...
LG: A Creole boy?
LeP: A Carib man.
AT-K: A Carib man.
LG: Oh, a Carib. Well, you see, Caribs...I don't...Caribs here...A lot of people don't like them. Is the lady Spanish?
AT-K: Yes, she's Spanish.
LG: 'Cause my father isn't too fond of the idea of us falling in love and wanting to marry a Negro.

LeP: A Negro?
LG: He's not fond of the idea, no. I think over the years he would probably accept it, but he does not...initially he doesn't like the idea at all.
LeP: Do you think in the younger generation that's breaking down?
LG: Falling in love?
LeP: The prejudice is breaking down?
LeP: But a lot of the Caribs are teachers of course.
LG: Yes...I don't know why people...well in our own family, you know, when we are joking we make fun of...the black people...of this thing or that thing. But em, as a whole we get along with them very well. Now the Caribs, a lot of people are prejudiced against them because they say that they do bad to other people. They believe in this obeah business. I don't know if you understand about that.
LeP: I understand very well...
LG: OK and I think that that's probably a primary reason why Spanish people and other Creoles are against them...and it seems that the Creole people are very jealous of them, because you know that they are quite...intelligent. The Caribs are usually very important people.
LeP: They have a lot of good jobs. So you think the Creoles might be jealous of them?
LG: From what I have seen, yes.
LeP: But nevertheless the Caribs talk Creole?
LG: Yes. Very well. And the Creoles don't speak Carib.
LeP: Do you think the idea of people being Belizean is catching on now? Rather than, rather than being Creole or Spanish?
LG: Oh, yes er, I know for National Day you know, they put out sweat shirts and posters and everything that says 'Belize is for ever', 'Belizeans for Belize'.
Br: 'Belize is for Belizeans'.
LG: 'Belize is for Belizeans', aha.
LeP: Do you think, you feel you are a Belizean?
LG: Oh, I definitely do. That was always my...my dream was to come back home...
LeP: Was it?
LG: And I don't want no other country taking over us all.
LeP: Well, that's very interesting indeed and very helpful to me. Andrée, did you want...
AT-K: Yes, your smaller brothers, what, what kind of language do they talk?
LG: He talks Spanish and Creole and English.
AT-K: All three of them, all three languages? So he would for example talk Spanish to his father?
LG: Mhm.
AT-K: With whom would he talk the Creole?
LG: With the other children...with them.
AT-K: Ah, yes and with this one? So within the same family you have, er, several languages used according to whom?

LG: Oh, yes. To me my brother that's in, in High School, he speaks proper English because...I teach him...and he...I usually speaks to...I usually speak to them in proper English because I don't know the Creole very well and they make fun. Because I find it difficult to talk Creole because.. just goes against my grain to use the proper English and then it isn't proper.

We have no means of knowing whether there is any innate component in our possible predisposition to find a mate physically similar to ourselves. It may be that any such predisposition – if it exists – is wholly learned through cultural pressures; or our mating patterns may be very largely the outcome of accidental or extraneous factors. Whatever their origins, the patterns certainly can break down when social circumstances strain them, and it seems that the threat from Guatemala to 'Belizeans', most of whom certainly do not wish to live under Guatemalan rule, has been among the social factors de-valuing racial or ethnic aloofness and leading to a greater sense of ethnic homogeneity among 'Belizeans' as 'mixed' people. Another factor has been the need for young people to travel the country in search of work.

It helps if we view the history of man as a history of more or less continual migration in response to ecological pressures, so that cultural and ethnic 'focussing' and 're-focussing' have taken place from time to time rather as eddies and whirlpools form as features of flowing water, affected by geography and the nature of contact between different streams. New streams are formed out of tributaries; new cultures, new ethnic loyalties, are formed out of the human tides; cultures and civilizations flourish and collapse; 'racial' identities change. Within the Caribbean, identities as African or European gave way to local and regional identities as Jamaican, Barbadian, Guyanese, West Indian etc., and such identities presumably tend to encourage some degree of fresh genetic focussing as proximity and mutual interest draw people together. In the Eastern Caribbean there remains in some territories (Trinidad and Guyana, for example) a fair degree of 'racial' separateness between, for example, Amerindian, East Indian and Creole. In St. Lucia we discovered in our survey a high degree of homogeneity in identity as 'St. Lucian'.

In Belize, in spite of the tendencies expressed by LG, the last cited informant, the processes of focussing around a 'national' identity, Belizean in this case, have still a long way to go, as they have in multi-ethnic communities in a great many other parts of the world. Possession of a Belizean passport would support a Belizean identity, but the mere use of the term will also put a stress on 'Spanishness' and on 'Mayaness' that in turn may lead to awareness that the borders of the 'Spanish' population and the 'Maya' population do not coincide with the borders of Belize. In Europe, the cases of Basque and of Catalan identity illustrate how populations settled on both sides of a political frontier, between the state of France and the state of Spain, may prefer to give first importance to their common identity as Basque or Catalan rather than to their identity as French or Spanish. In turn the example of the German-dialect-speaking population of Alsace in North-eastern France illustrates how a more general identity, that of French nationality in this case, is given first importance in spite of language use that links the area to a far larger German-speaking area. In each case, various factors intervene, mainly historical, political, economic.

Cultural focussing and national identities

It is worthwhile to look briefly at one or two other attempts at cultural focussing around national identity. Singapore is proud of its multiracial harmony, and a great deal has been done to stimulate progress towards a Singaporean identity while retaining the cultural properties of Chinese, Indians and Malays. There is today, however, no more miscegenation across these ethnic boundaries than in the past. The sharply-contrasting religions, practices and beliefs of Chinese Taoists or Buddhists, Indian Hindus, Muslims or Sikhs, and Islamic Malays not only in themselves provide barriers to intermarriage but help also to support contrastive attitudes to life and the activities of living which again maintain cultural and ethnic separatism. Even within the 'Chinese' community, however, (which the Government, as we shall see, is trying to homogenize through linguistic measures) older people tend to cling to separate clan identities such as Hokkien, Hakka, Teochew, Cantonese etc., and to have distinct stereotypes for each such clan. It has been claimed (e.g. by Benjamin 1976) that by constantly drawing attention to 'racial' identity in Singapore (Singaporeans are willy-nilly classified on their identity cards as 'Chinese', 'Indian', 'Malay' or 'Other' according to the classification of the putative father) the Government, while speaking always of 'multiracial harmony' in fact enhances ethnic separateness. Those who are the children of mixed marriages can claim the identity 'Singaporean' but this is not an officially recognized classification under 'race'. We shall see later what the linguistic concomitants of this situation are.

Most of the former European colonies are ambivalent on the question of ethnic and cultural focussing around their post-colonial national identity, and the integration or separate maintenance of 'ethnic minorities'. In the

schools of Australia children are classified as either 'ethnic' or 'Anglo';
as in the United States and Britain there is dispute as to whether a policy
of complete assimilation, or one of respecting the wishes of some to retain
their 'ethnic' identity, should be pursued (see e.g. Smolicz and Secombe
1977). (The aboriginal population of Australia, like the Indian population
of America, North and South, and the Negritos of Malaysia, frequently
gets ignored in the course of such disputes.)

It may be thought that in countries such as Brazil or the United States
new identities such as 'Brazilian' or 'American' might be leading to
greater physical and behavioural homogeneity, and indeed it may be so,
just as apparently happened under the Portuguese in Goa. But, nevertheless,
in Brazil and in the United States 'Negro' and 'Indian' communities also
remain identifiably separate. The persistence of various kinds of ethnic and
cultural boundaries and of 'racial' distinctions is remarkable, and may be
bolstered by religion, by the political system (as most obviously in South
Africa), by the educational system (as in Northern Ireland), by economic
and social organization (the Indian caste system) or any one of a host of
other factors; but it is frequently discussed and rationalized in 'racial'
terms. Boxer (1969: Chapter 11) deals at length with the importance of
the concepts 'purity of blood' and 'contaminated races' during the
establishment and maintenance of the Portuguese colonial empire:

The synodal constitutions of the archbishopric of Bahia, which were drawn
up in 1707...were based on those obtaining in Portugal and they reflect a
long-standing situation. They laid down that candidates for ordination must
be, among other things, free from any racial stain of 'Jew, Moor, Morisco,
Mulatto, heretic or any other race disallowed as contaminated'... The candidate's
purity of blood had to be proved by a judicial enquiry, in which seven or eight
'Old' Christians testified on oath from personal knowledge that his parents and
grandparents on both sides were free from any such racial and religious taints.

(1969: 260)

One can only but wonder what this 'personal knowledge' could have been
based on except for having heard that parents and grandparents identified
themselves and were identified solely by desirable identities such as
'Christian' and 'white' and never by non-desirable identities such as
'Jew' or 'black'.

2. The role of language in relation to concepts of ethnicity

Linguistic nationism

The equation 'a race = a culture = a language' is quite patently misleading,
both in terms of real biological criteria and in terms of popular stereotypes.
One has only to think of linguistic communities such as those who speak

English, or French, or Spanish, to see that the linguistic and ethnic boundaries are far from isomorphous. Nevertheless, linguistic nationism is a very common political phenomenon.

We have already discussed linguistic focussing in Chapter 5, and cultural and ethnic focussing in the previous few pages; for a parallel description of how social rules and concepts of group membership in general evolve, see Sprott (1958). (There have, of course, been other ways in which names for languages have come into existence; and also other ways in which languages have become associated with groups.) One fairly common progression in the relationship between isolating and naming hitherto unidentified groups and hitherto unidentified languages is set out below:

1. A group of people is named in accordance with one of the criteria we have set out, viz their common geographical provenance ('The Americans', 'Malaysians'), their common parentage ('the tribe of Judah'), common physical characteristics ('the Blacks'), common traditions ('the Christians').

2. The group's linguistic behaviour is denoted by an adjective formed from such a term, together with the noun for 'language'. Thus, *englisc gereord* – the way the Angles spoke; *lingua franca* – the way the Franks (in the Mediterranean) spoke; *Bahasa Malaysia* – the language of the country of the Malaysians; *papia kristang* – the language of the (Malaccan) Christians. These are divisions of the universal human faculty of language, according to the groups of which they are characteristic.

3. These adjectives become used as nouns; and the nouns not only denote the linguistic system felt to be the property of the group, language as used by them, but also connote the social values attached to the group – at this stage, in other words, the name of the language is inseparable from the sense of being the usage of a group of speakers. Thus we find, in Russell's *The etymology of Jamaica grammar* (1868):

The estates usually employ, besides Creoles, Africans, and these latter, even after they manage to speak 'creole', still retain the deep and harsh accentuation of their own language.   (*DJE* s. 1980: CREOLE 4)

It should be noted that the mere fact of naming a variety of linguistic behaviour tends to give it status as an isolate whose existence was previously subsumed under (possibly stigmatized, incorrect) versions of another variety. To describe the variety tends to raise its status, even if only for humorous purposes.

4. The system becomes detachable from the group, and comes to have some degree of autonomy as a linguistic system; the social values which

attached to the group now tend to be transferred to the system. Prestige, for example, tends to be converted into 'good, correct' (as with the French of the Isle de France), and parallel pejorative terms tend to attach to those systems whose users originally attracted stigma or to those new users who depart from the rules of the prestige system (hence, Creole is also known as 'bad talk' and 'broken talk'). Such values of course merely reflect the values of the users of the terms; they have no objective status.

5. Once the system has achieved some degree of autonomy in people's thinking it can be both *reified* and *totemized* – that is, it can be made into an object, and given iconic status. Reification usually involves some body of doctrine (grammars, lexicon, a literature) by means of which the system can be *taught*. For teaching purposes a standard variety must evolve, by one of the means we described in Chapter 4. The teacher who has learned and then teaches that variety will stigmatize other varieties as 'wrong' or socially unacceptable. Totemization brings us back to the language adopted now as one of the defining social properties of a group. Members of a group who feel their cultural and political identity is threatened are likely to make particularly assertive claims about the social importance of maintaining or resurrecting 'their language' (as, for example, in Wales, Quebec, Belgium, immigrant groups in Britain and Australia, and a thousand other communities throughout the world).

There are many other complex cross-connections between ethnicity, nationism, nationalism and language. Nevertheless, as we look around the world we find that a language is sometimes apparently of comparatively little importance to nationalism in a community. In fact, the vast majority of the people of the world live in multilingual communities in which the language of the law, of politics, of education – that is, the language (or languages) recognized as official, as the vehicle of government, is not the same as that of their own vernacular community. Sometimes the vernacular has equal prestige within its own domestic domain, as for example in German-speaking Switzerland. Sometimes the vernacular has comparatively low prestige or is even stigmatized in comparison: in a highly centralized state such as France, where the use of French was and is one of the assets of the power of central administration, that is, Paris-located, the use of regional languages tends to shrink and eventually they completely disappear (Tabouret-Keller 1981b). During the first half of this century Breton fishermen were confronted in offices by posters announcing *It is forbidden to spit and to speak Breton*. Not only that; they could only sell their catch in French, of which they had no command – or not sufficient to deal with French-speaking buyers who ruled the market as they wished. This meant that there had to be bilingual middle-men who were actually in the service of the buyers; fishing was all the fishermen could do in their own language (Floc'h 1981).

It has been claimed (by Eastman and Reese 1981) that language and ethnic identity should be related through the concept of 'associated language'. 'From the point of view of ethnic identity it does not make any difference whether we know, speak, or just claim an ethnically related language as long as there is one we can somehow associate with' they say (p. 109). 'We assert that the knowledge and use of language and the act of self-ascription are not strictly related behaviors. What language we know (*langue*) and use (*parole* or speech) and what self-identity we claim may be quite unrelated. Yet language is an aspect of our self-ascription' (p. 110).

Such a proposal raises problems within our own general hypothesis in this book. We have proposed that self-ascription is always accompanied by linguistic symptoms, within the constraints of our four riders. The problem seems to lie in treating as the same phenomenon *self-ascription* and *ethnic identity*. 'The group or groups with which from time to time we wish to be identified' may be many and various, and some of them may have very little of an ethnic component. For example, it would be hard to define Yorkshire people as an ethnic group, but there are very definite linguistic stereotypes associated with a 'Yorkshire' identity. The world-wide community of native speakers of English may view their ethnicity in such terms as 'Canadian' or 'Australian' or 'New Zealander', or in such terms as 'Italian-American'; the kind of association of language with ethnic identity is clearly a variable here. 'Jewishness' is usually regarded as an ethnic, as well as a religious, characteristic, and for some Jews the need for that ethnic identity and its association with Hebrew is so strong that they will learn and use Hebrew in order to proclaim their Jewishness – even in the absence of any religious belief either on their own part or on the part of their parents or grandparents, and even where only their mother was Jewish. Other Jews, however, are content to keep their Jewishness purely nominal and have little interest in Hebrew. Among the older generation in Alsace, an Alsatian identity is a matter of great concern, as the region has from time to time been forcibly annexed by Germany and from time to time, as now, has formed part of France. The domestic use of the Alsatian dialect is certainly of importance to them in asserting their ethnic identity, and this in turn may well have contributed to ethnic focussing. But today the younger generation are tending more to use French, without losing their Alsatian identity (Tabouret-Keller and Luckel 1981a, b).

There is therefore some truth in the concept of associated language, but it is not a *necessary* part of ethnic or 'racial' identity. It is even less a necessary part of national identity. In the Lorraine coal-mining region of North-eastern France the official language and nationality has changed five times within the last century from French to German and back again; the frontier between France and Germany has shifted seven times since 1815 and, as in many parts of Europe, the rural, traditional way of life has changed into an industrial, semi-urban one, due to the development of mining. As Pradelles de Latour (1983) illustrates, 'the complexity of this situation, in which French parents became Germans who bore German children who later became French and later again had German children, etc...is best summed up by a 65-year-old man's self-description: "I come from Lorraine, of Germanic culture, of French nationality and I think in *Platt*"' (the provincial Germanic dialect). He adds that he prefers to read in Standard German, watches German or Luxembourg television, but feels most at ease writing in French. This situation, already complex by historical necessity, became even more complex by the influx of successive waves of immigrants (Polish and Italian before 1940, Portuguese, Spanish and North African after 1945, and more recently Turks), hence the making-up of an entirely new population. The only common feature in a classroom of 23 pupils might then be, as Rebaudières-Paty (1985) shows it, to have French as the medium of teaching.

Language boundaries and group identities

It is evident that 'language' plays a very complex role in relation to ethnic or national or racial identity. Among the Chinese it is the written language that exerts the most powerful pressure on the ethnic stereotypes, although the spoken language or 'dialects' also matter. Not only is it the written language that is important, but the language as written in characters rather than in any alphabetic system or syllabary. The Chinese often claim that in spite of the lack of mutual intelligibility of a number of spoken Chinese dialects, they remain united by their written language. In one sense this is true. Even though very large numbers of Chinese are illiterate, and the character-writing system does not help to promote mass literacy (since the meaning and pronunciation of each character has to be learned to a large extent independently of one's knowledge of spoken Chinese – except to the extent that the order of the characters and that of the spoken morphemes corresponds, and also insofar as homophones are made use of in character-simplification), the existence and appearance of the written language is familiar to all, and the art of calligraphy is an integral part of Chinese painting. Thus efforts to introduce an alphabetic system for Chinese meet with constant resistance, rationalized sometimes in very curious ways (see e.g. Seybolt and Chiang 1979). A further example of the complexity of the relationship between language and ethnicity is provided by the history of Sikhism. A judgment of the British House of Lords (23 March 1983) ruled that the Sikhs were a race; the headmaster of a private fee-paying school in the north of England, having sought to exclude a Sikh boy from entrance to the school unless he gave up wearing a Sikh turban (which is enjoined on Sikhs by their religion), had been prosecuted on the grounds of illegal racial discrimination; the headmaster won the case in the Court of Appeal but this judgment was reversed by the Law Lords. As Rama Kant Agnihotri (1979) has shown, many Sikhs in Britain are losing any command of Punjabi, but their religious leaders try by every means to preserve the identity of the group by teaching in Punjabi, by promoting endogamy, and by insisting on patterns of behaviour felt to be central to Sikhism including hair styles and the wearing of turbans. The House of Lords upheld their view that they were a racial group with a distinct common genetic source; and this view has been hailed as a victory against racism by the Council for Racial Equality in Britain. However, neither the Punjabi language nor the wearing of turbans is peculiar to Sikhism either in India or Pakistan or in Britain. Nor is it really possible to maintain that endogamy has been so strictly preserved among the descendants of the founders of the religious group from among the Hindus of the Punjab in the seventeenth century that they constitute a 'race'. It is interesting to note that at the partition of the sub-continent in 1951 a great many Punjabi speakers, Sikhs and Hindus, moved out of Pakistan into India to avoid living in a Muslim state. Among them, those who were Sikhs continued to call their language Punjabi; those who were Hindus, to distinguish themselves from the Sikhs and to identify with other Hindus, began to call their language (the same language) Hindi. They settled in a sector to the west of Delhi in a region which subsequently became the State of Haryana. Their language was not identical with the Hindi of Delhi, but because of their presence and influence as 'Hindi' speakers, the concept of what is Hindi has been modified among all Hindi speakers in the region (see Le Page 1980a).

On the other hand, feelings of ethnic identity, certainly when buttressed by religion or by any institutional maintenance of political or cultural traditions, or by traditional economic roles, can survive total language loss, as we see among various immigrant groups in different parts of the world. The East Indians in the Caribbean have very largely given up their Indian languages except for ritual purposes (see e.g. W. F. Edwards 1977; Rambissoon Sperl 1980) in favour of Creole, but nevertheless identify themselves and are identified, within the wider 'West Indian' identity, as East Indians.

It has been claimed by one Bantu scholar (K. G. Mkanganwi, as reported in Le Page 1980a) that among the Bantu in Southern Africa concepts of ethnic or tribal identity may be strong, but that the concept of a tribe 'owning' a variety of Bantu as its own language was an invention of the British – in particular of missionaries and of the linguist Clement Doke. Clement Doke was sent out in the early 1900s to describe varieties of Bantu in an attempt to standardize teaching materials and he thus created a variety, e.g. called Shona, as distinct from other varieties – whereas the Shona themselves had been accustomed to thinking of the linguistic behaviour of all Bantu as one continuum of 'language'. At the other extreme are situations such as reported by Rigsby and Sutton (1982) in the Cape Keerweer region in Australia where language is owned and not merely spoken, and as reported by Jackson (1974, 1983) for the Vaupés Indians of Colombia, where individual settlements are multilingual speech communities. Both examples are cited at length since they are probably remote from the Indo-Aryan experience of most of us.

Ownership of language: the Cape Keerweer example

In the Cape Keerweer region of western Cape York Peninsula, as elsewhere in Aboriginal Australia, language is *owned* and not merely spoken. According to the Aboriginal model, one inherits a language from one's father, along with many other important forms of property such as land and major totems...

If we take a map of the Cape Keerweer region and mark on it the tracts of land claimed as 'own country' by the various Aboriginal families who come from there, and then we superimpose the names of the varieties claimed as 'own language' by the same families, we obtain a picture which, to most dialectologists, looks like a real mess. Owners of the same variety do not necessarily have adjacent countries but in many cases their countries are scattered widely over the region. If we then turn to community political life and observe the pattern of marriages past and present, the pattern of residence both in Aurukun settlement and on the eight or so outstations south of it during 1976–1979, the pattern of ritual alliances, the pattern of disputes, and the forms of corporate and informal social identity, we find that people in the region can be grouped and sub-grouped at various levels. These groupings have two dominant objective correlates: the proximity of the countries claimed by the people, and the closeness of their links through marriage and shallow descent. These two major correlates, in turn, are paralleled in broad terms by the landscape. There is, for example, a profound division between coastal people and inlanders. There is also a distinct clustering of allied families who come from the lower reaches of the river systems. All these groupings, including others such as local 'nickname' clusters (e.g. families with adjacent countries known by a single geographical term such as 'from along the beach'), ignore linguistic affiliation for the purposes of recruitment. Language is used emblematically for certain levels of grouping, but apart from land-holding units, these are among the least salient of all forms of social identification in the region. There is, for example, a use of linguistic labels for far distant Aborigines with whom contact was minimal in pre-settlement times. There is also the use of 'Wik-Mungkana' to refer to the Archer River people, most of whom are owners of a variety of language going by that name; this is in spite of the fact that two families who also own Wik-Mungkana come from the coast and have no special relationship to Archer River at all.

The social grouping in which language has greatest ideological prominence is that of the land-holding unit, which for the purposes of this paper we shall call the clan...

Language is emblematic of clan identity in a system akin to clan totemism. Because of clan exogamy, the smallness of some clans, the mobility of individuals, and other factors, local residence groups (or 'bands') normally include members of several clans. Because of the pattern of disjunction between the distribution of countries and linguistic affiliation, most local residence groups contain speakers of several languages. Shared linguistic affiliation does not of itself justify living together, and is not even often appealed to, among coastal people, in propagandistic statements about unity and exhortations for unity. Thus residence groups, task groups (such as ritual participants) and regional political groupings are formed largely independent of linguistic affiliation...

How do people cope with so many languages spoken around them? They do not simply acquire hearing knowledge of other languages and go on speaking only in their own. Most people are active multilinguals, although modern conditions may alter this in the future. Their multilingualism is limited to a subset of the languages with which they have contact. Comprehension, however, does exceed use in speaking. In view of the high degree of mutual exposure among the linguistic varieties of the region, and assuming that it has existed over a long period (there is much evidence for this), we conclude that the linguistic varieties have maintained their distinctiveness during the course of sustained dense contact. There is evidence that both diffusion and continuing divergence have taken place simultaneously.

The acquisition of multilingual competence has been a normal part of every child's socialization among Cape Keerweer people from time immemorial. It is not at present a result of the need to bridge the communicative gap between isolated trading partners, nor is it a means of enabling communication between socially, rather than geographically separate groups, for all the socially significant groups other than the exogamous clans are polyglot both by affiliation and by competence. The use of more than one language is, rather, part of an elaborate speech etiquette. There is not space to describe this etiquette here; it involves not only the use of different languages (i.e. code-switching) but also the use of different registers of the same languages.

Whatever its origin, the present complex and somewhat random relationship between social and residential groupings and language ownership in the region has probably been long established. This is a feature which extends along at least the 150 kilometres between Aurukun and Edward River. There is nothing especially un-Australian about such a pattern. A similar pattern obtains in the Princess Charlotte Bay area of Cape York Peninsula (see Rigsby 1980), and White and Parsons (1973, 1976; White 1978) describe a highly comparable situation for northeast Arnhem Land. These are areas in which so-called 'tribes' are, if anything, definable only by reference to ritual, war-making and marriage alliances, and not by reference to language ownership.

(Rigsby and Sutton 1982: 18–20)

Individual settlements as multilingual communities : the Vaupés Indians. The situation described for the Vaupés Indians of Colombia by Jean Jackson (1974) is again distinct from the Indo-European experience:

> If the Vaupés, or the entire central Northwest Amazon, is a speech area, then the individual settlements – longhouses or villages – are its speech communities... Although longhouses can have as few as two nuclear families, they are nonetheless multilingual speech communities. The Indians who reside there are always affiliated to more than one father-language, and more than one language is used in many speech acts. Furthermore, no rules create rigid boundaries, geographical or otherwise, which result in predictable combinations of languages... the degree of multilingualism in the Vaupés, in terms of the number of languages, verbal repertoires, and speech itself, is unusually extensive... language is by far the most important marker distinguishing the language-aggregates and their members... Indians not only deny, but are antagonistic to suggestions that language-aggregates are differentially valued or that members of a given language-aggregate are superior or inferior... Vaupés languages are not differentially esteemed or stigmatized...   (pp. 55–7)

Nevertheless, they *are* socially marked, and tokens kept carefully distinct. Jackson continues:

> Any anthropological research carried out in the Vaupés must eventually concern itself with questions such as the following: Why are over twenty languages spoken, given (1) the small numbers of Indians identified with each language, (2) the low population density, (3) the homogeneous culture throughout the region, (4) the lack of stratification along language boundaries, and (5) the lack of role specificity for the various languages? Why do Indians learn at least three languages, and some as many as ten, when they could all communicate in Tukano? Why do some places have separate names in all the languages? Why do Indians so strongly emphasize the mutual unintelligibility of the languages? It is very unlikely that such questions can be answered without postulating that Vaupés languages are emblems of the language-aggregates and badges of

membership in them for individual Indians. The possession of a distinctive father-language is important because the language-aggregates function as discrete units in the distribution of women...(p. 61)

Verbal evidence from informants indicates that Indians are aware of the emblematic nature of Vaupés languages with respect to language-aggregate identity. An example of this is from a conversation which I had with a Bará Indian about the relationship between sibling terminology and marriage rules. I was hoping to get an explicit genealogical explanation of the rule of exogamy as it applies to all Bará Indians, such as 'We are all brothers because we descended from a common ancestor and therefore don't marry our sisters.' However, after preliminary comments relating marriage rules and kin terms (such as 'We don't marry our sisters'), the fact of language affiliation immediately entered the picture. What emerged was something like: 'My brothers are those who share a language with me. Those who speak other languages are not my brothers, and I can marry their sisters.' Another time, when I directly asked an Indian why they spoke so many languages rather than relying on Tukano exclusively, he answered, 'If we all were Tukano speakers, where would we get our women?'

That Indians consciously try to maintain linguistic boundaries when speaking is further indication that language is the main badge of language-aggregate membership. Sorensen states that languages appear to be kept fastidiously apart, and that when two languages are closely related an Indian will 'carefully and even consciously keep them apart' (1967: 675). Sorensen also states that an Indian will not attempt to speak a language he is learning until he feels quite competent to speak it correctly. This suggests that interference in speech from a father-language or another language in an individual's repertoire is socially disapproved of. I observed instances where women were scolded for allowing words from other languages to creep into conversations which were being held in Bará. Other Indians would comment that such women were not setting a good example for their children, who should learn to speak their father's and mother's languages correctly. (pp. 62–3)

Many communities hold stereotypes based on the idea of strict correlation between monolingual language use and univocal identity. The mere fact that linguists want to talk about 'speech communities' betrays a bias related to such stereotyped views. The series of examples we have given illustrates what a complex and shifting set of relationships exists between language, as it is used but also as it is defined, and forms of social organization such as kinship systems, tribal systems, caste systems, land ownership regulations, etc. As Rigsby and Sutton emphasize, this should at the least lead scholars to the use of a technical vocabulary 'sufficiently basic and elemental to allow us to understand the structural and dynamic features of the social reality underlying folk models'.

It has been part of our preoccupation in this book to reach towards such structural and dynamic features.

Language and stereotypes

Language is frequently used as a defining characteristic of ethnic groups, and genetic inferences are made on the basis of those groups. Who are the Yoruba? Those who speak Yoruba as their native language. Who are the Chinese? Those who speak a Han dialect and use Chinese characters for writing. The latter definition does not however prevent northern Chinese from speaking quite contemptuously about southern Chinese as if they were to be genetically distinguished; the physical and cultural stereotypes of classical Chinese literature are very much stereotypes based on northern Chinese concepts and characteristics.

Stereotypically, members of ethnic communities are supposed to feel that their own community, and their membership of it, are well-defined; members of such stereotypical communities would be likely to dismiss Belize, where people speak of themselves as 'Mixed' or 'Mix-up', as a-typical, not being aware that this a-typicality, the most common feature referred to in that community, is in fact a type in itself. But the more one probes the supposed defining characteristics of any ethnic group the harder the groups become to define. Ethnicity is a concept each of us has learned, an extension of 'family' or 'clan' or 'tribe', but, like our language, it is a concept which may mean something slightly different to each member of a group, and its defining characteristics are composite.

A human population which has been isolated from other human populations for a long period may appear to be very homogeneous, very highly focussed in its genetic and in its cultural characteristics, and in its language. The appearances deriving from such a population have in the past provided the popular idealized model for people's thinking about both 'race' or ethnicity, and about language. The concepts deriving from such a model seem to answer the psychological needs of many people in relation to their identity: Who am I? What groups do I belong to?, and sometimes also, Who shares the language that I speak and hence project my self-concepts in? The model may in some societies derive strong reinforcement from concepts of family or caste or clan. It may also be strongly reinforced by certain physical traits. It may, or may not, subsume language differences.

London Jamaicans. When we turn to the 'London Jamaicans' we find that a culture appears to be in process of evolution which has definite ethnic, 'racial' and linguistic components, focussing not around national but around a stereotypical view of 'racial' and cultural characteristics ascribed to West Indians, and stimulated by the sense of rejection often felt by Blacks in Britain. One thing it has in common with Belize is that the drawing-together is partly positive – for common defence, an identity of interests – and partly negative, for lack of an alternative possible identity. The concept 'Jamaican' has been further bolstered by sub-groups such as the Rastafarians, 'Rastas' or 'locksmen'. The physical symbols of their group membership are reinforced by the wearing of 'dreadlocks', a hairstyle which trains 'hard' hair into long locks. (The Rastafarian movement originated in Jamaica, taking its inspiration from the leadership of the Emperor of Ethiopia, Ras Tafari Haile Selassie, against the 1936 colonizing war of Italy; it inherited earlier 'Back to Africa' and African renaissance philosophies, and provided the concept of an alternative society within which the full dignity and potential of black identity could be achieved. The movement has spread throughout the Caribbean and to England.) 'Dread talk' has had its influence on the argot of black teenagers generally; Roger Hewitt (1982, 221–2), describes its significance as follows:

The equation made here between 'dread talk' and conflict with the police and with educational aims as expressed in school life – the hard and soft faces of state authority – suggests that *one* of the uses of 'London Jamaican' is as a language of opposition, the dialect in which the registers of resistance may be most properly employed. The parental view of this dimension, refracted here through the boy's perception, indicates something of the concern many black parents feel about the terms in which 'success' is posed for their children and the fact that black adolescents have re-invested creole with an oppositional meaning. However, a 'generation gap' is, itself, part of the new dialect. 'London Jamaican' lacks many of the Jamaican parent forms. Rural idioms are shed and new items are generated exclusively with a metropolitan urban context. There is a high turn-over of new words and expressions and a high level of innovation. (These observations are not the result of any systematic study of the speech of black adolescents but are based on my own casual observations in the field, interviews with adolescents and conversations with teachers and youth workers.) Much of this linguistic growth is independent of the speech of parents and, despite parental reservations concerning its low prestige in the wider community, it has established itself amongst young people as a prestigious symbol of group solidarity, even where personal skill with it is limited.

Thus the situation with 'London Jamaican' is similar to that described by Labov (1972) in his accounts of the Black English Vernacular of pre-adolescents in New York, to Ramirez's (1974) comments with regard to the use of Chicano dialect of Spanish by adolescents, Ryan's (1979) evidence concerning Mexican American non-standard English, and other cases. It is certainly consistent with Lesley Milroy's (1980) view that: 'instead of positing a sociolinguistic continuum with a local vernacular at the bottom and a prestige dialect at the top, with linguistic movement of individuals in a generally upward direction, we may view the vernacular as a positive force; it may be in direct conflict with standardised norms, utilized as a symbol by speakers to carry powerful social meanings and so resistant to external pressures.' In this sense, therefore, many black adolescents have made their own 'provision' for improving their prestige and that of their dialect within the contexts that are most meaningful for them and in relation to the power structures in which they see themselves embedded. Indeed such is the prestige and 'street credibility' of this dialect that in recent years it has even attracted children of other ethnic groups. Cases of Turkish and Greek children using creole forms are not uncommon and Asian boys have been known to adopt the blazonry of black youth culture in dress, employing 'London Jamaican' in speech. However, the most notable trend has been the acquisition of creole by white British working-class children, as an additional linguistic skill, and it is in the context of this that some of the most significant social meanings of creole language use by black adolescents are disclosed.

However, both Hewitt and Sebba (personal communication) feel that the actual linguistic influence of Rasta or Dread talk on London Jamaican is more through the use of a few linguistic tokens from that argot than anything more systematic. London Jamaican would have very much the same form today, and very much the same social function, even were there no Rastafarians. Thus, a group solidarity which owes its impulse to the stigmatization of possessors of certain physical features by the host society, develops an argot as a symbol of that solidarity; the group gains prestige among adolescents generally, the prestige is transferred to the argot itself, which is then adopted by those who do not possess the stigmatized physical features but nevertheless wish in some way to identify with the group.

It is interesting to note that West Indian families with ambitions for their children tend to move out of city centres into areas where there is a low percentage of Blacks, and to send their children to the schools of such areas. This process of dispersal has been noted also for the Sikhs of Leeds (Rama Kant Agnihotri 1979). In South East London, we have anecdotal information about the concentration of black children in schools, from Brixton and Peckham (very high) to Catford, Lewisham and Deptford (fairly high) to Charlton, Woolwich, and Eltham (comparatively low). 'My mum and dad thought I would have a better chance if I went to this school, so they moved here for that' one black teenager at Crown Woods School told us. His friends were nearly all white. His parents, from Jamaica, spoke Jamaican at home 'so fast sometimes I can't understand them'. He had been able to 'talk Black' when they lived in Brixton, but now he had forgotten most of it although when he went to a disco with West Indian friends they sometimes tried to 'talk Black'.

Conclusion

In this book we have been working towards a general theory concerning the way in which linguistic performance – what people actually say – is related on the one hand to their competence – that is, the systems they have built up which motivate what they say and which they use to project their view of themselves in relation to the universe in which they feel they live and the social structures it contains; and on the other, to the stereotypes and abstractions and idealized models which both linguists and non-linguists have about 'languages' and about 'speech or language communities'. In other words, how is 'language' in our Sense 2 related to 'language' in each of the other three senses we have set out? We have tried to do this by examining in detail the history and current behaviour of some Caribbean communities and their descendants in London. In the process, we have found the need for a multidimensional model which would enable a general theory of linguistic evolution to subsume all the known facts about various language communities, and problems which are highlighted in Pidgin- and Creole-speaking societies but inherent in all linguistic studies.

At the same time, while advancing a theory which requires us to view all linguistic tokens as socially-marked – that is, as being used by an individual because they are felt to have social as well as semantic meaning in terms of the way in which each individual wishes to project his/her own universe and to invite others to share it – we have been forced to examine some of the most usual social groups to which particular kinds of linguistic behaviour are ascribed: those of 'nation', of 'race' and of 'ethnic group' in particular. We find that although 'race' and 'ethnicity' frequently do have strong linguistic associations this is not invariably so, and linguistic groups are not by any means always isomorphic with either genetically-conceived 'races' or culturally- or socially-conceived 'ethnic groups'. The relationship is a complex one.

Neither 'race' nor 'ethnic group' nor 'language' turns out to be a clearly-definable external object. Rather, each is a concept we form as individuals, and the extent to which, and the manner in which, we project our concepts on to those around us and establish networks of shared suppositions determines the nature of the groups in our society and their mode of operation. The processes of projection, of focussing or diffusion are very similar for all kinds of social behaviour through which we define ourselves, and a similar model is needed for social behaviour of all kinds, including language. Language however has the extra dimension in that we can symbolize in a coded way all the other concepts which we use to define ourselves and our society. It is true that we do this unconsciously in our eating habits, more consciously perhaps in other rituals and practices. In language however we are offered, by the society we enter, and we offer to others, a very overt symbolization of ourselves and of our universe, not only in the various grammars and lexicons and prosodies we can create for various domains of that universe, but also through the social marking which each occasion of use carries. Language is not only itself the focal centre of our acts of identity; it also consists of metaphors, and our focussing of it is around such metaphors or symbols. The notion that words refer to or denote 'things' in 'the real world' is very widely held, but quite misplaced; they are used with reference to concepts in the mind of the user; these symbols are the means by which we define ourselves and others.

Consider, for example, 'Professor Mary Brown' as a statement of identity. If we have known Mary Brown since she was a little girl, and her father and mother Mr and Mrs Brown, but we are not ourselves part of any university world, the concepts to which we relate these symbols 'Professor, Mary, Brown' are likely to be very different from those of her colleagues who know her only in the context of her university. By talking to them we may of course bring our concepts more into focus with theirs, and we may affect theirs, but there is no single referent, the 'real' 'Professor Mary Brown'. It has been stated by a distinguished geometer, Professor Sir Michael Atiyah (1976) that mathematics is the *science* of *analogy*, as man attempts to reduce the universe to a manageable set of principles. The language of mathematics is a special kind of language, but all human language partakes of this property; mathematical language is a very highly focussed kind of language, all the users of which try constantly to agree on the values they attach to its lexicon and syntax. Human language expresses views of the universe, and each individual has a different set of views.

National, ethnic, racial, cultural, religious, age, sex, social class, caste, educational, economic, geographical, occupational and other groupings are all liable to have linguistic connotations. The degree of co-occurrence of boundaries will vary from one society to another, the perception of the degree of co-occurrence will vary from one individual to another. There is a tendency in a number of modern nation-states to wish to make ethnic consciousness synonymous with national consciousness, and language is frequently seen as a major tool for this purpose, via the education system. As against that, many have tried to defend and protect cultural pluralism and to ensure that provision is made for the retention of 'minority' languages and cultures within the national education system – both out of respect for the individuals and groups who use them and from the argument that cultural pluralism is a source of strength rather than weakness in a society. It is possible that the best way to achieve cultural and linguistic and ethnic uniformity is through internal 'benign neglect' coupled with an external threat; but within any society various kinds of groupings will develop and will, if buttressed by vested interests or functional properties of any kind in their maintenance, prove, like the caste system of India, to be extraordinarily tenacious. Similarly, within any society linguistic groupings will develop and focussing will take place within them which may well lead to stereotypes about language coming into being which become reified, institutionalized and totemized and again extraordinarily tenacious. Thus both linguistic and non-linguistic groups will form; stereotypes will jell, and subsequently may decay; and the roles played by each kind of group in the formation and maintenance of the other are complex and of great variety.

Bibliography

Agnihotri, R. K. 1979. Processes of assimilation: a sociolinguistic study of Sikh children in Leeds. D.Phil dissertation, Department of Language, University of York; Ann Arbor: University Microfilms.

Agnihotri, R. K., Khanna, A. L. and Mukherjee, A. 1983. Variations in the use of tenses in English: a sociolinguistic perspective. New Delhi: ICSSR (Report of Project No. 1–120/78 RP).

Alleyne, M. 1980. *Comparative Afro-American*. Ann Arbor: Karoma Publications.

Anonymous. 1842. *Emigration to the British West Indies* (pamphlet). Liverpool: D. Marples.

Atiyah, M. F. 1976. Global geometry. The Bakerian Lecture for 1975. *Proceedings of the Royal Society of London*, A 347: 291–9.

Bailey, B. L. 1966. *Jamaican Creole syntax*. Cambridge: Cambridge University Press.

Bailey, C.-J. N. 1973. *Variation and linguistic theory*. Washington, DC: Center for Applied Linguistics.

Bailey, C.-J. N. and Shuy, R. W. 1973. *New ways of analyzing variation in English*. Washington, DC: Georgetown University Press.

Baker, P. and Corne, C. 1982. *Isle de France Creole: affinities and origins*. Ann Arbor: Karoma Publications.

Bal, W. *et al.* 1975. *Miscelânea luso-africana: collectânea de estudos coligidos por Marius F. Valkhoff...etc.* Lisboa: Junta de Investigações Científicas do Ultramar.

Barth, F. (ed.) 1969 (reprinted 1970). *Ethnic groups and boundaries: the social organization of culture difference*. Bergen: Universitetsforlaget; London: Allen and Unwin.

Batalha, G. 1977. *Glossario do dialecto Macaense*. Coimbra: Instituto de Estudos Romanicos.

Baxter, A. (to appear) Unpublished PhD dissertation on the Creole Portuguese of Malacca. Canberra: Australian National University.

Benjamin, G. 1976. The cultural logic of Singapore's 'multiracialism'. In *Singapore: a society in transition*, ed. by Riaz Hassan. Kuala Lumpur: Oxford University Press. pp. 115–33.

Bernstein, B. 1971. *Class, codes and control*. 2 vols. London: Routledge and Kegan Paul.

Berrenger, ?. 1811. *A grammatical arrangement on the method of learning the corrupted Portuguese as spoken in India*. Second edn. Colombo: Government Press.

Bickerton, D. 1975. *Dynamics of a creole system.* Cambridge: Cambridge University Press.

1981. *Roots of language.* Ann Arbor: Karoma Publications.

Bortoni de Figueiredo Ricardo, S. M. 1983. Urbanization of rural dialects in Brazil. PhD dissertation, University of Lancaster.

Boxer, C. R. 1957. *The Dutch in Brazil, 1624–1654.* Oxford: Clarendon Press.

1965. *The Dutch seaborne empire 1600–1800.* London: Hutchinson.

1969. *The Portuguese seaborne empire 1415–1825.* London: Hutchinson.

BPP, see *British Parliamentary Papers.*

Breen, H. H. (one-time Registrar of St. Lucia). 1844. *St. Lucia: historical, statistical, and descriptive.* London: Longman, Brown.

British Parliamentary Papers (Irish University Press edn). *Slave Trade,* vol. 61a. An account of all vessels which arrived in the British West Indies from Africa with slaves, 1 Jan, 1796 – 5 July, 1801; Exports from these islands, with destination, for the same period. pp. 35–6.

(Irish University Press edn). *Slave Trade,* vol. 61b. Abstract of imports of slaves into and exports from the British West Indies, for the year ended October 10, 1805. p. 447.

Brown, R. 1958. The original word game. In *Words and things.* New York: The Free Press. pp. 194–228.

1965. *Social psychology.* New York: The Free Press.

Burdon, Sir J. A. (ed.) 1931 etc. *Archives of British Honduras*...Government Archive Office, Belize.

Burns, Sir A. 1954. *History of the British West Indies.* London: Allen and Unwin.

Burrowes, A. E. 1983. Barbadian Creole: a note on its social history and structure. In *Studies in Caribbean language,* ed. by L. D. Carrington. Trinidad: Society for Caribbean Linguistics. pp. 38–45.

Carrington, L. D. 1967. St. Lucian Creole: a descriptive analysis of its phonology and morpho-syntax. Unpublished PhD dissertation, University of West Indies.

(ed., in collaboration with D. Craig and R. T. Dandaré). 1983. *Studies in Caribbean language.* St. Augustine, Trinidad: Society for Caribbean Linguistics.

Cassidy, F. G. 1966. *Jamaica talk.* London: Macmillan, for Institute of Jamaica.

Cassidy, F. G. and Le Page, R. B. 1980. *Dictionary of Jamaican English (DJE),* second edn (first edn 1967). Cambridge: Cambridge University Press.

Cedergren, H. and Sankoff, D. 1974. Variable rules: performance as a statistical reflection of competence. *Language, 50:* 333–55.

Censuses. For colonial census statistics see *British Government Census Reports,* 1801–1931 and 1945; also:

House of Commons Papers (Irish University Press edn) General Index, 1801–1852, Colonies:

1826 (350) XXVI, 377 (Returns relating to the populations of the Colonies of Barbadoes, St. Lucia, and the Cape of Good Hope, in each year from 1812 to 1820).

1831 (260) XIX, 171 to 1845 (49) XXXI, 31 (General statistics relating to each colony, including population).

1845 (426) XXXI, 329 (Population of each of the British West Indian Islands and British Guiana, etc.).

Annual Blue Books and *Blue Book Reports to the British Government*, for each colony.

1960 Eastern Caribbean Population Census. Port-of-Spain, Trinidad: Central Statistical Office 1963.

1960 West Indies Population Census. Kingston, Jamaica: Department of Statistics.

Charpentier, J.-M. 1979. *Le pidgin Bislama(n) et le multilinguisme aux Nouvelles-Hébrides*. Paris: Société d'études linguistiques et anthropologiques de France (SELAF).

Chaucer, G. 1957. *Complete Works* ed. by F. N. Robinson. Second edn. (first edn 1933. Cambridge University Press). London: Oxford University Press.

Chomsky, N. 1965. *Aspects of the theory of syntax*. Cambridge, Mass.: MIT Press.

Christie, P. G. 1969. A sociolinguistic study of some Dominican Creole-speakers. Unpublished D.Phil dissertation, University of York, Department of Language.

Clammer, J. R. 1979. *Ambiguity of identity: ethnicity maintenance and change among the Straits Chinese community of Malaysia and Singapore*. Singapore: Institute of South-east Asian Studies.

1982. The institutionalization of ethnicity: the culture of ethnicity in Singapore. *Ethnic and Racial Studies*, 5, 2: 127–39.

CLS I, II 1960, 1961. *Creole language studies* vols I, II, ed. by R. B. Le Page. London: Macmillan.

Community Relations Commission. 1975. *Ethnic minorities in Britain: statistical data*. London: CRC.

Craig, D. R. 1977. Creole languages and primary education. In *Pidgin and creole linguistics*, ed. by A. Valdman. Bloomington: University of Indiana Press. pp. 313–32.

1980. A Creole English continuum and the theory of grammar. In *Issues in English Creoles*, ed. by R. Day. Heidelberg: Julius Groos Verlag. pp. 111–32.

Craton, M. 1982. *Testing the chains: resistance to slavery in the British West Indies*. London: Cornell University Press.

CSP Col. Calendar of State Papers, Colonial.

Curtin, P. 1969. *The Atlantic slave trade: a census*. Madison: University of Wisconsin Press.

Dampier, W. 1697. *A new voyage round the world*, 1729 edn. ed. by N. M. Penzer. London: Argonaut Press. 1927.

Davies, K. G. 1957. *The Royal African Company*. London: Longmans, Green & Co.

Dayley, J. P. 1979. *Belizean Creole Grammar handbook*. Brattleboro, Vermont: ACTION/Peace Corps.

DBE, see Holm and Shilling (1982).

DeCamp, D. 1960. Four Jamaican Creole texts. In *Creole language studies* vol. I, ed. by R. B. Le Page. London: Macmillan. pp. 125–79.

De Sandoval, Fr. A. 1627. *De instauranda Aethiopam salute*. Seville.

De Saussure, F. 1916. See Saussure, F. de.

De Silva, M. W. S. 1979. *The vernacularization of literacy : the Telugu experiment*. Hyderabad: International Telugu Institute.

Devonish, H. 1978. The selection and codification of a widely-understood and publicly useable language variety in Guyana, to be used as a vehicle of national development. Unpublished D.Phil dissertation, University of York, Department of Language.

DGRST. See Le Page and Tabouret-Keller (1977).

DJE. See Cassidy and Le Page (1980).

Dobson, N. 1973. *A history of Belize*. London: Longman (West Indies).

Downes, W. 1984. *Language and society*. London: Fontana.

Dunn, R. 1973. *Sugar and slaves*. London: Jonathan Cape.

Eastman, D. M. and Reese, T. C. 1981. Associated language: how language and ethnicity are related. *General Linguistics*, *21*, 2: 109–16.

EDD. Wright, J. 1898–1905. *The English dialect dictionary*. 6 vols. Oxford: Oxford University Press.

Edwards, J. R. 1979. *Language and disadvantage*. London: Edward Arnold.

Edwards, V. K. 1979. *The West Indian language issue in British schools*. London: Routledge and Kegan Paul.

　1983. *Language in multicultural classrooms*. London: Batsford.

Edwards, W. F. 1977. Sociolinguistic behaviour in rural and urban circumstances in Guyana. Unpublished D.Phil dissertation, University of York, Department of Language.

Eliot, T. S. 1944. 'East Coker' in *The four quartets*. London: Faber and Faber.

Emigration to the British West Indies – see Anonymous (1842).

Escure, G. 1979. Linguistic variation and ethnic interaction in Belize: Creole/ Carib. In *Language and ethnic relations*, ed. by H. Giles and B. Saint-Jacques. Oxford: Pergamon Press. pp. 101–16.

　1984. The acquisition of Creole by urban and rural Black Caribs in Belize. *York Papers in Linguistics*, *11*, 1984, ed. by M. Sebba and L. Todd, 95–106.

Ferguson, C. 1959. Diglossia. *Word*, 15: 325–40.

Ferraz, L. (Ivens). 1974. A linguistic analysis of salient features of the Portuguese Creole of St. Thomas Island. Revised and published 1979 as *The Creole of São Tomé*. Johannesburg: University of Witwatersrand Press.

Fishman, J. A. (ed.) 1974–. *International Journal of the Sociology of Language*.

Floc'h, G. 1981. Emploi du breton et vente du poisson en Bretagne du Sud. *International Journal of the Sociology of Language*, *29*: 29–50.

Fodor, I. and Hagège, C. (eds) 1983. *Language reform : history and future*. 3 vols. Hamburg: Buske Verlag.

Fyle, C. N. and Jones, E. D. 1980. *Krio–English dictionary*. Oxford University Press.

Geggus, D. 1982. *Slavery, war and revolution : The British occupation of Saint Domingue 1793–1798*. Oxford: Clarendon Press.

Gibson, K. A. 1982. Tense and aspect in Guyanese Creole: a syntactic, semantic and pragmatic analysis. Unpublished D.Phil dissertation, University of York, Department of Language.

Gibson, K. and Levy, C. 1983. A semantic analysis of tense and aspect in Jamaican Creole. University of the West Indies, Jamaica (mimeo: 60 pp.).

Giles, H. 1979. Ethnicity markers in speech. In *Social markers in speech*, ed. by K. R. Scherer and H. Giles. London: Cambridge University Press. pp. 251–89.

1980. Accommodation theory: some new directions. *York Papers in Linguistics*, 9: 105–36.

(ed.) 1977. *Language, ethnicity and inter-group relations*. London: Academic Press.

Giles, H., Bourhis, R. Y. and Taylor, D. M. 1977. Towards a theory of language in ethnic group relations. In *Language, ethnicity and inter-group relations*, ed. by H. Giles. London: Academic Press. pp. 307–48.

Giles, H. and Powesland, P. F. 1975. *Speech style and social evaluation*. London: Academic Press.

Giles, H. and Saint-Jacques, B. 1979. *Language and ethnic relations*. Oxford: Pergamon Press.

Giles, H. and Smith, P. 1979. Accommodation theory: optional levels of convergence. In *Language and social psychology*, ed. by H. Giles and R. St. Clair. Oxford: Blackwell. pp. 45–65.

Gilman, C. 1978. A comparison of Jamaican Creole and Cameroonian Pidgin English. Amsterdam: *English Studies*, 59, 1: 57–65.

Gleason, H. A. 1965. *Linguistics and English grammar*. New York: Holt.

Goodman, M. 1982. The Portuguese influence in the New World Creoles. Paramaribo, Surinam: Fourth Biennial Conference of the Society for Caribbean Linguistics (mimeo).

Goslinga, C. Ch. 1971. *The Dutch in the Caribbean and on the Wild Coast*, 1580–1680. Assen, The Netherlands: Van Gorcum.

Gumperz, J. 1972. *Language in social groups*, a collection of Gumperz's papers ed. by A. S. Dil. Stanford, California: Stanford University Press.

Gumperz, J. and Hernandez-Chavez, E. 1972. Bilingualism, bidialectalism and classroom interaction. In *Functions of language in the classroom*, ed. by C. Cazden, V. P. John and Dell Hymes. New York: Teachers' College Press. pp. 84–108.

Günther, W. 1973. *Das portugiesische Kreolisch der Ilha do Principe*. Marburg: Universitätsbibliothek.

Haarman, H. 1983. Criteria of ethnic identity. *Language problems and language planning*, 7, 1: 21–42.

Haas, W. (ed.). 1982. *Standard languages, spoken and written*. Manchester: Manchester University Press.

Hague, R. (ed. and trans.) 1937. *La Chanson de Roland*. London: Faber and Faber.

Hall, R. A. Jr. 1953. *Haitian Creole: grammar, texts, vocabulary*. Philadelphia: American Folklore Society.

Hancock, I. F. 1969. The Malacca Creoles and their language. *Afrasian*, 3: 38–45.

1971. A study of the sources and development of Sierra Leone Creole.

Unpublished Ph.D dissertation, School of Oriental and African Studies, University of London.

1972. A domestic origin for the English-derived Atlantic Creoles. *The Florida Foreign Language Reporter*, Spring/Fall 1972: 7, 8, 52.

1980a. Texan Gullah: the Creole English of the Brackettville Afro-Seminoles. In *Perspectives on American English*, ed. by J. L. Dillard. The Hague: Mouton. pp. 305–33.

1980b. Gullah and Barbadian – origins and relationships. *American Speech*, 55, 1: 1–15.

1980c. Review of Fyle and Jones (1980). *English World Wide*, 2: 2.

1982. The fate of Gypsy slaves in the West Indies. *Journal of the Gypsy Lore Society*, 4th series 2, 1: 75–80.

1983. A preliminary classification of the Anglophone Atlantic Creoles. To appear in *Pidgin and creole languages: essays in memory of John E. Reinecke*, ed. by G. Gilbert.

Harlow, V. T. 1926. *A history of Barbados*. Oxford: Clarendon Press.

Harris, J. 1751. *Hermes*. London: T. Bolas. (Scolar Press Facsimile: Menston, 1968.)

Hartog, J. 1976. *History of St. Eustatius*. Aruba: De Witt Stores NV.

Hewitt, R. 1982. White adolescent creole users and the politics of friendship. *Journal of Multilingual and Multicultural Development*, 3, 3: 217–32.

Holm, J. 1978. The Creole English of Nicaragua's Miskito coast. Ph.D dissertation, University College, London.

1982a. *Creole English of Nicaragua's Miskito coast*. Ann Arbor: University Microfilms.

(ed.). 1982b. *Central American English: Creole texts from the Western Caribbean*. Heidelberg: Julius Groos Verlag.

forthcoming. *A survey of pidgin and creole languages*. Cambridge: Cambridge University Press.

Holm, J. A. and Shilling, A. W. 1982. *Dictionary of Bahamian English*. New York: Lexik House.

Hudson, R. A. 1980. *Sociolinguistics*. Cambridge: Cambridge University Press.

Huttar, G. L. 1982. *A creole-Amerindian pidgin of Suriname*. Society for Caribbean Linguistics Occasional Paper No. 15.

Jackson, J. 1974. Language identity of the Colombian Vaupés Indians. In *Explorations in the ethnography of speaking*, ed. by R. Bauman and J. Sherzer. Cambridge: Cambridge University Press. pp. 50–64.

1983. *The Fish people: linguistic exogamy in Northwest Amazonia*. Cambridge Studies in Social Anthropology No. 39. Cambridge: Cambridge University Press.

Jesse, The Reverend C. 1966. An hour glass of Indian news: a record of settlement in St. Lucia. *Caribbean Quarterly*, *12*, 1: 46–67.

Jones, J. S. 1981. How different are human races? *Nature*, *293*: 187–90.

Joyce, J. 1950. *Finnegan's wake*. London: Faber and Faber.

Labov, W. 1966. *The social stratification of English in New York City*. Washington, DC: Center for Applied Linguistics.

1972a. Negative attraction and negative concord in English grammar. *Language*, *48*: 773–818.

1972b. *Language in the inner city*. Philadelphia: University of Pennsylvania Press.

1972c. *Sociolinguistic patterns*. Philadelphia: University of Pennsylvania Press.

1972d. *Is the Black English Vernacular a separate system?* Chapter 2 of *Language in the inner city*. Philadelphia: University of Pennsylvania Press. pp. 36–64.

1972e. The linguistic consequences of being a lame. Chapter 7 of *Language in the the inner city*. Philadelphia: University of Pennsylvania Press. pp. 255–92.

1978. *Where does the linguistic variable stop? A response to Beatrice Lavandera*. Austin, Texas: Southwest Educational Development Laboratory Working Papers in Sociolinguistics No. 44.

1980. Is there a Creole speech community? In *Theoretical orientations in creole studies*, ed. by A. Valdman and A. Highfield. New York: Academic Press. pp. 369–88.

Lamming, G. 1953. *In the castle of my skin*. London: Michael Joseph. And later titles.

Lass, R. 1980. *On explaining language change*. Cambridge: Cambridge University Press.

Lavandera, B. R. 1978. Where does the sociolinguistic variable stop? *Language in Society*, *7*: 171–82.

Le Page, R. B. 1957/8. General outlines of creole English dialects in the Caribbean. Louvain. *Orbis*, *6* (December 1957): 373–91, and *7* (June 1958): 54–64.

1960. Jamaican Creole. *Creole language studies* vol. I, ed. by R. B. Le Page. Cambridge: Cambridge University Press.

1964. *The national language question*. London: Oxford University Press (reprinted 1966, 1971).

1968a. Problems to be faced in the use of English as the medium of instruction in four West Indian territories. In *Language problems of developing nations*, ed. by J. A. Fishman, C. A. Ferguson, J. Das Gupta. New York: Wiley. pp. 431–41.

1968b. Problems of description in multilingual communities. In *Transactions of the Philological Society* (1968). Oxford: Blackwell, pp. 189–212.

1972. Sample West Indian texts. University of York, Department of Language (mimeo).

1973. The concept of competence in a creole-contact situation. *York Papers in Linguistics*, *3*: 31–50. Reprinted in 1977 *Studia Gratularia in honour of Robert A. Hall Jr*, ed. by D. Feldman. Madrid: Playor. pp. 173–89.

1977a. Processes of pidginization and creolization. In *Pidgin and creole linguistics*, ed. by A. Valdman. Bloomington: University of Indiana Press. pp. 227–55.

1977b. Decreolization and recreolization: a preliminary report on the socio-linguistic survey of multilingual communities, stage II: St. Lucia. *York Papers in Linguistics*, *7*: 107–28.

1978a. '*Projection, focussing, diffusion' or, steps towards a sociolinguistic theory of language, illustrated from the sociolinguistic survey of multilingual communities, Stages I : Cayo District, Belize (formerly British Honduras) and II : St. Lucia*. School of Education, St. Augustine, Trinidad: Society for Caribbean Linguistics Occasional Paper No. 9. Reprinted in *York Papers in Linguistics*, 9, 1980.

1978b. Some preliminary comments on comparative lexicography in the Caribbean. Paper 12 in *Collected Preprints, Conference of the Society for Caribbean Linguistics*, Barbados 1978.

1980a. The concept of 'a language'. In *Festgabe für Norman Denison*, ed. by K. Sornig, *Grazer Linguistische Studien*, 11/12, Frühjahr 1980. Universität Graz: Institut für Sprachwissenschaft: 174–92.

1980b. Theoretical aspects of sociolinguistic studies in pidgin and creole languages. In *Theoretical orientations in creole studies*, ed. by A. Valdman and A. Highfield. New York: Academic Press. pp. 331–68.

1980c. See 1978a.

1980d. Hugo Schuchardt's Creole studies and the problem of linguistic continua. In *Hugo Schuchardt : Schuchardt-Symposium 1977 in Graz, Vorträge und Aufsätze*, ed. by K. Lichem and H. J. Simon. Vienna: Austrian Academy of the Sciences.

1983. Review of Philippe Van Parijs, *Evolutionary explanation in the social sciences*, London: Tavistock Publications 1981, in *Journal of Literary Semantics*, XII/2, October: 87–9.

1984. Retrospect and prognosis in Malaysia and Singapore. *International Journal of the Sociology of Language*, 45: 113–26.

(to appear) The need for a multidimensional model. In *Pidgin and creole languages : essays in memory of John E. Reinecke*, ed. by G. Gilbert.

Le Page, R. B., Christie, P., Jurdant, B., Weekes, A. J. and Tabouret-Keller, A. 1974. Further report on the sociolinguistic survey of multilingual communities, Stage I: Cayo District, Belize (formerly British Honduras) and II: St. Lucia. *Language in Society*, 3: 1–32. London: Cambridge University Press.

Le Page, R. B. and Tabouret-Keller, A. (Directors) 1977. Report to the Direction Générale de la Recherche Scientifique et Technique, Paris, on the sociolinguistic survey of multilingual communities, Stage II: St. Lucia. University of York, Department of Language (mimeo).

1982. Models and stereotypes of ethnicity and of language. *Journal of multilingual and multicultural development*, 3, 3: 161–92.

Lewis, M. G. ('Monk'). 1834. *Journal of a West Indian proprietor, kept during a residence in...Jamaica*. London.

Ligon, R. 1647. *A true and exact history of the island of Barbados*. London: Moseley.

Local, J. K., Wells, W. H. G. and Sebba. M. 1984. Phonetic aspects of turn-delimitation in London Jamaican. *York Papers in Linguistics*, 11 : Papers from the York Conference 1983, ed. by M. Sebba and L. Todd.

Long, E. 1774. *History of Jamaica*, 3 vols. London: T. Lowndes.

Lowenthal, D. 1957. The population of Barbados. Institute of Social and Economic Research, University of the West Indies, Jamaica: *Social and Economic Studies*, *6*, 4: 445–501.

McEntegart, D. 1980. *Final report and appraisal of the sociolinguistic survey of multilingual communities, Stage I: Belize and Stage II St. Lucia.* University of York, Department of Language and Université Louis Pasteur, Strasbourg. Section Psycholinguistique; ESRC, 1 Temple Avenue, London WC1.

McEntegart, D. and Le Page, R. B. 1981. An appraisal of the statistical techniques used in the sociolinguistic survey of multilingual communities. In *Sociolinguistic variation in speech communities*, ed. by S. Romaine. London: Edward Arnold. pp. 105–24.

Markey, T. L. 1982. Afrikaans: creole or non-creole? *Zeitschrift für Dialektologie und Linguistik*, *49*, 2: 169–207.

Matthews, W. 1935. Sailors' pronunciation in the second half of the seventeenth century. *Anglia*, *59*: 192–251.

1937. Sailors' pronunciation 1770–1783. *Anglia*, *61*: 72–80.

Mencken, H. L. 1919/63. *The American language...etc.* 4th edn and two supplements, abridged...with new material, by R. I. McDavid etc. London: Routledge and Kegan Paul.

Milroy, L. 1980. *Language and social networks*. Oxford: Blackwell.

Mittelholzer, E. A. 1941. *Corentyne thunder*. London: Eyre and Spottiswoode. And many later works.

Mühlhäusler, P. 1980. Structural expansion and the concept of creolization. In *Theoretical orientations in creole studies*, ed. by A. Valdman and A. Highfield. London: Academic Press. pp. 19–56.

1982. Language and communication efficiency: the case of Tok Pisin. *Language and Communication*, *2*, 2: 105–22.

1983. Review of D. Bickerton, *Roots of language* (1980). *Folia Linguistica.*

1984. Continuity and discontinuity in the development of pidgins and creoles. In *Studies in language ecology*, ed. by W. Enninger and L. M. Haynes. Wiesbaden: Steiner. pp. 118–34.

Mukherjee, A. 1980. Language maintenance and language shift among Panjabis and Bengalis in Delhi: a sociolinguistic perspective. Unpublished Ph.D thesis, University of Delhi.

Ndukwe, P. I. 1984. Planning for standard varieties in two Nigerian languages. Unpublished D.Phil dissertation, University of York, Department of Language.

Negreiros, A. de A. 1895. *História ethnographia da Ilha de S. Thomé*. Lisbon.

New Belize. December 1981. 'Asylum'. Belmopan, Belize: Government Information Service. pp. 4–6.

Niles, N. A. 1980. Provincial English dialects and Barbadian English. Ph.D dissertation (Linguistics), Ann Arbor, University of Michigan.

OED. Oxford English dictionary, and *Supplements*. Oxford University Press, 1933 *et seq.*

Palmer, H. E. 1924. *A grammar of spoken English*. Cambridge: Heffer.

Parry, J. H. 1963. *The age of reconnaissance*. London: Weidenfeld and Nicolson.

Parsons, J. J. 1954. The English-speaking settlement of the western Caribbean. *Yearbook of the Association of Pacific Coast Geographers, 16*: 3–16.

Patterson, S. 1963. *Dark strangers : a study of West Indians in London.* London: Tavistock Publications.

Piaget, J. 1952. *The language and thought of the child.* London: Routledge and Kegan Paul.

Pollard, V. 1983. The social history of Dread Talk: In *Studies in Caribbean Language,* ed. by L. Carrington. Trinidad: Society for Caribbean Linguistics. pp. 46–62.

Poussa, P. 1982. The evolution of early Standard English: the creolization hypothesis. Posnan: *Studia Anglia Posnaniensia, XIV*: 69–95.

Pradelles de Latour, M.-L. 1983. Identity as a complex network. In *Minorities : community and identity,* ed. by C. Fried. Dahlem Workshop Reports, Berlin: Springer Verlag.

Rambissoon Sperl, S. 1980. From Indians to Trinidadians. M.Phil dissertation, University of York, Department of Language.

Ramirez, K. G. 1974. Socio-cultural aspects of the Chicano dialect. In *Southwest areal linguistics,* ed. by G. D. Bells. California: Institute for Cultural Pluralism.

Rawley, J. A. 1981. *The Trans-Atlantic slave trade.* New York, London: Norton.

Rebaudières-Paty, M. 1985. Langues et identités dans le Bassin Houiller Lorrain. Une approche de terrain. *International Journal of the Sociology of Language, 53.*

Reid, V. S. 1950. *New day.* London: Heinemann. And later works.

Reinecke, J., Tsuzaki, S. M. *et al.* 1975. *A bibliography of pidgin and creole languages.* Honolulu: University of Hawaii Press.

Rickford, J. R. 1983. *Standard and non-standard language attitudes in a creole continuum.* Society for Caribbean Linguistics Occasional Paper No. 16.

forthcoming. Chapter 4 in *The Guyanese Creole continuum,* a volume in the series *Varieties of English around the world,* ed. by M. Göhrlach. Amsterdam: John Benjamins.

Rigsby, B. 1980. Land, language and people in the Princess Charlotte Bay area. In *Contemporary Cape York Peninsula,* ed. by N. C. Stephens and A. Bailey. Brisbane: Royal Society of Queensland. pp. 89–94.

Rigsby, B. and Sutton, P. 1982. Speech communities in aboriginal Australia. *Anthropological Forum, v,* 1, 1980–82: 8–23.

Robertson, I. 1974. *Dutch Creole in Guyana : some missing links.* Georgetown: Society for Caribbean Linguistics Occasional Paper No. 2.

1982. *Redefining the post-Creole continuum : evidence from Berbice Dutch.* Georgetown: Society for Caribbean Linguistics Occasional Paper No. 14.

Romaine, S. 1980. *On the problem of syntactic variation – a reply to Beatrice Lavandera and William Labov.* Austin, Texas: Southwest Educational Development Laboratory Working Papers in Sociolinguistics, 82.

1981. The status of variable rules in sociolinguistic theory. *Journal of Linguistics, 17*: 93–119.

1982a. *Sociohistorical linguistics : its status and methodology.* Cambridge: Cambridge University Press.

(ed.). 1982b. *Sociolinguistic variation in speech communities*. London: Edward Arnold.

forthcoming. The sociolinguistic history of t/d deletion. *Folia Linguistica Historica*.

Rosen, H. and Burgess, A. 1980. *Languages and dialects of London schoolchildren: an investigation*. London: Ward Lock.

Ross, A. S. C. 1950. Philological probability problems. London: *Journal of the Royal Statistical Society*, Series BXII, *1*: 31–6.

Ross, A. S. C. and Moverley, A. W. 1964. *The Pitcairnese language*. London: André Deutsch.

Runyon, D. 1950. 'Breach of promise'. In *Damon Runyon on Broadway*. London: Picador Books.

Russell, T. 1868. *The etymology of Jamaica grammar*. Kingston: De Cordova, Macdougall.

Ryan, E. B. 1979. Why do low-prestige language varieties persist? In *Language and social psychology*, ed. by H. Giles and R. St. Clair. Oxford: Blackwell. pp. 145–57.

Ryan, E. B. and Giles, H. (eds). 1982. *Attitudes towards language variation*. London: Edward Arnold.

Sahgal, A. 1983. A sociolinguistic study of the spoken English of the Delhi elite. Unpublished M.Phil thesis, University of Delhi.

Sankoff, G. 1974. A quantitative paradigm for the study of communicative competence. In *Explorations in the ethnography of speaking*, ed. by R. Bauman and J. Sherzer. Cambridge: Cambridge University Press. pp. 18–49.

Sankoff, G. and Brown, P. 1976. The origins of syntax in discourse. *Language*, *52*, 3: 631–66.

Sapir, E. 1921. *Language*. New York: Harcourt, Brace.

Satyanath, T. S. 1982. Kannadigas in Delhi: a sociolinguistic study. Unpublished M.Phil thesis, University of Delhi.

Saussure, F. de. 1916. *Cours de linguistique générale*, publié par Charles Bally... et Albert Sechehaye... avec la collaboration de Albert Riedlinger. Lausanne, Paris. *Course in General Linguistics*,... Translated by Wade Baskin. London: Peter Owen. 1960.

Scaglione, A. (ed.) 1984. *The emergence of national languages*. Ravenna: Longo Editore.

Scherer, K. R. and Giles, H. (eds) 1979. *Social markers in speech*. London: Cambridge University Press.

Schmidt, A. 1984. Young people's Dyirbal. MA dissertation, Canberra, Australian National University.

Schuchardt, H. 1882. *Ueber das Negerportugiesische von S. Thomé (Westafrika)*. Wien: Carl Gerold's Sohn.

1889. Zum Negerportugiesischen der Ilha do Principe. Beiträge zur Kenntnis des kreolischen Romanisch IV. *Zeitschrift für romanische Philologie*, *13*: 463–75.

Sebba, M. 1983. Code-switching as a conversational strategy. Working paper, University of York, Department of Language (mimeo).

Sebba, M. and Le Page, R. B. 1983. Sociolinguistics of London Jamaican English: Report on the pilot project (1981–82). University of York, Department of Language (mimeo).

1984. Transplanted parents, indigenous children: the linguistic symptoms of fresh cultural groupings. Society for Caribbean Studies Conference, 1984 (mimeo).

Selvon, S. 1952. *A brighter sun.* London: Allan Wingate. And later works.

Sessional Papers. 1842. *House of Commons Sessional Papers.*

Sessional Papers. 1892. *House of Commons Sessional Papers* for 1892, LVI, 207. Return showing particulars relating to immigration of Indian and Chinese coolies into British Guiana since the Commission of Enquiry in 1871.

Seybolt, P. J. and Chiang, K. (eds) 1979. *Language reform in China : documents and commentary.* White Plains, NY: M. E. Sharpe; Folkestone, Kent: Dawson.

Shephard, C. 1831. *An historical account of the island of Saint Vincent.* London: W. Nicol (printer).

Sidney, Sir P. 1586. *The Countesse of Pembroke's Arcadia.* London.

Smith, I. R. 1977. Sri Lankan Portuguese Creole phonology. Unpublished doctoral dissertation, Cornell University.

Smith, M. G., Augier, R. and Nettleford, R. 1960. *The Rastafari movement in Kingston, Jamaica.* Kingston, Jamaica: Institute of Social and Economic Research, UCWI (The SAN Report).

Smolicz, J. J. 1979. *Culture and education in a plural society.* Canberra: Curriculum Development Centre.

1982. Modification and maintenance: language among schoolchildren of Italian background in South Australia. Paper delivered at the Second Australian Conference on Italian culture and Italy today, The Frederick May Foundation for Italian Studies, University of Sydney, August 1982.

Smolicz, J. J. and Secombe, M. J. 1977. A study of attitudes to the introduction of ethnic languages and cultures in Australian schools. *Australian Journal of Education, 21,* 1: 1–24.

Sorensen, A. 1967. Multilingualism in the Northwest Amazon. *American Anthropologist, 69,* 6: 670–82.

Sprauve, G. Bilingualism and phonological filtration in the Dutch and English Creoles of the Virgin Islands. *Journal of the College of the Virgin Islands, II:* 5–19.

Sprott, W. J. H. 1958. *Human groups.* Harmondsworth: Penguin Books.

Stone, M. 1981. *The education of the Black child in Britain : the myth of multiracial education.* London: Fontana.

Sutcliffe, D. 1982. *British Black English.* Oxford: Blackwell.

Sylvain, G. 1901. *Cric? Crac! Fables de La Fontaine racontées par un montagnard haitien et transcrites en vers créoles...* Paris: Ateliers Haitiens. Second edn, 1929. Reprinted, New York, 1970. Kraus Reprint Co.

Tabouret-Keller, 1964. Contribution à l'étude sociologique des bilinguismes. *Proceedings of the II International Congress of Linguists.* The Hague: Mouton. pp. 612–21.

1968. Sociological factors of language maintenance and language shift: a methodological approach based on European and African examples. In *Language problems of developing nations*, ed. by J. A. Fishman *et al.* New York: Wiley and Sons. pp. 107–18.

1969. La motivation des emprunts. Un exemple pris sur le vif de l'apparition d'un sabir. *La Linguistique*, Paris, 5, 1: 25–60.

1970. L'enquête sociolinguistique à grande échelle. Un exemple: Sociolinguistic survey of multilingual communities, Part I, British Honduras Survey (A. Tabouret-Keller and R. B. Le Page). *La Linguistique*, Paris, 6, 2: 103–18.

1972. English translation of Tabouret-Keller (1964). A contribution to the sociological study of language maintenance and language shift. In *Advances in the sociology of language*, ed. by J. A. Fishman. The Hague: Mouton. pp. 365–86.

1975a. Un champ sémantique: les noms d'appartenance raciale au Honduras Britannique. *La Linguistique*, Paris, *11*, 1: 123–33.

1975b. Plurilinguisme: revue des travaux français de 1945 à 1973. *La Linguistique*, Paris, *11*, 2: 122–37.

1976. Ethnic names and group identity in British Honduras. *Rassegna Italiana di Linguistica Applicata*, Rome, *8*: 191–201.

1977. La notion de nation en défaut: le cas de Bélize. *Equivalences*, Bruxelles, numéro spécial *Langues et nations*, *2–3*: 85–99.

1978. Bilinguisme et diglossie dans le domaine des créoles français. *Etudes Créoles*, Paris, *1*: 135–52.

1979a. Origine et simplicité: des langues créoles au langage des enfants. *Enfance*, Paris, *3–4*: 269–92.

1979b. Le jeu varié de l'expression linguistique des enfants: le cas du district de Cayo à Bélize. In *Linguistique fonctionnelle, débats et perspectives*, ed. by M. Mahmoudian, Paris: PUF. pp. 57–75. Reprinted in *Recherche, Pédagogie et Culture*, Paris, 1979, *43*: 16–23.

1980a. A family case in San Ignacio, Cayo District, Belize: 'They don't fool around with the Creole much, as with the Spanish.' *York Papers in Linguistics*, *9*: 241–59.

1980b. Psychological terms used in Creole studies: some difficulties. In *Theoretical orientations in Creole studies*, ed. by A. Valdman and A. Highfield. New York: Academic Press. pp. 313–30.

1981a. Langues maternelles et langues secondes. *Dialogues et Cultures*. Québec, *21*: 241–59.

1981b. Introduction: Regional languages in France: current research in rural situations. *International Journal of the Sociology of Language*, *29*: 5–14.

1982a. Entre bilinguisme et diglossie: du malaise des cloisonnements universitaires au malaise social. *La Linguistique*, Paris, *18*, 1: 19–43.

1982b. Identités et évolution des situations linguistiques complexes. L'éducation bilingue dans l'école valdôtaine: conditions, problèmes et perspectives. *Bibliothèque Valdôtaine*, *21*: 35–41. Aoste: Musumeci.

1983. L'importanza dei fattori sociali nella realizzazione del bilinguismo e il problema dell' identita: studio comparativo. L'apprendimento precoce della seconda lingua. Trento: Nuova Stampa Rapida. *Educazione bilingue, 8*: 71–88.

1985a. Classification des langues et hierarchie des langues en Alsace. In *Le français en Alsace*, ed. by G. Salmon. Paris: Slatkine.

1985b. Plurilinguisme. *Encyclopédie de l'Alsace, 9*. Strasbourg: Publitotal.

Tabouret-Keller, A. and Le Page, R. B. 1983. A longitudinal study in the use of Creole and its relation to Belizean identity in Cayo District, Belize. In *Studies in Caribbean Language*, ed. by L. Carrington. pp. 277–99.

Tabouret-Keller, A. and Luckel, F. 1981a. La dynamique sociale du changement linguistique: quelques aspects de la situation rurale en Alsace. *International Journal of the Sociology of Language*, The Hague, *29*: 51–70.

1981b. Maintien de l'alsacien et adoption du français. Eléments de la situation linguistique en milieu rural en Alsace. *Langages*, Paris, *21*: 39–74.

Theil, H. 1972. *Statistical decomposition analysis with applications in the social and administrative sciences*. Amsterdam: N. Holland Publishing Co.

Thomas, J. J. 1869. *The theory and practice of Creole grammar*. Port-of-Spain, Trinidad: The Chronicle Publishing Office. Facsimile edition with introduction by Gertrud Buscher, 1969. London: New Beacon Books.

Traugott, E. 1981. The sociostylistics of minority dialects in literary prose. *Proceedings of the seventh annual meeting of the Berkeley Linguistics Society*. pp. 308–16.

Trudgill, P. 1973. Phonological rules and sociolinguistic variation in Norwich English. In *New ways of analyzing variation in English*, ed. by C.-J. Bailey and R. W. Shuy. Washington, DC: Georgetown University Press. pp. 149–63.

1974. *The social differentiation of English in Norwich*. London: Cambridge University Press.

1980. Acts of conflicting identity: a sociolinguistic look at British pop songs. *York Papers in Linguistics, 9*: 261–77. Reprinted in Trudgill (1983: 141–60).

1983. *On dialect: social and geographical perspectives*. Oxford: Basil Blackwell.

Turner, L. D. 1949. *Africanisms in the Gullah dialect*. Chicago: University of Chicago Press.

Valkhoff, M. 1966. *Studies in Portuguese and Creole with special reference to South Africa*. Johannesburg: Witwatersrand University Press.

1975. L'importance du Portugais comme langue mondiale avant le français. In Bal, W. *et al.* (1975: 72–85).

Venables, General. 1655. *The narrative of General Venables*, ed. by C. H. Firth. London: Royal Historical Society, 1900.

Voorhoeve, J. 1973. Historical and linguistic evidence in favour of the relexification theory in the formation of Creoles. *Language in Society, 2*: 133–46.

Walcott, D. 1950. *Henri Christophe*. A play. Bridgetown, Barbados: The Advocate Co.

1953. *Poems*. Cross Roads, Jamaica: The City Printery.

1958. *The sea at Dauphin*. A play. Extra-mural Department, UCWI, Jamaica. And later works.

Wallace, S. 1978. What is Creole? The example of the Portuguese language of

Tugu, Jakarta, Indonesia. In *Contemporary studies in Romance linguistics*, ed. by M. Suner. Washington, DC: Georgetown University Press. pp. 340–77.

Ward, W. E. F. 1948. *History of the Gold Coast*. London: Allen and Unwin.

Warner, A. 1982. *Complementation in Middle English and the methodology of historical syntax : a study of the Wyclifite sermons*. London: Croom Helm.

Weinreich, U. 1953. *Languages in contact. Findings and problems*. NY: Publications of the Linguistic Circle of New York. No. 1.

White, N. G. 1978. A human ecology research project in Arnhem Land region: an outline. Australian Institute of Aboriginal Studies, *Newsletter*, 9: 39–52.

White, N. G. and Parsons, P. A. 1973. Genetic and sociocultural differentiation in the Aborigines of Arnhem Land, Australia. *American Journal of Physical Anthropology*, 38: 5–14.

1976. Population genetic, social, linguistic and topographical relationships in north-eastern Arnhem Land. *Nature*, 26: 223–5.

Whorf, B. L. 1956. *Language, thought and reality. Selected writings of B. L. Whorf*, ed. by J. B. Carroll. Cambridge, Mass.: Technology Press of MIT; New York: John Wiley.

Williams, J. P. 1983a. Dutch and English creole on the Windward Netherlands Antilles: an historical perspective. *Amsterdam Creole Studies*, 5: 93–112.

1983b. A social history of White Saban English. Part of MA thesis, Department of Linguistics, University of Texas at Austin.

Winford, D. 1984. The linguistic variable and syntactic variation in Creole continua. *Lingua*, 62, 4: 267–88.

Wishart, D. 1978. *Clustan user manual*. Edinburgh University: Program Library Unit. (For details of our later cluster-analysis work see McEntegart 1980.)

Wurm, S. A. and Mühlhäusler, P. 1982. Registers in New Guinea Pidgin. *International Journal of the Sociology of Language*, 35: 69–86.

Young, C. 1973. Belize Creole: a study of the creolized English spoken in the city of Belize, in its cultural and social setting. Unpublished D.Phil dissertation, University of York, Department of Language.

Index